Chastity Shawl & Other Stories

By
Matt Hribar

Copyright 2023 by Matt Hribar,
Starvolt Studios
All rights reserved.

Table of Contents

Dedication	3
Foreward	4
The Weird Kid	7
Chastity Shawl	34
A Lack of Decorum	54
Trying To Have A Social Life	79
You May Now Be The DJ	104
Thank You For Your Service	145
Audioaddict	163
Audioaddict ii	175
(Pop Star Incoming)	175
Savanthood	194
A Collection of Random Notes Written In Passing (2019-2022)	223

Dedication

To everyone who has inspired the stories in this book, and stories elsewhere in my life. And to my mother, the one who supports my stories the most and edited this entire book. My thanks can't even be properly worded.

Foreward

"You're a writer? Have you published anything?"

It's a question that has been commonly ricocheted to me as soon as anyone finds out that I enjoy writing. It's a question that every writer gets asked, especially in a country that values commodification. You can't just love something, you have to be able to sell that love. If you're not *selling* what you do, are you even *good* at it?

For years I avoided labeling myself as a writer just to avoid this question of publication. More successful authors and talented writers would hopefully agree that they don't write material purely with the publishing aspect in mind. They write what they are called to write whether that's fantasy, reality, crime, romance, truth, falsity, self or other. Those who write purely focused on publication miss out on the beauty and enjoyment of writing.

A harsh truth is that so much of my lifetime's mass of writing will probably never see the public eye. Such a realization to a writer is both sad and beautiful. The collection of stories before you is not just mere slop delivered to feed farm animals in a trough. It is a process — an art, an emotion, something to share with the world.

After so many years of writing, and so many years of knowing I would like to publish, I decided to go through with it. What was stopping me? Quite often I faced challenges and obstacles I bulldozed through to accomplish goals.

Indecision got the best of me when it came to considering publication. What would be the most reader-friendly? Should it be a series? Should it be something that would require eons of editing time? Maybe I should save my best material for later when I can *publish* publish a book? Is that genre in? Is that genre out?

It got to a point where I was working on multiple pieces at the same time — like a polygamist, but for writing. Instead of partners left and right, it was manuscripts, drafts, new books, and concepts — and there I was — in the middle of a good ten projects wondering *how did I get here among all this crap?*

So I focused on creating this book. I've been wanting to write short stories based on real-life experiences for a while. I wrote this book in an intentional, methodological sequence. I summoned my own memories and conducted casual interviews. The more people I talked with, the more stories flooded back to me. It doesn't just feel like a personal patchwork quilt — I feel like I have taken aboard so many other people's stories as my own. I've always joked that I was a succubus-type creator for stories. I want to know the stories of others, of the world. I gather them like jewels to display in window boxes.

This book evolved quicker than a turtle on the Galapagos. It started as observational humor and personal anecdotes. It then became a diary, a recollection, and a history of myself; the original comedic spin tilted a little to other emotions in an effort to resonate truthfully. I didn't want to paint sad stories with humor — or tell sad stories without something that makes the reader go, "oh thank God I can chuckle because that story got *dark*."

Not everything is shared in these essays. My memory is awful, and I'm sure there's future essays about the past that will resurface eventually. I kept some personal stories for myself, and for certain friends. Some essays make others look better than they were, and make myself look more justified than perhaps I was. History teaches us that the victor decides the story and context. As my own victor, I demand that same rule in my work and offer no atonement if you disagree.

Maybe I'll save some of the scraps I've taken out of this book for another collection. Maybe it will forever hang like a pressed blazer in a personal vault. Or maybe what was so presently unshareable will find itself forgotten. What's the bigger sin — to share such ultimate truth with the world? Or to forget the ultimate truth altogether? I'm a public person that is quite open about most things. But I'm weirdly private at the same time about special things.

So enjoy *Chastity Shawl and Other Stories* — and if you don't like the book, pass it on to someone who might enjoy reading the following depravity and insanity. Or it might be easier to give it to someone you hate, which would make poetic justice in gift-giving.

The Weird Kid

No parent wants to admit they have a weird kid. Or at least they didn't want to admit that back in the 1990s-2000s era that I grew up in. These days parents are proud to brag that their four-year-old daughter Blueberry Sage is vegan and anti-capitalist. But back in that 21st-century cusp, you wanted an ordinary kid with a few featured fun facts that made them seem distinguishable.

"Well, Jeffery has a penchant for his colors, enjoys dancing to Motown, and loves turtles!" It's like fun and bubbly dating profiles, except instead of matching for love, you were swiping for points with other parents.

No parent wanted to say: "My 4-year-old son has an obsession with Madonna, hates waking up early to open Christmas presents, and is reading at a 3rd-grade level at age 4." That sounded cringy back in 1998. It's like finding out that the mozzarella platter that looked so good in the restaurant menu photo is no more than frozen mozzarella sticks heated up with canned tomato puree.

Those above descriptors are accurate when it comes to little Matt Hribar. Apparently, and I say apparently because I don't have the memories, I made a scale-sized version of Madonna out of plastic food. We then mailed a picture, along with some beads, to Madonna? I don't know how my mom found an address — this was just shy of when we would sell our souls to Google.

Another time, I asked my principal in kindergarten if, for my birthday, they could play "Holiday" by Madonna over the morning announcements. The principal apparently wished she could — but then would have been bombasted by other students who wanted music played during their birthday.

I'm fascinated with people who can actively remember large chunks of their youth. One friend had a memory of when they were two years old. I can't tell if they're just brilliant or lying. I discovered my earliest memory was a lie (or so my mother says). I have a clear distinctive recollection of being slapped across the face as a child by my mother in the kitchen of our first home.

"I *never* slapped you across the face!" My mother gasped when I shared my earliest memory, which didn't happen.

"Well, you definitely spanked us a couple times." I pointed that out as if a butt smack was the same as a full-arm rotated swing face-slap.

"That's *different*. I only spanked you a couple times."

"Doesn't that feel adjacent?"

My mother gave me an 'adjacent my ass' look.

One of the things my family and close friends are aware of is that my memory is comparable to a fish. I will forget names and events, mix up details and definitions, and actively rearrange reality. Notice how the title of this piece is called *The Weird Kid*, and not *The Smart Kid,* nor *The Semi-Normal Kid With A Functional Memory of Reality*. I don't have a publication house to confirm this, but that latter title feels too long.

I was partially placed into kindergarten at the age of four because I could name the planets and the order of the planets and distribute fun facts about the planets. This was before Pluto was annexed for being too small — size does matter gentleman. There were other signs that I was decently bright. At least smart enough to push into kindergarten right away. But I like the idea that someone knowing the planets is enough to prove one can skip a grade.

"Liz knows Neptune is a blue planet named after an old Roman god, so we'll have her skip preschool and start her in kindergarten immediately."

"Liz doesn't seem able to comprehend basic addition..."

"So? She knows about *Neptune,* for God's sake!"

My mother once again found my memory to be lacking in this department.

"They moved you on because of your social skills." My mother recently told me over a glass of grape cider. "You were emotionally intelligent."

In 1998, being emotionally intelligent was not a thing a parent would brag about, but if I had been a young child of 2023, I would have been treated as a modern-day Socrates.

My only memory of kindergarten was when the class got in trouble. Consequently, we couldn't play with the plastic kitchen and house set in the corner of the room. That toy system was the elite cream of the crop. It was the Chanel of all the toys in the kindergarten classroom. Because of bad behavior, it was roped off like a crime scene had happened. Like there was a police investigation happening due to an assault by plastic food items.

Before technology ruined my ability to read literature, I quickly crushed a book or two a week. A few of my elementary school teachers would softly complain about how I'd hide novels within textbooks. It was hard for my mother to take their complaints seriously because while the rest of the class was doing second-grade phonics, I was smuggling Harry Potter into my textbook and reading at a fifth-grade level. The indiscretion usually went ignored.

Back in grade school, we had an Accelerated Reading program. You could read various classic books and take a quiz on a school computer. It was a semi-optimal reading test in which students needed a breezy ten points per year. I remember constantly logging my points so I could be one of the year's top students. Besides, I was continually reading anyway.

Toward the end of the school year, I'd make a mad dash for extra points by looking through eligible quizzes to see if there were any short books I could read and test myself on. Or maybe books I had read in the past that I hopefully could bullshit myself through a test on. One book, *The Hundred Dresses,* was worth four points and had less than 100 pages. It was a book I could crush in a day — and a book that other students did to get their bare minimum points.

Most people did Accelerated Reading because if you collected enough points, you could trade them in for prizes: 30 points got you a pen, 50 points accumulated you a toy, and 75 points got you a dress-down pass. Having a dress-down pass in a Catholic grade school with a strict dress code was like having access to the best drugs in prison. Quite often, we'd have two-dollar dress-down days, where the student body would *pay* the school just so we could wear jeans and t-shirts.

When I was in first grade, you could trade in your Accelerated Reading points for an exotic prize: lunch with the librarian. I was the only student who claimed the reward of dining with Sister Eitien. I had assumed that lunch with the librarian included a *provided* lunch. Like Sister Eitien would whip up something at the convent for us to dine over. I put in an actual food order — as if she was a private chef I had hired: cheese broccoli soup, entree options, and even a dessert course.

"I don't think Matt understands that I don't bring lunch for us," Sister Eitien told my mother. "He gave me a whole food order..."

I was still pretty excited to have lunch with the librarian, even if it was just peanut butter and jelly.

Having your mother be a teacher at the school you're attending was never a problem for me. My mother didn't treat me differently just because I was her son. If anything, she probably treated me a little more harshly just to prove a point. And because my mom was both a great teacher and considered cooler than the other teachers, it was more of a benefit for me. Although there were times my mom had to lay down the law, people considered me deputy sheriff behind my mother.

My favorite moment of being the teacher's son was when it was my mother's birthday. One of the faculty had brought in a cake for my mother's birthday. I was walking by the library, which had turned into the faculty room, halfway through my time at school. The old faculty room had to be converted into a classroom following the expansion of kindergarten into two separate classes.

"Matt!" One of the teachers called out, and I turned to see a flock of teachers having lunch in the library. "This birthday cake is for your mother. Could you go see if she will let us have some? We're about to finish lunch..."

I was taken aback at the request but walked to my mother's classroom. She was proctoring an assignment.

"The teachers in the library were wondering if they could cut into your cake," I said, a bit neutral but with a look of *the audacity*?'

"Sure." My mom said without a care in the world. My mom wasn't that much of a dessert person anyway. She appreciated that someone got her a cake, but she wasn't dying to eat the whole thing.

I arrived back in the library with permission from my mother, only to find that the birthday cake had been sliced into.

Pieces were already being distributed to the teachers on early lunch.

"My mother said it was okay," I meekly informed the room.

"We figured she'd say it was!" Said the teacher cutting out another slice with a brimming smile. I turned around and left. For the most part, I'm a goody-two-shoes who wants to avoid conflict and problems — I still am to this day.

In my eight years of elementary and middle school, I was only written up three times for **bad behavior**. Classmates would get into squabbles or act out in rare situations. But my three demerits came from three ridiculous situations.

Fourth grade, picture it. The weird time when you don't feel like an older kid, but you don't feel like a younger kid either. My teacher was Marian Patterson, an old-school academic who could deliver information successfully and had a sharp whip tongue that didn't take prisoners. Her big obsessions were clowns and penguins. We decorated laundry hangers with old pantyhose to make freaky hanging clown mobiles. She was also a notorious smoker. She'd hand back essays that smelled like nicotine.

I remember we read The Wizard of Oz during class, and we'd often be told by Mrs. Patterson that the *book* came before the movie. And that the book was better than the movie. Another memory of Mrs. Patterson was when I accidentally, or maybe purposefully, but I genuinely can't remember, left behind an assignment with a lousy grade. Every week we bunched and stapled our papers and assignments to give to our parents. It was like a flower bouquet of grades.

"You could have placed that bad grade at the back of your packet," Mrs. Patterson said, raising a stapler to staple the rotten grade on *top* of the packet. "But now that you tried hiding the grade, we're going to put it right on the top."

That was an excellent and aggressive way of demonstrating responsibility. It carried the shame that Cersei probably felt in *Game of Thrones* when the nun rang the bell and cried out s*hame* for her entire walk through the city. People ask me why I feel guilty, upset, or shame over specific actions. I point back to my Catholic schooling and upbringing. It has me in a tighter grip than the Suez Canal had on that ship that got stuck for a week.

I wished some modern grade-school teachers had Mrs. Patterson's blend of tough love and real-life application. I always found her sound, except when she wrote me a demerit.

I was sitting next to Gus, a goofy and friendly classmate. Someone in our quad of desks had farted, so Gus turned to me.

"Matt, you farted!" Gus said, beginning typical fourth-grade blame and attack games.

"I didn't fart!" I retorted back — both truthful with a shade of defensive. Getting accused of a fart was the grade school equivalent of murder. Naturally, kids avoided this charge super defensively. And human nature makes us think the super defensive are often guilty of the charged crime.

"You farted," Gus shook his head, as if he was defending his position on global warming.

"I did not fart!" I repeated — this time a bit loudly and firmly. Mrs. Patterson overhead and immediately zeroed in.

"What kind of LANGUAGE are we USING in the CLASSROOM!?" Mrs. Patterson yelled like I had dropped a significant no-no term. The room was confused at this point. Those who hadn't heard me probably thought I had declared a dirty comment in front of Mrs. Patterson.

"We do not speak bathroom language in my classroom," Mrs. Patterson said, taking me to her desk. She pulled out the pink paper of death — a demerit. I didn't feel bad for what I said — but now I had to explain to my poor mother what had transpired. Years later, my mother recalled the incident with relish.

"I really didn't care," My mother said with a chuckle. "It was *fart*. You didn't say a bad word — but what could I say? I wasn't going to punish you, but you were too young to say, 'this demerit is bogus.' So I just let you take the punishment without much comment. I actually laughed about it in private..."

In sixth grade I got a demerit because I wasn't wearing a belt. Back then, I was apt to forget that my blue navy pants *demanded* a belt per the school uniform. Miss Oliver was a stickler for rules. She was also known for her ancient history lessons where we would mummify oranges in Ancient Egyptian burials and play Ancient Greek Olympic Games.

"No belt again; that's a demerit!"

I don't recall my mother complaining much about that demerit either.

I definitely was building up a reputation for bending the rules. When tasked to read a chapter out loud in Miss Oliver's class, I'd create remarkable voices.

"Matt gave an interesting voice to a ten-year-old girl," Miss Oliver muttered to my mother once. "She sounded like a Southern truck-driving cigarette-loving woman in her fifties."

The third demerit happened in seventh grade. I had Ms. Pokorny, an older, thoughtful, and kind woman. She had trouble with authority — especially as pre-teenagers and budding teenagers are apt to rebel against some figures. She had been convinced that students couldn't hear her at some point. I don't know which students tricked poor Ms. Pokorny into believing that. But lo and behold, Ms. Pokorny invested her cash into getting a Britney Spears-style microphone attached to a speaker at the hip. I don't think it helped much — because while her vocals were a bit louder, the cheap speaker offered crinkles and feedback.

After school, my classmate Ryan and I stayed back because it was our turn to clean the classroom. We were given watered-down solutions and rags to wipe down desks and seats. Ryan jokingly sprayed me, and that turned into a spray war between the two of us. We let loose — watered-down cleaner flying across the classroom. Bullets of spray flew at each other like two werewolves tossing salvia haphazardly.

Ms. Pokorny walked in right when I sprayed Ryan right in the face. She howled as if we had been shooting each other with real guns and ran to Ryan's side.

"WHAT are you two DOING!?" She cried, before making Ryan flush out his eyes with water. Both of us went home with a demerit for biological weapon warfare — or whatever Ms. Pokorny described in the demerit sent home to our parents.

Eighth-grade graduation was a colossal deal at my elementary school since the cream of the crop was leaving and never coming back. My friend Sarah cried in the parking lot during the last moments of our pre-high school life.

"We'll have to have a five-year anniversary and see everyone again — right?" Sarah said a few times to the agreeance of some and the indifference of others. It would soon become impossible to bring that truth to fruition — two of my classmates would commit suicide, one committed a murder-suicide, and another would go on to overdose. Four deaths in a class that was somewhere around 50 strong. I can't help but feel a bit eerie over that statistic.

I wouldn't love to see half of my elementary class. Some of my old elementary classmates were really problematic apples. The biggest irony was that the class suck-up during the DARE anti-drug education became the biggest drug users. A couple other people grew into fundamentally twisted ideologies — and while I can appreciate the memories, I have no desire to open up the modern can of worms just to say, "*Remember when?*" fifty times over in a church hall.

I vaulted into high school with the same weirdly popular personality, but not in the traditional sense. At an all-boys high school that valued sports over art, academics, and anything that didn't involve physical combat, my interests and activities were not high on the cool scoreboard. But I was active (*too* active) in clubs that I probably had no business leading. I was actually the president of the Relay For Life Club, and I still don't know why? I had no background in running nor any personal connection to cancer. But someone needed to step up, and I have always been a 'yes' person.

This sounds terrible — but I don't remember much of high school. I remember trading any shards of math and science skills for English, history, and art. I took additional art and English classes and dropped my language during my senior year (you only had to take three years). I was taking Latin and barely learned the subject. The only word I remember is Agricola, which means farmer.

It's not a traumatic reason why I have forgotten. But high school makes us anxious and wrapped up in perception. For a short while, I donned a cocoon that I shed upon college. I carry no regret, for it is part of the natural order of modern schooling and adolescence. You start off open, become closed quickly, and then slowly become open again.

When I was in college, I quickly felt a bit worried about my image. I had spent high-school ugly and un-sexual, but now I was finding that I desired self-beauty. I hit the gym pretty quickly. I was constantly eating salads in the college cafeteria. Those salads were often made with kidney beans, black beans, chickpeas, egg, and tomatoes over spinach with a thousand island dressing. I don't even think that the salad was that healthy — but it was less about the actual calorie count or the health of the salad and more about that I was just eating *a* salad.

It was like saying, 'we're going to go to the best winery in Cleveland.' But in reality, you were going to some lady's garage where she poured you glasses of Aldi. I was blind to the situation as if I were a contestant on Netflix's show *Love Is Blind*. I didn't marry someone sight unseen. I just fooled myself into thinking my habits and current state were optimal.

Freshman year felt like a weak version of 90210. Not only had I been eating salads around the clock, but I actively walked over to the CVS to buy weight loss pills on a shelf for twenty bucks. I used them, but they failed to do anything. That motivated me to go, "oh, this is useless?"

Before my transformation, I layered many clothes as if I were Amish or an Italian grandmother who was always cold, no matter the temperature. My hair was long, curly, and mopish. Add glasses that didn't fit my face, and I looked like that ugly nerd in an 80s movie who got bullied by the mean jocks.

However, there became a quick turning point — March or April of my college freshman year. I shaved the mop down and got contacts — taking the ugly duckling and evolving into a decent 7/10. Who knew you needed contacts and a Great Clips coupon to meet society's expectations?

With the confidence given to me by new hair and contacts, I tried on my first pinnie — a mesh tank top. It's the kind of look you would wear as a basketball athlete. But for some reason, I enjoyed it. I displayed my creamy shoulders as if they were Versace. I liked the jock look — it felt different. And maybe it wasn't necessarily about coming across as a jock but just doing something different.

The pinnie was the gateway clothing item to my impending and current obsession with tanks. Before the tank, I would wear t-shirts to the gym. But now, I'm most likely attending workouts with the gun show open for business.

I've always admired my thighs the most. Thick, strong, and muscular, my thighs are clearly the top-shelf liquor of my body. They're like two security guards at the club: formidable and possibly overbearing. Those elephant trunks really do an excellent job of holding me up. And if my thighs were real people, they'd probably question my tank choices.

"I'm sorry..." My thighs would grunt. "We've ALWAYS been hot. And yet you choose those decent shoulders over *us*?"

I go through ensemble phases like a character on *Riverdale* or other cheap, tawdry shows. There was 'varsity jacket Matt,' a phase where I wore a $45 Urban Outfitters knock-off varsity jacket. I wore that varsity jacket to the point where the faux leather was cracked and wouldn't button to cross my slightly increasing gut. My stomach and chest were like continents breaking away from Pangea — there was slight movement gradually over time. I never woke up to find my chest noticeably bulkier.

There was bandana Matt, who took up his massive curls and slid a bandana over them. This was when I kept my hair long and looked for ways to style it properly. My optimistic yet naive self didn't realize there was no way to properly wear that hair. Looking back, Bandana Matt was the most brutal. I looked like a Yankee trying to be a southern peach farmer or a wannabe biker who would probably do better if they played with Hot Wheels or grabbed onto a biker Lana Del Rey style. Best to leave bandanas to leather daddies and bald men.

It should not have been a surprise that when, upon finding the hidden beauty, I began to show off that beauty by shedding clothes. And in that cycle of wearing sexier clothes, it was evident that jorts would eventually roll up in my ensemble. Homemade jorts, to be specific. I was a college student on a budget. I still rock a jort, but not as aggressively as I used to. Bandanas are to jorts like how people complaining to the manager are to those who directly write refund demands to companies. Both seem like a waste of time, but one does seem classier than the other.

My thighs were happy to see some sunlight and a few peek-a-boo eyeballs. I was unstoppable and indestructible: husky, giant shoulders and formidable, iron thighs. Feet draped in work boots — sometimes a tank to add more skin. People would turn their heads, wondering if they had witnessed Jesus' return. A more prominent man, confident about his body? I was no Paul Revere who rode while screaming that the British were coming, but I'm sure my tube tank, low-ride jorts, and work boot combination might have caused a wayward scream here or there.

My fashion sense evolved somewhat over the years. Years of sexless fashion resulted in a bit too much show. Eventually, in my mid-twenties, I would find the correct balance. My friend Billiam recently pulled out a photo of us at a dance formal.

"Oh my god, WHAT am I WEARING!?" I texted back. The image of me — short militant hair, sunglasses, a green blazer, a blue and orange shirt, bright green pants — was way too much color and style for one single look. I can imagine fashion stylists poking their eyes out.

I don't have the confidence that it takes to be a nudist. Nor do I get pleasure from being nude. I love tanks and shorts because they provide privacy while allowing breathing room. My voluptuous body tends to overheat.

I wear tanks as much as possible. I have all sorts of tanks, some perfect for a casual picnic, others so lowcut that they're almost to my navel. My body feels freer when allowed to sometimes spill casually out of the thin fabric. And when you have shoulders that bounce off your chest due to their size, you appreciate tanks more than shirts. My tanks become a superior meter in whether I've lost or gained weight. "Oh...this tank used to be loose, but now it feels tight," would be the story of what would lead me to a week of mere salads.

I hit the gym early on in college. I started going late to avoid the competition over weight racks and bars. At John Carroll, the gym space was called the 'Corbo Room' — named after some weightlifter long ago. It should have been called the 'Cor-no Room' because it was a constant battle to grab a cardio machine or any weight equipment.

I actually worked at the gym, and it was one of my favorite jobs of all time. You swiped cards, did whatever you wanted on your laptop, and occasionally cleaned some gym equipment. I wish I had a job where I did minimal work and could crank out stories or surf the web.

The other college job I loved was working for the campus coffee shop, The Cubby. I don't even know why I was hired. I had a little catering experience and retail experience, but I was far from being a barista. That's where I met Karyn — one of my closest friends to this day. Karyn and I would spend hours inventing drinks and designing posters advertising our beverages.

There was always drama happening at The Cubby — sometimes because of the student staff, but more so the non-student staff who worked at the sister establishment. There was an employee who was caught stealing food on the security cameras. There was a disagreement over a chicken wing special. Employees coming in drunk or high.

My favorite non-student employee was Miss Donna, an older, quiet woman who slowly waltzed around the place. Miss Donna liked her work, but she wasn't a fast worker. She would take minutes to make a single drink. But everyone, including me, loved her. At the time, I thought she was just old. But she probably was performing the amount of work correlated with her pay rate.

Midway through my tenure as a campus barista, the administration decided to have a non-student work a new morning shift at the Cubby. Before that, our shifts ran from 5:30pm to 9pm and from 9pm to 12:30am every night. It was a simple nighttime establishment. But now, a morning employee would open the place up around 7am and keep it running till 2pm. I don't even remember the original name of the Morning Lady — but she quickly became crowned with the title of "The Morning Lady."

I would never meet the Morning Lady — but I had heard stories of her prowess. She dyed her hair a Ronald McDonald red and apparently had a very jittery appearance. She would put forth rules for all nighttime student employees and considered herself management (she was never a manager). The Morning Lady changed display cases and would 'clean things' but made them dirtier during the cleaning process. She even made a drink called "The Flying Monkey" that she would push onto people — so much so that we received complaints for how often people were asked to have her disgusting drink.

The Morning Lady was eventually let go and replaced with Adrienne — who became a bossier yet more put-together version of the Morning Lady. My favorite Adrienne story was that she started a 'communication folder' which turned out to be a series of diary entries by Adrienne blaming the student employees for everything that was wrong with the place. A squashed blueberry on the floor? It was the student employees! Dust underneath one of the tables outside The Cubby? It was the student employees! Adrienne made a drink wrong? It was the student employees!

The biggest frustration I would have as a barista had to be people who didn't know what they were ordering. A cappuccino is typically espresso with a bit of milk and a giant cup of foam. Half of a traditional cappuccino is nothing more than milk foam. Quite often, we'd have people order them and be upset when it wasn't sweet and milky like you might get at a self-serve gas station. With that in mind, I would grill everyone who ordered a cappuccino.

"Could I get a cappuccino?" Girls would ask.

"You know it's mostly foam and doesn't have a lot of milk?"

"Oh. Can I have a latte?"

The biggest rush of the week would be Sunday following night mass. With prayers handled, the next thing people needed was their late-night caffeination or a smoothie situation. Sometimes the meanest people are indeed the ones sitting in the front row at mass.

"Why is it so slow?" Someone might mutter from the back of the line. Cindy, forty people are ordering expensive coffee beverages — and most don't even know what they want when they arrive at the front of the line. They spread themselves out in a position to indicate that they're relaxed. They eye the menu slowly in the mannerism of a rich, entitled person who might examine a box of fabergé eggs.

"Can I? Mmm, no, maybe not that. I can't decide...well, should it be *that* drink, *this* drink, *that other* drink, or *this other* drink, or maybe THAT drink over there..."

Sometimes the indecision made no sense. Sure — should I have chocolate or white chocolate in my latte would be a toss-up.

But some people had no clue if they wanted hot or frozen, caffeinated or caffeine-free, or maybe they just wanted a smoothie instead of a coffee. I'd have to parse through their decision-making, like a classroom aide helping a child put together a block tower.

Midway through my last semester, the shop transformed into a capitalist nightmare. Instead of serving organic products, we would start selling Starbucks. Creativity on the drink menu had been sliced out altogether. Phenomenal boss Rachel Friend (a friend to all) left for better (coffee) grounds. Her absence made the incompetence of other managers spiral out of control. I was thankful for not only graduating from college but graduating from this job. And while I haven't made a latte since 2016, if you got me back in front of an espresso machine, I'd have no trouble cranking out a double.

My frustrations as a barista became tenfold in practicum when it came to serving. Upon graduation and completing my year of service, I decided to look for options for some good side money. Cleveland was gearing up to open a Margaritaville, undoubtedly a weird geolocation for the brand. When I thought tropical getaway, I did not think of Cleveland. Weirder yet, the site of the Margaritaville was in the popular kids' party district. And nobody is trying to get drunk and club at Margaritaville, especially when they close at 10 PM.

That summer was a soft trauma for the staff. We'd get slammed and would overseat people. The kitchen was too small for the whole restaurant. Things would get more backed up in that kitchen than in a colon-cleansing commercial. Because of how much we worked, we would steal quick bites of nachos and appetizers in the back during long shifts. Our tables got cranky for the wait because the small kitchen and limited staff would become indifferent over the multitudes of orders. The food wasn't even that good — think Applebee's, but you're paying more. When people would get pissed at me over their frozen appetizers taking a half-hour, I'd internally believe it was *their* fault for eating here in the first place. I don't believe in victim blaming, but you can't blame the cheesy establishment for having bad food.

One of my defining love languages is map exploration and creation: I love analyzing maps and roads and looking up places and geography. It's not even for some weird geography quiz fetish — although I could probably tell you a few state capitals and locations of countries. My family jokes because, on the state standardized testing, I scored in the 99th percentile on maps and directions. My pedigree is never used; I always map my way to destinations. I couldn't even tell you the names of highways, and I've been regional to Cleveland for almost three decades.

"Did you take I-90?" This is a question that quite often ends up with the answer:

"Which one is that again?"

Like most kids who grew up in the 90s and early 2000s, I loved Rollercoaster Tycoon. For those who missed out, it was a computer game where you could design rollercoasters and manage a park.

"One of the teachers in your old school thought you'd be excellent at city design," my mother explained.

"That kinda makes sense," I said. "But it's not because I scientifically know how to design a city. I would just have the *aesthetics* down."

Don't ask me to make sure the plumbing and electricity work. But I would make sure the city looked pretty.

I love developing my own fantasy maps with coastlines, mountains, port cities, fields, and volcano craters left abandoned. I created maps for stories I would eventually write and would share these creations with my classmates, denoting where they would live and rule. I remember one map featured towns named after my friends' first and last names: "Sammyville, Mace City, Serowickin Town, Blazevic Town." At the time I thought it was the *coolest* thing. Looking back, I cringe when reminiscing about my on-the-nose artistry.

It isn't just maps that make me weird. I have an amusing attitude when it comes to inanimate objects. Take cars, for instance. My first car was a Chevrolet from the 90s. I remember it was thick and brown, the kind of car that could take up two spots and not for any good reason. It was a gas guzzler. Hummers get more gas than these cars. There weren't any fancy buttons or dohickeys, this car was meant to drive, and that was it. I was nineteen, and driving a car that crappy seemed part of the standard human experience, alongside experiencing buffalo chicken dip or having a bad experience with one type of liquor and never drinking said liquor ever again.

The concept of driving was still new to me. I had skipped the whole phase of getting my temporary driver's license at sixteen. Mainly because I didn't want to spend money taking the classes. I would watch the driver's education classes, which were an afterschool, almost extra-curricular, in a shanty classroom that looked more like a basement storage facility in the school's basement. There would be slideshows of what car accidents looked like and some serious discussion. A lot of the time, it looked like they were watching movies, like *Fast and the Furious* or something. "Don't drive like this, *kids,*" the teacher would say to a bunch of high school juniors and seniors as Van Diesel flipped a car over the highway like some Tony Hawk skateboard move.

I took my driver's exam at eighteen when I didn't have to take or pay for the class. By that point, I had plenty of experience. Driving with my dad was too easy. He'd fall asleep occasionally in the passenger seat while I sweated nervously. *Was that turn too sharp? Was I okay to run that green light?* I remember one time I missed the exit, so I had to get off at the next exit to turn around. My father, awoken by the brakes, was quite upset that we had driven past the intended exit.

"How did you miss the exit?" My father asked in a tone that implied I had not only missed the exit but rammed down five cars since and was on a destructive driving rampage that could not be stopped. Needless to say, we were back on the road, and he was back asleep soon enough.

My mother was always the more encouraging type. She was helpful early on and explained fundamental driving tips without the *Fast and Furious* visuals. After practicing in the parking lot, she wanted me to drive on the street. Nervously, I turned onto the road and went zero to forty. We screamed for a few seconds before I pulled into the next driveway, which, ironically, was the police station.

I've only had three speeding tickets in my driving history, one of which was bogus. I was caught going 40 in a 25, but every time I drive by the scene of the speeding crime, the speed limit sign says 35. Add that to my list of 'things I may never get over.'

My father is notorious for getting a speeding ticket a year, a fact that he almost boasts with bravado. While some might topically talk about their trips to Maui or their interest in medieval feudalism, my father loves to mention that he's Cleveland's equivalent of John Wayne with speeding tickets.

People say I'm reckless when driving, although I don't see it. I'm not a fan of those 'let me pump the brakes and go two miles per hour on this turn' turns. I'm not a horrific speeder, but I believe in efficiency. If the off-road route saves me two minutes, then that's the route I'll take. I'll also avoid tolls, but that's not reckless. That's economically smart. I have a habit of blaring music, podcasts, and audiobooks, but if that's reckless, then it's just as irresponsible for someone to drive in silence which is unthinkable.

My first car, that thick Chevrolet, went out with a story that my parents still hold over my head. I basically was unaware that cars needed oil changes, neglected that car like it was Oliver Twist in the orphanage, and it soon died on me. I wasn't stupid enough to *not know* about oil changes. More so...forgetful that I should do my due diligence to get an oil change. After killing that car, I was blessed to find a family friend who sold me their beat-up Trailblazer for three-hundred bucks.

I made that Trailblazer last for about two or three years. Like the Chevrolet, the truck was a gas guzzler. Taking a trip down the block was about one-eighth of the tank. It was a bit beaten up, but it had character. You'd look at my Trailblazer and think, 'Well, that car has plenty of stories. After the bumper fell off due to rusty nails, the car looked like it came out of Mad Max or some apocalyptic movie.

Having a Trailblazer meant that we frequently used my car to Shepard groups of friends to various weekend events. Most specifically, Thursday nights out to Coventry, a ten-minute drive west of campus. Coventry is like a miniature San Francisco: some drugs, some coffee, some gays, some fashion, and plenty of alternative cultures. This culture's most Caucasian college element included a local chain featuring audacious Thursday night specials, a nearby hookah bar, and some weird basement arcade place. I was more of a fan of the now-extinct La Cav, an underground wine bar that initially didn't have phone service. You had to see if your friends could talk without needing their phones.

In my Trailblazer, we could fit anywhere from seven to nine, not as comfortably, to twelve in emergency situations. We'd barrel down Cedar Road like the first space mission: cramped in and holding our breath as the Trailblazer whirled to life. If you asked me to list everyone who rode in those Trailblazer Thursdays, I'd only be able to come up with one-third of the crew. Sometimes it was friends from 'Group A,' and other times, 'Group B.' Fraternity brothers would come alongside their current romantic interests. Random friends of friends would come, people, I would never see again. It was like SNL in a car — you never know who would show up, and sometimes even when they showed up, you have no clue who they were. They would take any ride, even if the car seemed like it was going to fall apart by the wheels at any moment.

After college, the Trailblazer began to show signs of fast age. There were steering wheel issues and brake issues. Hell, the whole car was an issue. My remedies included shrugging and assuming that the vehicle would explode one day. Not in a ball of fire, but more of a soft sigh, like, 'well, sorry, Matt, it's time to be hitting the old dusty scrapyard.'

It got to the point where my mother demanded I stop driving the Trailblazer. The *'I'm driving a deathtrap'* jokes had gotten her too riled up.

"I'm afraid you're going to die in that thing." My mother confessed. "It's been keeping me up all night..."

"Really?" I questioned, doing that thing where you raise your eyebrows in a way to say, 'this sounds a tad over-exaggerated.' Many things kept my mother awake like she was some ghost medium who was visited by spiritual hauntings every night. "I thought about that part-time job you took...it kept me up all night," "I thought about where we went for lunch the other day...maybe we should have gone elsewhere, it kept me up all night."

It finally got to a point where the Trailblazer was practically undrivable. It got traded for what probably was only two cents, and I got a used Nissan Rouge 2008. The Rouge was quite an upgrade, a bit sleeker than its two predecessors. It was like when your first two college classes were with ancient old men, and then your third college class was with a younger professor whose eyes sparkled with possibility.

Like a relationship bent for a destructive finale, I was initially in pure love with my car. I loved it even when the radio died (something familiar within the car species, I'd find out). I loved my Nissan even when it had a leaky transmission, which meant I had to give it weekly oil-ups. I loved it even when the A/C and heat fan went out. That meant I drove a giant ice cube in the winter. I loved that car even without a left mirror, with its broken taillight, bumps, and dents, and even when someone smashed the entire passenger window to steal a roll of quarters out of my car. I would rather have paid the guy fifty bucks to not touch the vehicle in the first place.

My Nissan, like the Trailblazer, involved a rusted-off front bumper that gave it a Mad Max look. I decided to trade in my rolling hunk of metal to get four grand off a brand new Mitsubishi — which was an incredible deal considering that my Nissan Rouge was more like a beaten down, unhoused rouge.

It didn't take long for me to dirty the brand-new car. Like the cars before, I treated the vehicle as more than a transportation tool. It was an emergency closet — filled with clothes shed throughout the day as the sunlight kicked in and gym clothes that had been changed into or out of, left in the car for the future Matt to utilize.

Another aspect of my car that close friends and family can attest to is that it's full of recycling. My parents instilled a heavy sense of personal responsibility in me regarding recycling — to the point where I will gather my recyclables and leave them in my car to form a dumping ground of spent plastics and papers. It will get so bad that people look in my vehicle and gasp.

Part of me wonders if it's less about recycling and more about just dumping things in my car and handling it later. Recently I came across a post on social media that talked about ADHD. I had always wondered if I had ADHD but had managed to train myself to easily overcome the obstacles. So what if I couldn't swim in a straight line? I'd just learn to move straight but swim in different directions!

The post discussed how those with ADHD will only complete something if it features uniqueness, challenge, or urgency. The post explained that washing a single dish isn't unique, challenging, or urgent. A pile of dirty dishes isn't unique or challenging, but it poses urgency. So, when it becomes critical, the plates will get done.

Reading that made me gasp — for there was a giant pile of dishes that I had been ignoring — and would forget — until they absolutely consumed the kitchen, leaving me without clean plates for future meals. I had chalked up so many quirks to personality and artistic tendencies. But maybe I was justifying questionable behaviors? And the recycling in my car — was that being altruistic, or just a sign of undiagnosed things happening under the roof of my brain?

There are a few things about me that do seem a bit *different*. Some of them are little things — a penchant for asking complex or nuanced questions to strangers, talking to co-workers about personal matters way too quickly. But maybe it's not a matter of being different, but I have too much to give.

Throughout my life, I have created six alter egos who fully flesh out the ever-evolving persona of Matt Hribar.

The first persona was a music one: Hribstar, my persona that focused on my entertaining and artistic side. Hribstar would eventually become Rybar. Hribstar is the bold showstopper who sets off with a vision. He's the one who wants to put on a show and makes everything grand and opulent.

Reebs came second, unlocked like a video game avatar in freshman year. He's the competitive jock, obnoxious and loud. He will probably scream and yell throughout the match if you have him on your volleyball team. Reebs likes to work out, which is a bit too much for some people.

Father Time came out of a student union meeting where I was berating people for not having enough time. My good friend Molly has used Father Time as a nickname ever since. Father Time is the philosopher and balancer who manages time and space around him. He's quieter and harsher than the other personas — filled with my ever-abundant sense of justice and the occasional hard stance on a rule. Father Time reflects how I bind myself to specific and particular norms that the other personas otherwise ignore.

Matilda is the justice warrior and logistics queen who enjoys a good coffee. She's the one planning events and theme parties, the one sitting on councils, and the avid activist. Matilda came to be when my old roommate Dariga had to fudge that she was living with men. Instead of living with Matt and Dan, she resided with Matilda and Danielle. For Dariga's family, I became Matilda. But Matilda eventually became part of me.

Todd was created out of a discussion I had with someone random at a bar called O'Reilly's. O's was an Irish dive pub-type establishment close to college grounds. It was an excellent place for a weekday drink or five — and there were darts in the back of the bar that seemed like an incredibly risky aesthetic for drunk college people. I don't think I was ever carded at O's. They either trusted you were twenty-one or trusted you to 'shuddup about it.' I told someone about the previous four personas, and they countered with a question.

"So, are you not normal?" The stranger asked with a joke.

Is the Pope Catholic? At that time, he might have been before there was a Jesuit Pope.

"Well, I can be normal," I explained as if normality was like some hyper-final form in a cartoon where I had to unlock and push myself to some ultra-final dangerous form.

"Ya know, normal, like professionally. Or if you were to meet someone's parents, ya know?"

We all have to gloss over our personalities sometimes. And that's Todd. The traditional facade, the family-friendly archetype that wouldn't embarrass you. He wasn't the most prevalent persona, but he was deep inside and part of my personality.

Honeysuckle Ginseng is my persona who loves design, social media, drama, and gossip and is a master of relationship and sex advice. I think of her as having pink and blonde hair — done up curly and bold in a time when hairspray ruled the streets. Honeysuckle is insightful, poetic, and sensual. Like most of my other personas, she is also strong-minded and stubborn. But

Honeysuckle can easily woo you into compliance with hidden aggression.

Yung Matt came from my boss's comment, which inferred that I was young. The character that came out was aggressive, the rule-breaker, the one who got in your face. He's the boldest version that will stand up for those who cannot stand up for themselves.

I used to believe that wearing masks or framing ourselves was wrong. Why would we hide our genuine selves? We shouldn't feel like we have to put on a mask for someone, right? But then, part of me thinks that a complex soul or personality uses covers and frames to present a specific version. When I become the bland Todd — he's not taking over my whole essence. He's a slice that I'm currently utilizing for the situation. And I don't think it's fake — it's just how the world is.

You might think — but isn't that a *terrible* way to perceive the world? I might agree with you if I wasn't having fun.

My mother and I ran into an old family friend at a baseball game, Mrs. Fisher. Mrs. Fisher has two kids of her own, Eric and Erin. They are similar in age to my sister Annaliese and me. We go back to when we were younger, having met at a theater camp. My mother and Mrs. Fisher were both educators, and they bonded over that, along with having kids that got along. I can't imagine having a child be friends with another child whose parents I can't stand.

Erin, Eric, my sister Annaliese, and I ran thick as thieves at pre-teen and youth theater camps, art camps, science camps — anything enriching for some pretty challenge-needy kids. We hadn't spoken to them in a long time except for social media interactions.

"I've been meaning to reach out, but I don't have your number!" My mother exclaimed to Mrs. Fisher. Mrs. Fisher began reciting her digits, and my mother gasped.

"Oh my gosh — you're in my phone." My mother looked mortified, like she had accidentally backed over and injured a bald eagle. "I can't believe it."

Mrs. Fisher has one of those laughs of character. You know the type — a distinctive laugh that denotes an individual. You can hear that laugh and immediately recognize the person. For Mrs. Fisher, it's a quick staccato of deep-throat yet high-pitch bursts of barks.

One of the clearest moments I remember with Mrs. Fisher was when Eric and I watched television and came across *Family Guy*. Mrs. Fisher walked into the living room and was absolutely aghast. Upon sharing that story, my mother pointed out that even though my memory was awful, I seemed to remember memories with high emotional value. Back then, I wasn't just putting on my goody-two-shoes — I was runway walking and showing them off constantly. The idea of making my friend's mother upset was scary to a young kid like me.

"You know, Eric's getting *married*," Mrs. Fisher stressed the word married like she was the pastor from *The Princess Bride*.

"I think I saw that on Facebook!" I said. Eric was one of the twenty-five people that Facebook decided I should know everything about. I often disagreed with Facebook's choices, but this one was correct. I liked seeing what Eric was up to.

"Eric's making bagels now!" Mrs. Fisher exclaimed. Instantly I was both hungry for a bagel and desiring the chance to make bagels myself. One thing I loved about Eric was that he was constantly reinventing himself — whether by personal desire or the world around him. I liked to think I had the same aptitude.

It didn't take long for my mother and Mrs. Fisher to bond over childhood stories and memories of simpler times. Their favorite story involved my six-year-old self having a wardrobe malfunction. According to my mother, I often rocked commando as a youth. My poor mother had to be told one day that I should have underpants on so I didn't flash anyone while changing. Poor six-year-old Matt didn't know that he was technically flashing his child junk at many innocent bystanders.

"I remember Annaliese's starring role," Erin added. "She was one of the alcoholic angels in *Joseph and the Technicolor Dream Coat*."

"That play had *alcoholic* angels?" My eyebrows shot up in a puritan-Esque disbelief that such a wonderfully colorful, family-friendly play shouldn't have angels who have hit the bar for happy hour.

"The rendition we put on did!" Erin chuckled. "It was one of the creative decisions Mr. Schultz made."

Mr. Schultz was the director of the plays — a very bold, happy guy who knew how to put together a production and send a sassy lash against someone. He was actually the one who donned my theater camp nickname: Billy-Matt. Saying the name out loud makes me think of a version of me that sports a mullet, shoots gigantic guns, but also loves musicals. It's the name you might see on a modern re-telling of *The Little House on the Prairie*. I don't even *know* the origin of the name. I'm guessing I played a character named Billy.

"Erin's nickname at camp was Princess," Mrs. Fisher mused, which caused Erin to roll her eyes in memory. Erin might be strong and bold, but she wasn't a princess. Unless she was one of those modern Disney princesses who transcended the stereotype.

"Did he have nicknames for everyone?" I said — and if he did, were they all a bit rough?

Before we left, Erin commented how it felt like a decade hadn't passed, and I had to agree. Time is weird — you never know when the last time is. Or if it's the last time. And that goes for venues, friends, families, activities, and places... no one is actively saying, "ah, today is the last day I'll ever visit Lake Erie." You don't return and probably don't actively reminisce about it on a chaise lounge like a dramatic Jane Austen character.

Sometimes the ribbon that's been running long naturally runs out. Or it's cut dramatically, and you see the possible length of the ribbon fall to the ground. But so often the ribbon keeps rolling. Or it's reconnected — what is cut becomes glued together or taped. Or it's just a new ribbon with the same old person, place, or pleasure.

"We'll definitely see each other soon," I said, hugging Erin close. How often do we say this to figures, acquaintances, or workplace friends, who have faded into the past? We rarely know when it's the last time we see a casual friend. But this time, I meant it and hope I'm not reading this essay years later, having left another ribbon on the table, unrolled.

"You and Erin vibed more than you and Eric or Erin and Annaliese," my mother commented after we left. Maybe it was an age thing, or a gender thing — but who has time to parse demographical query about an old friendship.

That was an interesting comment from my mother, and I mused about my friendships over the years. I had friendships that spanned the gamut of diversity — but it felt like I was probably pushed to have more male friends. My closest male friend in grade school was named Joey — and he was kind of a weird kid as well. My favorite memory was when we made nachos at his parent's house, which were burnt to crisps.

"I want to be a chef when I'm older," Joey told me as we waited for charred-black nachos and cheese. The nachos had evolved into the plastic I would eventually horde in my car. My parents didn't love my friendship with Joey. I wasn't sure why until I discovered that Joey's father was a dirty forensics scientist. Maybe that was why my parents discouraged the friendship? I ended up looking him up, and he looks married, so I'm glad he didn't melt that marriage like those nachos.

"You know, Mrs. Fisher had quite the compliment for you," my mother said with a sparkle as we left the baseball park.

"What was it?" I asked — ready to hear that I was friendly, fun, or funny.

"Well, her compliment was interesting to me." My mother continued. "Because originally, I was thrown off, but the more I thought about it, the more I understood what she meant."

"Now you have to tell me what she said!" I was like one of the Willy Wonka Factory kids standing in front of the most tempting candy I've ever had.

"She said you were always listening to others — you gave them all your focus."

I agreed with my mother — I had never considered myself someone who focused in general. If anything, I had a lack of focus. What was missing from my life was a severe strain of stress. But maybe Mrs. Fisher had identified something in me that I had overlooked. Did I give others unconditional attention — focusing on their conversation and needs? Maybe sometimes.

Even in the mid-late twenties of my tiny human lifeform, I'm still confounding the binaries inside me. I'm still confronted with my own personality — as large as a giant serpentine and often shedding old skin off of itself. Add on top of that the perceptions and comments of others. Each person in my life would probably say different things — maybe similar words, but with different assigned emotions. I think they could agree, if not on the word 'weird,' that some synonym is applicable.

Chastity Shawl

For my sister's 21st birthday, my mom and I decided to plan a legendary getaway. We would take my sister to Las Vegas to celebrate her legal drinking age and see family-favorite pop artist Lady Gaga during her residency. Who wouldn't want to pound drinks, visit one of the best modern pop artists, and travel for their big twenty-first? To make it more exciting we were taking my sister's gay best friend Declan and my best friend Monica was meeting us out there. My father jumped in on the trip idea as well. June in Vegas was going to be hot, but so were we when we hit the strip.

My mother had helped plan the trip but had decided to stay behind and babysit for my sister's two young girls. Someone responsible had to lead the charge; my mother was the only option. My sister's fiance worked a lot, and my father would be flying in that Sunday (even if my dad wasn't flying in, I doubt he could fully hold down a responsible title). My dad wanted to travel to a national park, so my mother decided to reserve a rental car for us. At this point in life, I hadn't had that much experience with rental cars — mainly because I was 24 at the time of this story. I thought it was a great idea because who doesn't love national parks?

We got plane tickets on Spirit, which didn't cancel or push the flight back. It was a rare form for the cheap airline. For the first time flying on Spirit, I felt confident. Not because of Spirit, but because of the spirit of adventure that lay before us. I was correct that there would be a spirit of adventure. But the picture I had on my flight to Vegas differed from the soon-to-be reality. It would be like one of those paintings made out of dots. While making the painting, you'd think it was the best piece ever. And when the hard labor is complete, you see it looks like slop.

The Las Vegas airport is partially better than the average airport because it's clean and has bright shiny neon slot machines. I'm not a gambler; I'm merely attracted to shiny things like a bat, a moth, or someone who has taken too many party drugs. We exited the airport to arrive at the place where you pick up rental cars. I didn't have experience, but my Hollywood movie background told me that you usually just went to a desk in the airport to rent a car. We had to take a shuttle which would take us to a nearby building that housed the various car rentals.

"A shuttle doesn't seem too bad!" I said, a bit thrown, but it seemed easy enough. We'd hop over next door, grab a car, and soon find ourselves driving down the strip, hair tossed in abandon. However, when the shuttle arrived at the car rental stop, I discovered that we had to take a *second* shuttle to our car rental place. I felt like I was in the lowest class on the Titanic. While others who went with the big rental car companies were rolling to the reservation desk of their choice, we waited fifteen minutes before a more minor, cramped shuttle arrived. This shuttle wasn't as efficient or classy as our first one. This second shuttle was the offspring of a bus and a square car. Annaliese, Declan, and I would be boarding along with a couple of others, all with luggage. Talk about a clown car of people and suitcases.

"Oh my gosh," I told Annaliese and Declan. "The car rental place we're going to must be so cheap that it's even *further* away from the airport."

Annaliese did prefer the finer things but adapted well, but you could tell Declan was a fancy salmon that did not want to schlep in this country bumpkin river.

I checked the name of the car rental company—Economy. I had never heard of this brand in my life. The company name did imply cheap, so maybe I should have spent extra money on the name brand. I was curious — are we being shuttled to our deaths? Is this what happens when you're too cheap, you fall victim to a rental car scam? Imagine this second shuttle taking us to a deathhouse of horrors.

Of course, none of this happened; I can't even blame my obsession over true crime podcasts because that would blossom the following year. Soon enough, there would be a financial murder, but no physical harm would happen.

To make the situation weirder, the bus driver decided to masquerade as a tour guide. While I appreciated his attempt to entertain, he pointed out the worst things one could mention on an impromptu tour. I think it was his way of elevating the experience or apologizing for the state of the shuttle.

"This CVS right here to our right is *actually* open twenty-four-seven!" He mentioned that as if I planned to revisit the outer banks of Vegas just for a CVS.

The car rental place was in the middle of an oversized lot in the middle of the desert. Imagine a giant mall-type lot filled with gravel and used cars.

"Where are we?" I asked as we stepped out of the shuttle. The place looked deserted. It was now around 9 pm on a Friday, and I had assumed I would have had the car by now. However, this car rental place was more packed than an authentic burrito at a Mexican restaurant. We were behind at least five or six groups of people looking to get a car. Annaliese, Declan, and I joined the cue, and I could feel my energy slowly draining out of me. The older couple in front of me began to mutter.

"Do you see how the employees at the counter keep chatting with people?"

Usually, I would find fault with older adults regarding their opinion of retail and customer service workers. But I tuned in like a radio signal to the nearest reception counter to hear the car rental employee say:

"Where are you staying for your trip?" the employee behind the counter asked the couple he was currently helping. The couple genuinely answered with a couple of minutes of banter. I was aghast — this line was out of control, and the employees and customers were wasting time talking about the Hilton Hotel's benefits packages?! This was not the time for a trip to *Small Talk City*; this was the time for a speedy journey on, *Let's Hurry It Up Town*! It's one thing if the small talk is happening during the transaction, such as when a Trader Joe's employee asks if you've had the new mango guacamole while they ring out the fifty pre-made meals I've added to my cart.

While I waited for the customers to finish giving their life stories, I was mentally preparing to quickly get through the eventual conversation with my future reception employee nee discussion partner. My mother had booked the car for the trip and had told me she had gotten it for a hundred bucks. All I had to do was show up and pay for the vehicle. Easy. And at this point, the hassle for a hundred-dollar total car rental seemed worth it, even with Annaliese and Declan mewing like cats. Except at least cats don't keep saying, "*ugh*, this is so *slow*; I just want to get to the hotel room."

Finally, we approached the counter, and the employee explained that I had to put down a two-hundred-dollar deposit. No stress! And then he calculated the remaining fees, which came to a total of six hundred and twenty-eight bucks. I felt my body buckle under the pressure as if the jury had found me guilty of murder. I should have known that a hundred-dollar car rental for four days was impossible. But even a more conservative estimate of four or five hundred bucks was instantly shattered by this 'economic' price point. Technically, I was going to get two-hundred dollars back (or was I?). But I still can't believe I was about to put this much on my card.

Reasonable people might ask, "why did you spend the money on the car? Why didn't you walk away and order an Uber?" The thought didn't cross my mind at all. Annaliese and Declan were now muttering how they were hungry and thirsty and wanted to change and hit the strip. They were like two adult children; I was the sober chaperone ready to abandon them at a fire station. We were in the middle of *Nowhere, Nevada* — potentially even across the state border. Best fried Monica had flown in earlier and asked for travel reports. Monica was worried because it was getting close to club time at Caesar's Palace, and if we got there too late, we might not make it in.

I could feel the stress building up, and I was willing to do whatever I needed to do to get out of that car rental place in the middle of nowhere. I begrudgingly handed my credit card over like submitting ransom money for a WASP's young child. Moments later, we were in the car and on the way to the hotel.

Driving that decently nice car down the strip was worth some of the money I spent. And trust me — I made sure we got our money's worth. We did a drive through the desert that weekend that was gorgeous — soaking up the desert as if making an artistic interpretation of *A Horse With No Name*. We also drove up to the classic Las Vegas sign that everyone knew. My dad and I would even take the car to Utah. But I still didn't know if the rental car was worth the financial compensation. My wallet vehemently disagrees.

My mother also handled the hotel booking. It's not that I was incapable of handling the hotel booking. We had planned that my mother would come, and we split some of the pre-vacation work duties. My mother booked the hotel and found the hundred dollars total car rental was actually six hundred and twenty-eight bucks. I got the Lady Gaga tickets. There was a clear distinction between our skills and abilities.

"The hotel is Travelodge." My mother had informed me before I had left. "It's close to the airport."

The proximity of the closeness to the airport didn't bother me, considering we had an expensive rental car that was going to shuttle us around. The hotel could have been forty miles from the airport, which would have been okay because we had a shiny rental car. Any decently-knowledged Vegas tourist knows precisely where the Travelodge is. It's in the middle of the strip and was the only simple hotel around for blocks. The vast majority of the Las Vegas strip hotels were the physical embodiment of the phrase: *"the party's here, boys."* The Travelodge on the strip stood stoic and plain around the peacocking hotels. This hotel was like a nerdy girl in an 80s movie who takes off her glasses to reveal a subtle cuteness. To me, this was the perfect win: we would be in the heat of the action without paying for access that my poor, middle-class bank account could not afford.

We arrived at the Travelodge in our rental car, and I recalled the information that the hotel had free parking, which felt like my first win since landing in Vegas. We took our bags and belongings to the front desk reception to check in. The hotel and our group quickly discovered that we did *not* have a reservation at the hotel.

"What do you mean?" I said in a half-Karen approach. "Isn't this the Travelodge?"

"Can I see your reservation email confirmation?" The receptionist cooly asked. I handed over my phone with a tinge of satisfaction. He will see the email and apologize by blaming the system. To apologize, we might be upgraded to the Presidential Suite equivalent that the Travelodge offers — maybe the Mayoral Chambers? The Comptroller's Lounge?

"Ooh, I see the problem." The receptionist said with a nod. "This happens on occasion. We're the Travelodge on the *Strip*. You've reserved a room at the Travelodge by the *airport*."

My bruised pride and ego accepted the mistake graciously and thanked the man. We piled back into the rental car and headed to our actual hotel. As we left the strip, we could see all the fun amenities twinkling goodbye as if saying, '*you* could *have had this*.' The Travelodge on the strip was in the *middle* of the Vegas strip. The Travelodge by the airport was out in the boonies of Las Vegas, *right* next to the airport. You could walk to the protective airport fencing in two minutes from our room. The hotel probably qualified as one of those hotels the airlines would put up people in if their flights were postponed for a day. The hotel wasn't just off the strip; it was off the strip and then ten blocks over.

Even for a minimal hotel, the Travelodge by the airport was depressing. The parking lot was covered with broken rundown cars next to an abandoned swimming pool closed for construction that I feared wasn't coming. People hung out outside their rooms as if searching for prey. It wouldn't surprise me if this was a place that dealt with drug distribution or illegal sex work. Arriving back at this hotel to find a murder scene would have felt on brand for the hotel as well.

Our room was also sad. It was the hotel a recently divorced man might stay in after his wife says to get out of the house. I would have been worried had the hotel room come with a mini-bar. Declan and Annaliese were the people who would accidentally crack open a ten-dollar bottle of water or go on a candy binge and fail to realize the stack of charges coming our way. I liked cheap stays — but even I would have shelled out Economy-car rental cash to stay in a slightly better situation. For four nights — I was paying over four hundred for this dump. And we didn't even have a *pool*. In *summer*. In *Vegas*.

In this moment of realization, I felt like I was in an early 2000s comedy movie. All these friends gather for a fun Vegas weekend only to discover the illusions they believed in had fallen to waste. This set-up was rife with natural comedy and growing conflict. Monica was still continuously texting me because we had to hurry to see Zedd at the Coliseum. Monica had booked a cheaper hotel which was *actually* on the strip. Her hotel was a fifteen-minute walk from our hotel, which meant we were fifteen minutes off the strip. I was jealous that Monica was *on* the strip, but mainly that she had paid less for her stay.

After looping to grab Monica, we arrived at Coliseum moments later — looking pretty decent for people who had completed a plane trip, an extensive car rental hassle, and a hotel switch-up. It was a summer Friday night in Vegas, so the place was slammed. People were here to party, drink, gamble, and celebrate a few vices. It didn't matter if the DJ was Zedd or your cousin who gets the aux cord and ruins the mood with his music choices.

"Let's get in line," Monica pointed to the line of people waiting for Zedd. We discovered that while Monica and Annaliese would get into the club for free, Declan and I would have to each pay a hundred bucks to get in. On my previous trips to Las Vegas, I had only hit a little of the nightlife. I would go out late at night and bar hop, but I wasn't trying to be part of the young, hip, boozy culture of Las Vegas.

In a world that continuously bolstered men and demeaned women, I liked the idea of a reverse-patriarchal system where women were free, but men had to pay. Even if the justification was that women were sexy and could lure men in for money. It still felt like the patriarchy was benefiting somehow in this whole system. If you are a man who wants to know what it's like being a woman, visit the Las Vegas nightclub. It's just super hashtag fun! You will be disrespected, ripped off, and abused — but don't worry.

I'm way too frugal to pay a hundred dollars to get into a club to dance. If I had been drunk, I would have paid that much or had casual amnesia about the fact that I had paid that much. I would have paid if I had only spent a hundred bucks at the car rental place. Declan also bowed out, so we decided to gamble and walk around for the evening. Eventually, my sister decided it was late and left the Zedd concert. Monica would go on to work her way to a great seat in the show; her words and beauty a persuasion that no VIP ticket holder could refuse. That was a whimsical night. Annaliese, Declan, and I cruised the strip at midnight, taking many photos like the Kardashians and creating content.

Part of the reason I love visiting Las Vegas isn't for the clubs, or the strip clubs, or the clubs that are half club and part pool. I attend Vegas specifically for the club sandwiches and various crudité of a Las Vegas buffet. This story was pre-pandemic. While a pandemic made me swear off buffets for a long time, I will forever buckle under the beauty of a Vegas buffet. They're full of lush desserts, brimming salad bars, meats of all designs, seafood delights (none for me), and international cuisine that tastes pretty good for what I'm assuming is not an international kitchen. It is the best hour-and-a-half you can spend in the city of sin. You could pay twenty bucks for a burger in Vegas, but why not pay forty or fifty for a fountain of food?

    I'm a systematic buffet eater — I always go for expensive foods, foods you can't get at home, and meats. I *love* a good salad but never waste my time with dollar bag-lettuce at a Vegas buffet. You have to take advantage of the system by getting steaks, sous vide, and Eggs Benedict for breakfast. And sometimes, you could smuggle an apple for a snack later in the day if you don't appear too conspicuous.

    Saturday morning, we decided that the first buffet on our to-try list was the Wynn. The Wynn is classy and decorated with flower arrangements and a significant waterfall feature. There was no comparison to venues like Hooters that hosted dollar blackjack. We weren't staying at The Wynn because we were fresh out of sugar daddies who could afford the room price. But you didn't have to stay at the Wynn to eat at the buffet. We were hungry due to the booze, and it had been roughly ten or twelve hours since last night's Taco Bell Cantina stop. The line was long, as if we were waiting to ride a roller coaster at Cedar Point. The main difference was that we weren't waiting for a two-minute adrenaline rush on a steel monster. We were preparing to open our jaws wide like miniature steel jaws of life to eat. The goal was always to eat more than the price of admission. It's almost an ancient art form to internally calculate a rough idea of what you ate versus how the food you ate at the buffet could be charged a la carte.

    We paid for our buffet table and waited too long to sit. Something was wrong, but I wasn't sure what it was. It's probably the feeling soldiers have in movies when they think there's a bomb, and it turns out to be a bomb and said bomb explodes. The tragedy is that had the soldier followed his gut, the bomb wouldn't have killed members of his squad.

    A woman who reeked of managerial talent approached us. She was holding a shawl in her left hand, and her knuckles were gripped more than my anticipation to wreck this buffet. The shawl within her grip resembled something an old lady might wear to church or a shawl you would confuse for a fancy napkin at a French restaurant. It was a retched mustard yellow color like grade-school puke or cheddar cheese past its prime. The shawl desired to be gold but fell into a murky mustard yellow that would never be welcomed on any hot dog. One glance at the shawl told me that whoever previously owned this ancient artifact was not disappointed in leaving it behind. This was a piece of clothing you could easily abandon in your travels or best lost in the far reaches of your closet. You would be disappointed to find that you even *owned* this shawl. You'd look at the shawl and wonder: *How did I get here? Why would I purchase this in the first place? Had I ever worn that shawl? It may be true what the locals in the town village say; I have no fashion sense.*

And how had this supervisor come into possession of the shawl? Was it her personal shawl? If this was the case, I needed the Fashion Police to arrest this woman on the spot; no arrest warrant required. And where had this shawl been? Was it used to wipe spills at tables? A fancy rag the cleaning staff utilized when customers weren't around? Had the shawl been a lost item, and the manager held it on behalf of lost and found? Maybe the manager was trying to run after someone who had left their vintage shawl behind the table.

"Ma'am, ma'am!" The manager cried out with a croaky broken voice of desperation to find the shawl's original owner. "You almost left without taking this ugly piece of fabric with you! Don't worry. Here at the Wynn buffet, we will always ensure you don't leave anything behind."

But instead of any of those scenarios that had quickly whipped into my creative yet arguably neurotic brain, something unexpected happened entirely. The manager aimed her sights at us, locking on us like a cartoon villain ready to unleash their plan. We were like the enemy submarine, and she was the missile launching. The manager held the shawl like a young man might pick up a sock that he had disgustingly utilized for dirty shenanigans. Finally she spoke, addressing Monica individually:

"Miss, I'm going to have to ask you to wear this." The manager's tone and eye glance were both judgmental in nature, as if we were kissing cousins or demanding to bring cannibalism back in vogue. It was a judgment that both disapproved of our existence and suggested we were utterly ignorant of her and society's perspective. I could see her clocking out of her shift, driving home to her lovely condo, and venting to her partner, sibling, roommate, neighbor, or cat: "you wouldn't *believe* what happened at the Wynn hotel today."

Monica accepted the shawl, holding it like it had anthrax. I can't believe Monica grabbed onto the shawl in the first place. The shawl carried foreboding energy that made me instinctively back away. Looking into it was like staring into a hole that led to hell.

"*Where* am I supposed to wear this?" Monica guffawed, looking between me, Annaliese, Declan, and the supervisor. Annaliese, Declan, and I had no answers to give Monica. I felt like I was on a game show, and it was my turn to provide a solution. I genuinely was speechless and doing a poor imitation of the shrug emoji. Monica had a bare midriff, an open stomach and backside, and booty shorts. There were multiple skin locations, all of which qualified for the supervisor's shawl. If there was an issue with Monica's bare skin, many places could be the problematic region. And for the record, Monica looked fantastic.

The supervisor sighed as if the answer to Monica's question was evident and we were too stupid to piece together the logic. We were tempting her customer service skills to break out into hellfire. The supervisor did a small closed roll of the eyes on the verge of opening their lids for the entire roll effect. The supervisor pointed her finger at Monica as if pointing to the town witch and signaling everyone to grab their fire, rocks, and rope.

"We have a dress policy, and those shorts are too short for our policy."

The supervisor demanded that Monica wrap this crusty shawl around her waist to hide her tanned upper thighs from the room. I looked around the room to see what the enforced dress policy was. A lot of brunch guests were wearing sweatpants. Some of those sweatpants had text scribbled across the cheeks in various proclamations like 'Wildcats' and 'Juicy.' Some proudly wore tattered rags, while the average buffet attendee had donned short pieces of clothing with something on display. It was well over a hundred degrees — and most people had dressed accordingly. Monica and Annaliese had forgotten to bring their robes to keep men's wandering eyes in check. I doubted anyone was worried about seeing Monica's upper thighs at the buffet. Most men were so full from the limitless buffet situation to become *fully* aroused.

Our arrival was an emergency for the Wynn hotel buffet staff. Walkies Talkies crackled with, '*code red, code red! Improper dress code situation.*' Men donned SWAT gear designed to stop sexy women from arousing them. Mr. Wynn *himself* would be abreast of the situation revolving around Monica's almost visible lower butt cheek. Whoever had allowed us to pay already for the buffet would be fired for gross incompetence.

"What happened to Shirley?" a staff member would ask.

"Shirley let some harlot wear shorts and almost allowed some trash through," a different staff member would explain.

"We can't have someone at the Wynn allowing a clothes-denying tart through the buffet line!"

The mustard shawl had been locked behind glass like a fire extinguisher, imprisoned like Han Solo in Star Wars. Or maybe the shawl was stuck at the bottom of a lost-and-found pile. Employees scrounged around to find something respectable for Monica to wear. Possibly they had borrowed the shawl from a visitor or employee.

"Ma'am, you're well dressed today like a *proper* woman," The supervisor had said to someone. "May we use your shawl to turn this scarlet-lettered slut into a mustard-shawled woman?"

Did The Wynn *themselves* sell the shawl? Maybe it was from the 1980s, and nobody had purchased it, so it was in the back storage room of the gift shop with the audacity to be on sale for an exuberant forty dollars. But that situation felt too fancy for such a musty-looking shawl. Instead, I bet the supervisor ran to the kitchen, sweat pouring down her neck:

"Kitchen staff," she called out, trying to remain calm about the Defcon-5 situation brewing at the pay desk in the front of the buffet. "We have a woman who has decided to dress like any woman you'd see on the Vegas Strip. Does anyone have *anything* we can wrap her in to hide her from God's heavenly sight?"

But maybe I was overthinking this whole situation. What if the shawl had come out of the supervisor's mammoth-sized knockoff-brand name purse? The supervisor used her manicured nails to dig deep, bypassing a Luna Bar, some crumpled receipts, and some compact that she didn't bother putting on in the first place. And there, shining with a halo, was the shawl. It sat at the bottom of the purse like a murky, mysterious underground lake. And with the shawl in tow, the supervisor confronted the whore who dared to wear booty shorts to a Las Vegas buffet.

At this point, Monica still held onto the natty shawl with as few fingers as possible. Monica pushed her hand forward, offering the shawl back to the manager.

"I'm not wearing this," Monica muttered with an outstanding balance of reason and sass. The supervisor looked offended as if Monica had tossed the rag in her face. Before the supervisor could take a deep breath and blast Monica to the next dimension, Monica came up with a shawl-free option:

"What if I just pull my shorts down a bit?"

Monica probably had a good inch of fabric that could hide some of her upper thighs without exposing her other sensitive region. The supervisor grabbed the shawl and held it as if she was Mary Magdalene clutching the cloth used to wipe Jesus' face. Monica rearranged her shorts, which didn't evoke that much of a difference. The supervisor cocked her head twenty degrees to the right as if she was a curious bird or if she needed to crack her neck. Was the head-cocking supposed to help her in any way?

"Well, are the shorts going to *stay* that way?" The supervisor asked, implying that Monica was lying merely to eat roast sirloin. Once free of the clutches of the modesty police, Monica would slide her pants up to showcase her assets.

"Yes..." Monica said, a bit thrown off but willing to do anything for food. I was stifling a laugh and nodding as if I was personally going to watch Monica's shorts for any possible shenanigans. I was the Night's Watch, but for shorts. The supervisor balled up the shawl and then allowed us to be seated.

We were then led through the Wynn buffet, filled with people who barely met the dress code themselves. People who had their own battles against Modesty: thin spaghetti straps, bras hanging a bit loose and wild, shorts that were just an inch lower than Monica's own, sandals that displayed an assortment of feet. Everywhere you looked seemed to host a violator on the cusp of their own chastity shawl.

I felt like one of those creepy older men who stare down at a beautiful woman — with or without proactive clothing. But I noticed more violations that had gone unnoticed.

I felt the supervisor's eyes for our entire buffet stay. The supervisor must have been worried that her classy Wynn buffet establishment would fall apart due to one beautiful woman's derrière. I imagined her gritting and grinding her teeth as if she were sanding down corn in a mortar bowl with a pestle. This disapproving stare from the supervisor wasn't the first of its kind. But her attitude that we would ruin everything known to man was humorous. All around us, people shoveled buckets of food into their mouths, most likely unoffended by the flesh. Unlike the supervisor, the fellow buffet attendees were aware that worse sins happened in Las Vegas.

Monica spent her Saturday at the pool while Declan, Annaliese, and I explored and eventually saw Lady Gaga. There is beautiful magic to a Las Vegas residency. Especially with a famous artist in a cozy small theater. We ended the night earlier since Annaliese and Declan had an early flight. My dad, the king of Vegas, would fly in tomorrow morning. Monica was staying through till Tuesday along with my dad and I.

My father and I planned to spend Sunday going to Zion National Park.

"I specifically want to go to this place called Angel's Landing," my father told me leading up to the trip, "I heard it's nice."

I didn't have any knowledge of the park or its specifics. But I loved nature even though I wouldn't declare myself a hiker; I enjoyed walking amongst nature. Usually, the hikes I love are flat and filled with gorgeous scenery. For some reason, we only brought a couple of bottles of water, no snacks, and no proper gear. I was dressed as more of a tourist wearing activewear than someone trying to accomplish a hike.

We arrived at Zion around 11 or noon to find a bustling park. When we arrived, the sun was beginning its afternoon peak. The sun was beating down on people like a landlord looking for rent money. Hikers would tell you that starting your hike this late in the day is a bad idea. The idea is that you're finishing the challenging parts of your trek by the time the sun gets decently high in the sky.

The sun and I don't have that great of a relationship either. I'm quick to burn thanks to my Irish ancestral blood, which probably comes from a history of cave-dwelling humans and natural grey and cloudy skies. In the past, I've blistered, burned, seared, and cooked my way through hazardous and painful situations that make me cautious.

Zion itself is free, but the parking is not. It feels a bit of a tease — like a free appetizer, but the entree is double the price to offset the cost of the free appetizer. After paying way too much to park, we climbed into the shuttle ride to go deep into the Zion wilderness. The shuttle ride was non-eventful, but I was constantly perking up due to the overhead voice-overs. A series of messages came over the muffled low-def shuttle speakers featuring everyone who worked at the Zion National Park.

"Hi, it's Mark from the recycling plant at the canyon. Just a reminder not to throw bottles in the park!"

"Hey, it's Janine from animal rescue. Please don't feed the animals in the park! They survive on their natural diet!"

Some of the voice messages felt like a bit of a stretch:

"Hi, this is Julie from concessions! The perfect meal to eat here is our new seasonal pumpkin bread."

The reminder about park recycling felt valid. The message about the seasonal slices of bread felt gratuitous.

The first stop was where we got on — at the visitor's center. Here you could spend tens of dollars on Zion-related merchandise and various hiking and camping gear. The second stop was for a museum; not a single soul exited to visit the little building.

"We're here at the museum!" the pre-made voice message exclaimed — but no one matched the excitement in our shuttle. I felt badly because while I did love a good museum, I didn't *come* to Zion for a *museum*. It was like going to a wine night, and someone suggesting a whole bottle of beer — not the mood or on the agenda.

The third stop was a two-minute walk from the museum, which didn't warrant a separate stop. The third stop didn't need to exist at all. Why stop twice in the same tenth of a mile?

The fourth stop was a rest center — but if the museum and visitor's center acted as resting areas, why would a rest center also be needed? Don't the places that have benches and water count as rest centers? Finally, the shuttle lurched forward into the actual park.

"It's Lindsay from Marketing, here at the park —"

The bus could explode into giant cartoony flames, but the voice-over and speaker system would survive the wreckage. While human bodies fell in scarlet flames, the speaker system continued to droll on and on about the park.

Stop seven is finally around the corner, and VoiceOver explains that to the left is a beautiful riverwalk with a waterfall.

"And to the right is Angel's Landing, which is a more strenuous hike," the lady said in a relaxing tone.

When I hear the word strenuous, I think hard but accomplishable. For instance, trying to do a Costco run and pay less than a hundred dollars was strenuous. An hour on the elliptical was harrowing. Both those examples allow you to fail, but it would be okay. Spending one hundred and fifty bucks at Costco or exercising for 30 minutes on an elliptical would be *fine*. But the description of this hike as strenuous felt wrong. This hike deserved a more accurate title: murderous.

The road to Angel's Landing tricks you because the journey starts with a flat route that slowly inclines into the canyon overpass. You realize there's been an incline at some point, but you've been powering through it nicely.

"Is *this* the strenuous trail?" I wondered, feeling confident in my amateur hiking ability.

Then the elevation increases, but it's still decently flat. You've begun to notice the incline difference and are slowing down. The word 'strenuous' might come into play here.

The third leg of the hike is the switchbacks. Switchbacks are zig-zag paths carved into the canyons. You'd steeply walk twenty feet upwards to your left and then stop at a landing. You'd turn around, walk twenty feet upwards to your right, and stop at a landing. This would repeat multiple times in a grueling monotonous way. You're zigging and zagging, swinging up the canyon in a straight upward line. The hike was *definitely* strenuous at this point. Part of me wondered why my father thought we could accomplish this hike.

There was some competition playing out here. Both my father and I didn't want to be viewed as 'lesser.' I purposefully and continuously set my hiking pace, so I was always faster and ahead of my father. My father quite often jokes about things that he has issues over. He would never think of himself as robust but would constantly point out that I have a voluptuous figure. In my defense, thick is trendy at the moment. For me, this was not a father-son hike. This hike was a significant chance to prove that my young vigor was no match for his older, fragile self.

We arrived at what I thought might be the halfway point. We were over an hour in and now incorporating breaks. Other hikers around us heading down the mountain were encouraging us, but also gave us their estimation on how far we had left in our hike.

"Oh, you're halfway there!"

"You're like one-third through the hike."

"I'd say two-fifths finished with your ascent."

Time is not art. The varying estimates in the grand scheme of the hike left me more confused. It was like asking for an estimate on how many eggs one needed for a batch of cookies. You might need three or four eggs for the recipe. One wouldn't say it could be two, three, five, seven, or ten eggs. You'd look stupid and unknowledgeable. But people confidently provided outlier time estimates to the point where I had to scrap all the data and assume we were far along.

We reached this point in the hike where a natural wind tunnel formed — cooling our faces down under the afternoon sun. This stranger explained to my father and I what was to come.

"You'll have a flat road for a bit, then switchbacks, and then *many* switchbacks."

I was grateful for the flat road, and the next switchbacks turned out to be easier than the former ones. Maybe I had grown accustomed to the switchbacks? Had these cursed path patterns turned me into a better hiker? Those superhero movies always feature people whose training kicks their butt yet makes them the best in their field. Perhaps I was going through my superhero training. Any confidence I had was shattered upon the final series of switchbacks which proved to be steeper, more in number, and simply crushing. I was constantly stopping to catch my breath. My muscles were on fire. The sun was now at its maximum height and beating on me as if whacking me with its purse I tried to steal.

All the agony washed away as soon as we arrived at the top plateau. It was one of those moments where you were thankful to be on this earth and see the creation spread before you. God forbid, but my hike wasn't too bad compared to what *could* have happened. But even a sprained wrist, a hungry stomach, or a couple of bruises would be easily made up for this view of heaven on earth.

From this plateau, you could see a smaller mountain ahead where you'd rappel on chains to reach the mountain's true summit. We were at the 'pre-summit,' where most people climbed to and returned. The remaining chain-rope climb to the top was not recommended for anyone unless they were advanced hikers. Considering my father and I had both the personality and look of the two old men from The Muppets, I instantly ruled that out for us.

"Should we go on?" my dad said, a small glimmer of excitement in his eyes as he looked at the bare chain rope dangling and dancing in front of us.

"We can't do that!?"

"Are you sure?" My father looked skeptical as if I doubted our ability to crack a joke or drive a car in a straight line. At that moment, one of us was pretty sure of our limitations. The other was ignorant at worst and naive at best.

"It took us three or four hours to get here," I muttered, swiveling a burnt hand to indicate that we were currently three hours deep on one-half of our climb. "There's just no way we are going to make that. We would *plummet.*"

While I sometimes bend reality a bit to my visions, my father can have a misguided sense of what is achievable and what isn't. I remember one family trip he convinced me to throw some stock in crypto. It was right when crypto was hitting a solid peak. Thanks to my dad's investment advice, I lost a couple of hundred dollars. (I took that advice because he usually knows what he's talking about when it comes to money.)

Thankfully, I convinced my father that we should return to the earth's crust and not chain rope our way to the sky. For all I know, my words had no effect on my father, who just noticed exclusively fit people going further up the chains. I'm sure if you talked to my dad now, he'd say: "Well, we *could* have climbed to the top." Blindside my father with evidence, and he'd say, "We made the *right* choice to abandon our hike."

I can't even say I hiked down to the bottom. It was more of a rolling and falling trip, like a minor snowball bouldering down a blizzard mountain. I don't even remember the car ride back to Vegas — that's how overcome I was by my heat stroke. I remember being slumped in the passenger seat, spread out like a body you might find at the beginning of a true crime show. I flirted with death that day. There are only a couple of times in my life when I briefly believed I would die. Once, a friend gave me a weed gummy that was 400mg of THC. That's the equivalent of handing a missile launcher to someone who has never even held or operated a handgun.

I found out more about Angel's Landing *after* we did the hike. People fall off of Angel's Landing *all* the time. Multiple deaths were attributed to people falling off the chain or sections of the path that were a bit lackluster. My friend Paul told me that he and his wife were training to do Angel's Landing, and even they decided that the hike would be too much for them. Knowing my father, I doubt he knew Angel's Landing was chaotic. I bet he saw a beautiful picture and decided he wanted to see it.

That night, we celebrated with the best buffet in Vegas — the Caesar Palace's buffet. Monica joined us, and between my father and Monica, six crabs found themselves defaced and ripped apart and served with butter and sauce. While I sat looking comatose and burnt, Monica was being hit on by two guys as she pounded down crabs.

"I'm with my family," Monica said — pointing to my father, who was also eating crab legs as if we had been stuck in Zion for the last week. I probably was serving Blair Witch Project with my spaceless eyes that had seen much on our hiking adventure.

"I'm not your dad," my father misread the situation like a typical white father in his forties.

"You're silly," I told my dad, trying to cover his error so that these boys didn't try and steal Monica away. Later that night, Monica and I got into a pool party club situation. Since I was a guy, I was paying twenty dollars a drink. Monica continued using her shawl-less thighs, bright smile, and fantastic personality to siphon free drinks from men. She even managed to get me a couple — which proves how excellent she is at flirting and what a great friend she is to me.

The following morning we were all heading back home. Monica was the flyer who wanted an accurate time of when she would arrive via plane. She didn't care if she had to spend a couple hundred more if it meant that there would be no delays and a bit more legroom. Meanwhile, my father and I didn't mind a couple of hours lost if it meant that the plane ticket cost under one hundred dollars.

I was desperate to get back home so I could adequately rest. My desire was a jinx because Spirit Airlines delayed our flight. I leaned back in one of those uncomfortable airport chairs from the 1960s. A lady with a small child and dog was distraught at this natural phenomenon of lateness. She complained loudly to the front desk agent as if she had never heard of a late flight. I noticed she was dragging her dog on the leash and upon closer inspection, saw that the dog had three legs. Instead of giving the animal time to walk, she decided to drag the dog behind her. She looked like a toddler who wasn't strong enough to lift an object thoroughly. Thus, she had no choice but to move their own body and allow the thing to billow after them.

"That poor dog," I muttered to my dad who was napping in the airport. While I needed the proper space, time, mood lighting, background media, and mindset to nap, my father could fall asleep anywhere. He was notorious for napping during his lunch in his workplace's auditorium, sleeping in cars during the daytime, and even napping while sitting in uncomfortable chairs or on old sofas. It was genuinely admirable that he slept peacefully while jackpot machines blared with alarms and clinking coins in front of people complaining about their flights.

Eventually, Spirit Airlines was able to get themselves together, and we boarded the plane. I sat down and pulled out my media devices. While listening to music, I heard a soft commotion and people staring heavily at the front of the plane. I remember seeing a few hostesses gathered, positioned around the lady who had dragged her dog from earlier.

"What's happening?" I asked, curious as to what was happening. This was before masks and the Karen memes.

"Her son wouldn't stop kicking the seat in front of him, and his mother is *defending* her son's kicking!" the person across the aisle summarized for me. Sometimes I feel badly for kids who have bad parents. But then I remember bad parents often raise *bad* children. Even if I paid a hundred dollars on a Spirit airplane that showed up three hours late and was held together with duct tape, I would expect a kid-kicking-free flight.

The stewards, who had gathered together to form a Justice League of customer service workers who had enough, were now asking the lady to leave with her dog and child. The plane's attitude was shifting from curious fervor to demanding blood. If this were the Roman Coliseum, the plane's hand would signal a lower 'to-kill' position. Finally, with direct threats involving an air marshal or police officer, the woman stood up with her child.

At that moment, I began to clap. The entire plane joined in with me, a cacophony that indicated that the aircraft was right to remove this woman, her kid, and her poor dog from the flight. They left to the sound of applause — although I like to think, in some weird way, I was applauding the fact that I had made it out of Vegas. I might not have had a lot of money and lost some years due to the heat of Zion. Hell, I might always shame myself in the mirror because of that buffet supervisor. But at least I wasn't causing a scene on a plane because I had *some* dignity and knowledge. Just not enough grace and wisdom to arrive fully clothed at a buffet.

A Lack of Decorum

    I've been called out on several occasions for my unprofessional attitude. I take pleasure from the criticism as if it's a secret compliment. My strengths include a genuine, authentic, and sometimes raw personality. Sometimes people confuse these things with 'mean.'
    "I'm just being honest!" Says a person who is just soul-suckingly rude.
    I believe that I just eschew traditional professionalism. My niceties are also part of my genuine self. I only become rude when someone is rude to me. That's when my New Testament ideology gets thrown out for some classic eye-for-an-eye rumbling.
    Besides, who is labeling or describing themselves as 'professional' anyway? Who conveys their personality as 'professional?' Are people defining themselves as professional and clean-cut? Do people love wearing a suit and tie and selling something to a client around the clock? I get enjoying your work, but I doubt people want the politico *around* their work.

People can dress up, put on fake smiles, and pretend to be elevated demigods. But I prefer someone nice with the occasional smack. Or a polite individual that has a rare uncouth moment. Some of the nicest people I know have their moments, whether it's tough love, genuine upset, or little anger that piles into a volcano that happens to explode for the first time in a long time. There's a saying that everyone is born with an internal instinct to kill. So if that's true, we're just savages pretending to wear proper clothes and diamonds, right?

My viewpoint was confirmed by my first '*corporate*' job. Even the word corporate feels like depression put on a horrid disguise in word form. This company really prided itself on its corporate attitude. The irony was that this company was messier than a wig store after an extensions sale. One of the main focuses were digital assets, but our digital media department was understaffed, regionalized, overworked, and out of touch. When COVID hit, we fired — I mean, '*furloughed*' — that division to bones. It's like a shoe store not having people to make, sell, promote, distribute or handle shoes.

Like a good chunk of awful corporations, this company tried to pass around duties like they were leftover food. "Would you like to do Sandra's old job? We're firing Michael, but if anything, we need people to do *double* Michael's old duties."

Recently, I talked with a restaurant supervisor who told me about all the things he had to 'give up' to become a supervisor.

"I miss the basic things," he sighed, as if imagining a lost Atlantis or an old dog who had since passed. "I can't go out for a smoke in the parking lot anymore..."

In leu of professional advancement, this poor young man can no longer vape nicotine in the neighboring paved lot. Truly a lost American dream.

I've become increasingly disillusioned with working in America over the years, but the pandemic made me start seeing red. Increased responsibilities and demands paired with stagnant, if not decreased, wages due to inflation. This, coupled with the 'essential' labeling were quickly discarded as soon as things became 'normal.' I used to go the extra mile across the board. But now, in a beautiful small personal resistance, I decided I didn't feel obliged to go the extra mile if organizations, people, or events warranted it.

And there were plenty of things that I didn't even need to go half a mile for. Too much time in corporate workplaces is focused on the mundane or idiotic. Instead of devoting time to achieving valuable work, we'd have ridiculous long-winded conversations about motivation. Issues as big as sugar packets would evolve into problems the size of a whole sugarcane field.

An example was when a *whole* department complained that I dressed too 'skimpy' for work. Imagine that the entire Finance Department at your workplace complained about you wearing a tank top. HR sent me an email saying, 'hey, love you, but this is a business, not the Aéropostale summer clothing advertisement.' If Elon Musk offered my company millions of dollars to expand our clothing policy to include tanks, I'd be free to become a borderline nudist at work.

My boss talked to me about what was called "TankGate." And just to clarify — it was not a thin-strapped tank. It was an ordinary tank that showed off a little upper shoulder and peak of the chest. And for reference: I don't see or talk with clients, and I'm alone in an office. There's no reason to dress up since the only people that see me only see me walking by them in the halls.

"I get that clothes can be expensive on your salary." My boss began. "But maybe you can go thrifting or something?"

Maybe if the company paid me a livable salary, I could afford some nice clothes. I will not wear *nice* clothes when the company pays me poor-middle class wages. That feels like I'm *encouraging* the piss-poor pay. I imagine my boss witnessing my professional outfit and saying, "Wow, look what he can *afford* on the abysmal salary!"

Management made it clear that they believed we were overpaid. As if we were millionaires doing thousandaire work. Half of the time, the staff made it so minuscule that they had no choice but to get extra work for cash. It's pretty sad for a 'successful' company to be paying unlivable wages. Some companies seem hellbent on making sure their employees' *look* the part. Standardized uniforms might be one of the worst things in America. Why can't people wear a hat or a name tag? Why do we need to look like the company molested us in branding?

"You should dress for the job you *want*." My boss added in the meeting carved out to discuss professional dress wear. I *was* dressing for the job I wanted. The job I wanted was to not be here at all. If you think I'm dressed 'poorly' but don't pay me money to buy clothes, you have two choices: let me dress how I want, or pay me more, and I'll buy the clothes you want. And if I presented that scenario to my boss, he would have been like:

"You know what, dress like a prom dumpster, baby. I'll talk to Linda, Linda, Linda, and Linda over in Human Resources. You can wear tank tops as long as we don't have to pay you a living wage!"

These professional optics and demands came from the same company that *refused* to have a proper working bathroom. I don't expect the Hilton Hotel VIP bathroom with homemade poo pourri, scented candles, wicker doors, and walls instead of stalls. But our work bathroom was sloppily constructed and smelled like raccoon urine. One time, someone from the national branch walked into our office, pinched their nose, scoured their face, and exclaimed, "this office smells like urine."

"We are fixing the bathrooms!" My grand-boss announced one day. I was surprised that he was excited to spend money. Like Ebeneezer Scrouge and Scrouge McDuck, my grand-boss was notorious for penny-pinching and frugality. He would constantly brag about how he was saving the company money while we fired people simply to save money and left their jobs vacant.

"What's the plan to fix the bathrooms?" Someone asked casually, knowing the bathroom discussion was a sensitive topic. It was the equivalent of small or big boobs — we didn't talk about them.

"Well, the first thing we want is a massive fan to suck all the scent out of the bathrooms so it doesn't leak into the office."

And as my grand-boss doted on the dreams of the bathrooms, I don't think he realized that none of the bathrooms dreams would come true. The fan, which was supposed to suck the shit out of the room, was more of a soft breeze. Simple bathroom equipment like the soap dispenser just didn't work. It was as if we time-transported someone from the 1700s to build the bathroom. You could wave your hand in a thousand different ways like a Janet Jackson choreography routine, yet the soap dispenser refused to hand over its bubblegum pink sticky medicinal goop. The best part was that the soap container would be cracked open as if someone was trying to steal the soap. To receive soap, you'd have to milk the bag of soap from within the dispenser.

The paper towel roll didn't roll out of the canister. You'd often see wet hand and palm prints on the paper towel roll as if we were playing a murderous game of Clue. Today's mystery: who left their bare-ass palm on the thinner-than-a-pencil shaving paper towel roll? You probably have noticed a theme: the toilet paper would get stuck in the holder, which of course, didn't work either. Consequently, the toilet paper looked like my hair during humidity: a mess of rolls and strips. It was as if Wolverine was wiping his derriere and shaving the toilet paper for the other staff members.

We lived with a medieval European bathroom — that is, out on the streets in shit rivers peddled away from the city but constantly swallowing and sticking around like a perturbed familial guest in your spare room.

A coworker of mine would *fund* out of her *own pocket* fancy soaps for the staff bathroom. These weren't dollar-brand or Christmas clearance soaps. This coworker brought in lemon rind thyme sassafras soap and ginger-orange tea blossom. It wasn't seasonal sale soap; this was *full-price* Bath and Body Works soap. It was an upgrade over the provided strep medicine that was disguising itself as soap. Imagine going from Walmart-brand ramen to authentic ramen in downtown Tokyo.

It was nice of my colleague to provide soap. She was like Robin Hood, but instead of stealing from the rich, she just gave to the poor. But I couldn't believe someone was regularly throwing down multiple dollars to provide soap for the heathens. I wouldn't give a *penny* to the workplace, let alone meet the bare minimum bathroom standards a corporate company should provide.

The one thing I assumed worked was the self-flushing toilet until one morning, my colleague approached me with a worried look.

"Did you just go to the bathroom?" Morgan asked.

"...yeah." I wasn't going to lie, but I was worried about what would happen next.

"Because you DIDN'T FLUSH!"

Waves of horror and embarrassment hit me like a natural disaster in one of those Dwayne The Rock Johnson apocalypse movies.

"Aren't the toilets *self-flush*?" I questioned — in 2022, on this planet Earth, what corporate bathroom didn't have an auto-flush?

"Nope, because I saw what you *left behind*."

I have a very high-fiber and eclectic diet of cuisines and knew that whatever healthy deposit I had left behind, it was not designer or museum-ready.

"Wait, I thought the toilets were automatic?" I asked. "Because I haven't been manually flushing for months."

Imagine finding out you've been leaving bathroom treats for your colleagues over the last few months. I usually had my headphones in, blaring some audio to keep myself active and awake. Had I not been hearing the sound of the flush?

I immediately investigated as if I were Sherlock Holmes. Upon inspection, the toilet was indeed an automatic flushing toilet. So why wasn't it flushing? Turns out, it was just defective because *sometimes* it flushed and *sometimes* it didn't. It was like a game show: *WILL! IT! FLUSH!?*

I had another coworker who discovered a lopsided tile that created a tripping hazard. Imagine arriving to work and hitting your head on the sink because of a jutting bathroom tile? Part of me wondered, was it worth seeing if I could try and trip? See if I could get workers' comp?

When I was training a new hire, they went to the bathroom as a person and returned as a ruin.

"What is with that bathroom?" The new hire exclaimed. "The toilet was clogged...and there were pubes on the toilet."

I wasn't even surprised; I just nodded in a proletarian resolution. I felt like a character smoking a cigar in a leather chair, asking: "Where have you been?"

And that iconic urine smell...it just never left. Like a witch who constantly outwitted the town, the urine smell permeated the office. It felt like we had an office cat who refused to use the litter box. So, instead of upping the fan's suction power, using heavy-duty cleaning supplies, or even going to Dollar Tree and grabbing something to put into the bowl, we admitted defeat.

However, the most 'effective' move that the company came up with was just adding a bottle of Febreeze in the bathroom. We live in that Febreeze commercial, except there's a giant turd in the toilet, and not even a momentarily lingering smell of Hawaii is enough to handle the vast issues. Did management really believe that the *presence* of a Febreeze bottle would dismantle decades of urine corrosion? Imagine waking into a house where the carpets are filled with cat urine and thinking a single cylinder-bottle of scent product will permanently change the situation.

One time I went to use the executive-approved purchase of Febreeze to discover it was *empty*. I had a lot of questions: why would someone not throw out the empty bottle? How long had this bottle been empty? Didn't this bottle just get placed in the bathroom, so we have a problem if we're going through a whole Febreeze bottle in less than a business week?

The irony is that the people constantly calling you out for being unprofessional tend to do some absolutely bonkers things that are just as unprofessional. The big boss in charge of my corporate gig sent an email titled "Meeting with [Boss's Name]." Instantly, I felt my asshole tighten three sizes that day like some anxious millennial Grinch. Nobody *wants* to meet with their boss, and you *certainly* don't want to meet with the grand-boss. In my entire time working for the company, I had never been called to a meeting with the big boss.

The grand-boss was an individual who would bite with sharp comments about wearing sandals as if only poor people wore sandals. This was someone who slashed a budget as if he were a slasher murderer. I could practically hear the 1990s from the old Dell computer that slogged onward and upward like a confederate soldier who had not gotten the memo that the war was over. They were the individual who casually flaunted their wealth and success, nothing super overt like gold bars being brought to the office. But there were mentions of penthouse living, fancy watches, and clothes that looked like full-sale price Men's Warehouse in a subtle 'look at me, I'm Sandra Dee.'

After my heart attack subsided over the email's subject line, I clicked inside to read the message. The email had been sent to all the production staff. The production department was the lowly of the heavenly angels. While we worked for 'heaven,' we were so close to falling off the clouds and tumbling into hell. We were regularly disrespected both in mistreatment and financial compensation. Think of hazing the freshmen when it came to a college fraternity but withholding money instead of pushing beer.

    The production staff were the shovelers of shit. We held onto the ladder so others could climb in lifeboats before the boat sank. We were coming in during COVID, the ones who, when sick, get told to work through it, never get small gifts — no, not the producers! That would be like giving a gift to 'the help'. Even *after* the COVID-19 pandemic, when I got sick, my employer told me to 'power through it,' like I was on the last mile of a 5K race. This, of course, after the leagues of emails, training, and personal conversations about the ever-importance of taking sick time. Now, if someone *important* at work got ill, we rolled out the five-star treatment for them. Need a week off to deal with your cough? Take two to be safe.

    My first thought upon seeing this email was, "oh, this is it." It was the firing that I wanted so I could claim unemployment while I applied and waited to land my next dream job. That dream situation echoed when you and your first date mutually agreed there was no need for a second date. You both release a sigh of relief, smile brightly, and mean it when you say, "I wish you the best."

    Getting let go from this job would have freed me from the toxic capitalist culture crammed with ego, outdated machinery, and the constant squeezing of job roles into my role. Letting me go meant they could save money by not paying out a meager wage that would be considered low-class. Oh, and I wouldn't have to smell the urine again.

    The worst part of this mystery meeting was how a few production team members went to their direct supervisors for appeasement and just found it more confusing. When pressing higher staff members on the content of the meeting, they giggled as if they were schoolgirls hiding secret crushes. 'Don't worry about it,' 'It's fine,' are things I want to hear when a surprise birthday party is planned for me.

    The next day, en route to the meeting, the production staff clucked like chickens who figured we were off to slaughter. We didn't see the sharp guillotines, a production line, cellophane, or styrofoam packaging. But we could *smell* it. The company's stock was lower than a dollar per share. A single piece of gum was more expensive than a share of our company. Of course, the entire production staff seemed unlikely. Who would schlep the shit if not the shit-schleps? Could they really outsource our jobs to India?

My grand-boss began the meeting like the lord of the manor, ready to yell at the servants. The production staff sat around the conference table like the cheaper Walmart edition of the Avengers. Management sat with Cheshire-cat grins as if they were employees at Disney and were being threatened by gun-point to smile.

"Well, I heard some of you thought this was a mass firing! Let me assure you — that's not happening!" My grand-boss chuckled. "If anything, that would be a one-on-one conversation!" cue the canned sitcom fake laughter over the track from the present supervisors and some of the production staff.

My grand-boss thought this was the comedy club and was testing a tight five minute set. At this point, I just kept sipping my giant jug of water. I knew it was essential to keep my colossal mouth shut. I have a tendency to spew with no filter. But I knew I would remain pretty quiet if I was constantly sipping water.

The news was that my office had acquired limited free parking passes, and the production staff would share them. Most of the production staff parked at meters and would trek down every two hours to quench the meter. It sounds expensive, but I only spent two to three dollars a day at a meter versus the seven to eleven price of the nearby garages. And since we were paid so low, literally every penny counted. Think about it — saving four bucks a day is twenty bucks a week, eighty dollars a month! It wasn't that bad of a deal, and I was impressed that, for once, we received a benefit.

My mood forever changed when my boss dropped an asshole quip:

"Think of this parking pass as a raise!"

The whole room did a half-groan, half-laugh combo that sounded like the live audience on the set of *Friends*. At best, it was just a clueless blunder. At worst, it was insensitive and stupid. It was like my grand-boss believed he was buying us a drink at the bar when they were grabbing a lemon wedge for our glass of water.

I have a whole list of terrible things about the professional workplace that I will write about here. If you're not interested, skip a couple pages for less-complaining segments of this essay.

One of the worst parts of the professional workplace is the amount of stupid, redundant, pointless meetings. These meetings were bloated, similar to the previous sentence in this paragraph which used three-similar adjectives. It inspired me to write the song, "Coulda Been An Email," in which I sing: *this could have been an email*. I don't think Shakespeare could write that — granted, explaining email to Shakespeare would probably make him pop a blood vessel. Life really does inspire one's Magnus Opus.

Most of the meetings I had at my first job were more social catch-ups than momentous work-related discussions. People would talk about weekend plans, develop ideas that they would be too lazy to accomplish, and let us know what streaming program they were watching. I didn't hate the light chat; I just hated the guise that we had an important meeting while praising or bombasting the latest Netflix original.

Sometimes that meeting gets canceled, and your initial euphoric wave is replaced with anxiety. Maybe the staff is still having the meeting, but now it's about you. *You*, your work, personality, choices, abilities, and skills are now the main reason there's a meeting that you're doing a terrible job. But in reality, even if the meeting *was* happening, it would have people talking about the new falafel place they went to or whether Julie Garner from Ozark deserves every single Emmy.

But it wasn't even at my workplace; I had frustrations with many corporations I didn't work for. I was like Cleveland's Martin Luther — except I replaced religion in the 1700s with current worker conditions. There are plenty of jobs that didn't post the salary (ridiculous), with terrible expectations.

I hate companies that make you wear a uniform. Most companies' work uniforms look like they asked Ayn Rand to create the uniform with a 1980s jail in mind. It's as if companies design their uniforms just so customers judge the staff. If you're a company proud of your products and brand — wouldn't you want the wage-slaves to look hot and sexy? Target's law of having employees 'just wear a red shirt' can be confusing. Talk about a fun game: is that a Target employee or just a customer wearing red?

There are two types of job interviews. There are interviews where it's not an interview but a conversation that ends with you being hired. I imagine it's like when those rich boys get their internships at daddy's firm:

"Hi, can I get a job? Yay!"

I just did an interview for a part-time job, and they were so impressed that they said, "We don't know how but we're going to make it work. We want to bring you on full-time." It was the equivalent of when you go on a first date, and they propose. And if you're a bit attention-seeking and a little low on esteem, your instinct is to say:

"STAWPPP, oh my gosh, you're so sweet, thank you...."

The second type of interview is where they do not give a single fuck. They don't want to interview you. They don't want to be doing their job. You're *why* they have to work today, and they hate you. And no matter what you do, they make a stank face as if you are only doing this interview to destroy them.

I wish I had more epic stories about handing in my two weeks' notice. When I worked at a tropical restaurant, I wrote 'Dear Diary, I'm handing in my two weeks' notice on a piece of paper to the manager on duty. The assistant manager told me, "I can completely take you off the schedule if that's easier?" Shocked, I agreed. For some reason, I was waiting for them to beg me to stay. I wanted them to feel the hurt of my departure. I wanted them to beseech me, toil for a relationship repair. I imagined managers fawning over me with compliments, pay raises, and the assurance that my demands would be solved. But Pink Floyd was the real winner because I was just another brick in the wall!

I've had tons of odd jobs over the years. I momentarily worked in a bookstore chain that we shall refer to as Harnes & Fable. I thought working there would be excellent because I love reading, writing, and being surrounded by books. I have a lot of childhood memories of reading books in the Harnes & Fable Darnbucks Café and using birthday and Christmas gift cards to purchase books. I can close my eyes and smell the non-caffeinated frappuccinos, the pages of books, and my father talking about how buying books was a waste of money when you could read them in the bookstore or get them at the library. My father was definitely the type of customer that Harnes & Fable hated, but could you call someone a customer when they never purchased anything?

My nostalgia was quickly bulldozed by asinine standards. One of the standards we were judged on was the number of memberships we could close on the unsuspecting public. The membership was a twenty-five-dollar program that only made sense if you spent a lot of money at the bookstore. Granted, you'd get 10% off all retail and café and 30% off hardcovers, but you'd still have to spend a couple hundred bucks for the membership deals to kick in. To the average college student buying Hamlet or the uncle trying to pick an educational present, this was *not* a reasonable membership price or benefit.

The best time to push the memberships was during the holiday when people came to shop for their massive families and friends. Some people got a free membership just because by the time they bought over two hundred dollars of products, the members' coupons deducted their total by thirty or forty bucks. Occasionally a guest would refuse the basically free membership — perhaps thinking they were being enrolled in some credit card scheme or auto-enroll product. So we'd just *apply* for the membership credit but give the membership to someone else. And why? Because we had a *quota* of memberships to meet. We wouldn't let a *free* membership go unspent!

The best part of that job was the four adult women managers who formed their apocalyptic horseman quartet. One was the lovely, motherly type, another stern and emotionless. The third was quick to anger and snappiness, while the last would just try to get things done. It was like witnessing a sitcom in real time. I'll never forget my favorite colleague — although I have forgotten her name. She always had some sad relationship but spicy sexual stories that made my nine dollars an hour worth it. Eventually, when I went full-time at my first professional job, I explained that I needed to temporarily be taken off the schedule and that I might return in the future. I knew I wouldn't return in the future, but my Libra personality felt confrontational saying otherwise.

They reached out during the holiday season later that year, and I brushed them off with an excuse of how busy my full-time job was. I received a dismal email later in the week that offended me at the time. I was (and still am) very bad about letting bridges be closed and sink into the lake. I always feel I need to keep my bridges in stasis if I want to return to them. I knew I would never return to the bookstore — but part of me wanted the *option* of returning. I do this with relationships all the time. In situations of mutual neglect, I'll refuse to fully cave in out of some sheer justice.

    I once had a colleague, not-her-real-name Demi, who had a bold personality. She was half protective mother cub who could bake a mean cake and half destructive minx who could destroy you tenfold. She is an inspiration to seize what you want, give what you can, and not let anyone tell you otherwise. After months of tenacious battling with management, things came to a grand finale during a heated discussion revolving around Demi's employment. She told our boss to 'kiss her fat ass,' and tossed her staff credentials at him before exiting. He watched, wide-eyed as she left the building.

    I was really nervous putting in my two weeks' notice at my first professional job. I had heard stories of workplaces that went ballistic. But the staff handled the situation well. I could feel my sphincter lessen, and finally, I felt a deluge of stress and drama leave my body. I had unlocked the ultimate level of un-motivation. I began to blatantly scrimp on my duties. What could they do at that point? Fire me? In the past, I had anxiety about messing up, which consumed me to the point where I became a living anxiety bomb due to explode. But in those last two weeks, my stress had deflated, leaving an empty balloon chilling through the final stage.

    The 'final exit' interview was *hilarious.* I pointed out that my absence would leave giant holes in the department. I was the only one certified in specific applications and programs. I hadn't showcased complete initiative lately, but I knew they wouldn't quickly fill the amount of enterprise, expertise, and hunger I brought to the table. My boss, ever a skeptic, got the new hire into the exit interview. My boss didn't even know what programs we used, so-referred me to quiz the new hire. He had minimal experience in many programs and applications that I utilized daily around the office. Not all of these things were needed or mandatory; but losing out on the only one capable would create an enormous gap. Nobody was OK when the only sushi chef left the Japanese restaurant staff.

While I don't have many 'storming-out' stories about leaving a job, I have plenty of botched job interviews. One time I interviewed for what sounded like a non-profit. It was one of those scammy organizations that sent people door-to-door collecting money. The money you collect is part of how much you get paid. Luckily we were in the neighborhood of my grandmother — so I crashed my grandmother's church to pretend to get signatures. I refused to get money out of people for this corporation, so I wrote four or five faux signatures, which impressed the crew.

"No one gets money on their first time out." The others said with a shrug. "You did great."

On my way out the hiring manager told me she would reach out in a couple of months. I nodded, not having the heart to tell her I wouldn't take the job. I spent the rest of the month worried that I would have to confront the hiring manager and turn down the job. Thankfully, they never called me again. I suppose they filled the position with someone who enjoyed the scam.

I had a few job interviews which framed themselves as event management only to be gigs working stalls at stores with samples or surveys. I hated that my time was purposefully misused and each time ended the interview giving them the professional equivalent to mess off. It doesn't feel accurate to say that the position is event management when in reality, it's giving samples, presenting surveys, or asking people to schedule an appointment for a large-scale product.

One job interview for one of these survey jobs dared to lump me with another candidate.

"We'll just do a joint interview for time." The manager said as I sat down with a mousy woman who looked like she was waiting for the cops to bust us at any time. I was so hot-tempered that I thought I had momentarily become a Taurus, ready to show the world what a raging bull I was. This company had the audacity to mislead me on this job, and *then* want to save time bullshitting that you place me with someone else?

Another job blatantly lied — saying they were looking for marketing positions when they were clearly looking for management for their abysmal retail spaces. The worst part was they got me twice with the *same* interviewer. I told them the second time to take me off the listing — but they had the audacity to reach out the following week about an upcoming group interview.

"I'm sorry," I texted back. "You completely misrepresented the position. Please never call me back."

The most frustrating job situation I've had wasn't with strangers but with an acquaintance. A fellow wedding DJ — let's name him Shane — was hiring hosts for the trivia side of his business. I interviewed and was, of course, super qualified. I clarified that I wouldn't be DJing weddings for him and that my supervisors at the company I DJ weddings for would be fine if I did trivia for Shane. Shane ghosted me over the position at the time — which was okay. I always have multiple blowpokes in the fire. My boss later told me that Shane had declined to hire me out of 'respect' and 'as a favor' to the company I worked for.

I have yet to confront Shane on that information, but I want to. It makes me feel like a piece of meat that others can utilize. My agency was destroyed — for what? Brownie points with the company that I worked for and who didn't care? How is this a favor, Shane? Your company isn't a threat to anyone — if anything, *I* was doing *you* a favor. Also, why not say something to me? I may engage in unprofessionalism, but ghosting a friend and colleague in the industry is probably rock bottom. Maybe one of these days I'll say something — but I'll probably chicken out. Instead, I'll secretly roll my eyes whenever I see a Facebook post about his integrity and character.

I've been ghosted on a few fantastic opportunities. One lady bought me a drink at Market Garden for a part-time job with her company. After emptying the glass and saying goodbyes, she too became empty on the news. I was beyond qualified, but I think my schedule made her anxious. People look at my two-page resume and think I work one-hundred hours a week. Once in a while, that might be the case. A vast majority of my current various side roles might only be for one or two evenings a month. It looks more impressive than it actually is.

When I was on the job hunt in early 2022, I managed to make it to many final interviews for jobs in the content creation/social media world. I would meet with CEOs who left me feeling sour.

"We work 9-5, no exceptions around here." One CEO explained. "We're trying to make sure people WORK."

Funny because your social media is deader than a Civil War graveyard, and your current logistics plan feels like it's run by freshmen in a frat house.

One job turned me down because the CEO thought I was overqualified.

"Your background seems to be in content creation, and we're looking for someone to do more social media management," the CEO said, as if he knew what he was talking about. Unfortunately, while he might have had accolades, awards, and degrees, I knew he did not understand the field in particular. Also, he was an older man — what older man without specific experience really knows what they're talking about when it comes to digital media?

I discussed my CEO woes with Monica, my best friend and expert on business matters.

"Well, what is the CEO going to say?" Monica muttered. "*Don't* work hard? *Have* boundaries in the workplace? The research shows that a lot of them are sociopathic anyway…"

Although I detest acting professionally in a capitalist workplace, I conform to decorum while teaching. Especially when teaching today's youth. It's one thing to be a blaggard in a professional workplace or with friends, but I'm not trying to be on Fox 8 for corrupting children with improper language.

I spent a semester teaching English and poetry to students who didn't want to learn the subjects. It was a constant uphill battle, and the only thing that got me through the semester was promising free time upon completion of lessons and practicum. While waiting for students to leave, a fourth-grade student asked me if I was celebrating Columbus Day. This was back in 2021, so I had already discovered via social media that Christopher Columbus was terrible.

"No, I don't think there's a reason to celebrate," I explained. "Also — he wasn't that great of a person."

My fourth-grade student smiled.

"That was a test." She declared. "And you passed."

"Oh, thanks!" I said nonchalantly.

"He's a bad man." She continued. "Did you know Christopher Columbus *raped* animals?"

You could hear the large machine brakes going off in my head.

"He...did that?" I didn't want to know why a fourth-grade girl understood the concepts of rape and bestiality. But you can tell in my tone that I was intrigued and aghast simultaneously. Part of me wanted to hear no more of it — but there was a more prominent part: the tonal version of *'spill the tea!'*

"He did!" She continued. I did some casual research and found that Columbus probably was a rapist of Caribbean women and young girls. Columbus did mistake manatees for mermaids, perhaps the only relatable-ish element of Columbus' persona. But *raping animals*? Even an excellent historical figure would be questionable under such a claim.

Another fourth-grade student joined my writing club because she was passionate about writing. I was super jazzed that she was engaged on a subject I dedicated personal and professional time on.

"Are you working on anything currently?" I asked as she pulled out her notebook.

"Yes — it's a ghost story."

Ghost stories can be PG. I deduced it would be a cute spook situation. Kids lost in an abandoned house, maybe a vampire or zombie. No ghost story I was aware of involves knowledge about or creativity of historical figures and sexual escapades with animals.

"What's your story about?"

"It takes place at the Cecil Hotel." The girl explained. Immediately all the air left my body, and I saw sunspots in my vision.

"The Cecil Hotel?" I questioned. For those who don't know, the Cecil Hotel is a haunted hotel that featured many acts of depravity — including being the home of many serial killers. A girl most likely committed suicide in a water tank on the roof. It was a whole Netflix documentary — and material that was definitely not suited for a fourth grader. I was twenty-six going on twelve and thought that the material was too heavy for me.

"Have you heard of it?" My writing student asked if she had been discussing a rare kids' anime show instead of a murder hotel.

"Um, yes." I nodded. I didn't know what to say. I wasn't an education major, just an educated man trying to educate. And besides, I doubt education majors have a specific class that addresses how to talk to fourth graders about historic bloody hotels of hate.

She read me the story — which was very good for her age group. It featured drawings decked with blood and other true crime elements. In the end, I thanked her for sharing and gave her a tip about how she could replace the word 'said' with various dazzling synonyms.

I was part of a film camp that was more strenuous than boot camp. I was tasked to lead fourteen student films, finish the shooting, and oversee the editing in eight days. To say the job was stressful would be like saying it's 'slightly uncomfortable' to sit on the spikiest cylindrical cactus.

One student immediately made themselves known as a bold personality. Their name was Malice. And since you might be reading this, I must clarify the pronunciation. It's not *malice,* as in "my boss has malice for the receptionist." It's Malice, as in "my lease is up next month."

I actually had no problems with Malice throughout the camp experience. I'm confident in the assumption that Malice grew up — whether with family or in school — having to be tough. They enjoyed TikTok and KPop and branded brutal honesty as a personality trait. I always treat younger kids like adults until you make me treat you like a child. The other adults in the room were quick to demonize Malice and would always watch like a priest looking for sin in his congregation.

Malice's proposed film was rough. I wasn't sure if the writing, the overarching confusing narrative, or the off-camera elements made certain moments underwhelming. It's like creating a superhero movie, but all the action scenes happen off-camera but are constantly referenced in the film's final cut.

"That battle was wicked." Says the superhero who continues and constantly references a fantastic match that the audience doesn't see.

We shot Malice's film in the last two days. And by "we," I mean other people. We legitimately had two days to finish editing ten other pieces (by that point, a few of the stragglers had fallen to the wayside). I had no choice but to send surrogates off to battle to execute Malice's piece.

Drama ensued on set. It was the type that would land us a deal at Bravo. Students complained to Malice about the problems with the script and production. Malice ricocheted back devastating aggression that knocked large holes in the S.S. Morale. Malice was upset because people seemed to be pushing back on particular problems with the piece.

"You're the director," I remember telling Malice while chopping footage because there was no time to stop editing. "You have to lead, but be effective. Listen to concerns and decide whether to fix them or overlook them."

When you ask people to work on your creative projects for free, you basically become a servant to them in the compliments department. My friend Nonnie pulls out the stops with food spreads and drinks for her crew. I compliment people so hard you'd think I was trying to bed and wed them.

I remember trying to film a music video with a friend, and they accidentally didn't record a whole sequence. I didn't notice we were missing the footage until after we shot it and I was editing it. Instead of being upset, I accepted it as part of the process of having free labor. Sometimes you mess up a shot, you spend a few hundred on snacks, and other times you're pulling out a thesaurus so you can successfully compliment people.

Malice, who could manipulate malice like a pro, did not ease the concerns but set fire to them. I could hear the yelling from the hallway — all because Malice couldn't find a few people needed for the scene they were about to film. Moments later, the door to the editing suite opened, and Malice sat down with a huff. I didn't say anything — what was I going to say?

"Hey, I heard that giant fight in the hallway; I assume everything is fine?" That's how you know I'm an optimist. The stomping, huffing, and puffing clearly indicated a few houses being blown over.

Moments after Malice entered the room, the camp leader not-her-real-name Patty came in. I could tell that Patty was ready to lay down the law like an old sheriff in a western movie. I continued editing footage as if I wasn't in the room.

"First thing: this is my camp. If you don't like it, then you can leave." Patty threatened. I let out a small piece of air like a tire popping. Patty had a homily of rules, expectations, and criticism to spew over Malice. People either pulled out lists in discussions for organizational purposes or throw-downs. And I doubted this was about how to organize their piece.

I didn't know exactly how this would play out. I doubted Malice would remain calm. I buckled down but continued trying to add music to one of the students' films.

"Fine, then I'll leave." Malice grabbed their bag in a mannerism that was basically an "F you" before leaving the editing suite. Patty was shook — there were definitely a couple seconds where an internal thought went, 'oh no, they didn't!' I didn't come from a traditional background on how to be an educator or an educational leader. But I knew telling a student like Malice, "if you don't like it, you can leave," was an invitation for them to leave. Patty followed Malice, and the editing suite was momentarily quiet. Suddenly, other students burst into the editing suite to discuss the drama. One student even ripped up the script for the shoot in a funny, dramatic fashion. I tried not to listen in or ask questions, but that was like asking the Cocoa Puffs mascot to not go insane over the presence of his favorite thing: a good story.

Since graduating from undergrad, I have been dreaming of the chance to teach a college class. I finally got the opportunity at the beginning of 2022, having been called in to teach a lesson on the *first day of class*. By a serendipitous strike of wonder, my mentor and friend Lisa had taken a new job and had mentioned that I should take over. This opportunity ended up being one of the best I ever received.

On my first day, I told the room that I had been asked to teach the class less than a day ago and that we would officially start on the next day of class. One student then asked:

"Well, if the class doesn't start till the next class, do I have to be here?"

My eyebrows rose two inches at that moment, and it took so much restraint not to verbally slap this man across the face with a sassy comeback. In some of my more uncouth moments, I would have countered with statements as extreme as, "Well, don't be here at all and drop the class," or sassy ones like, "Remind me not to attend *your* class." But instead, I kill them with kindness. Kill them with kindness equivalent to emptying out innards and letting beach crabs feast on a half-alive, half-dead version of your former foe. But with kindness.

My lack of class becomes most apparent in social structures. Without an institution to semi-please or represent, my natural raw energy blossoms like a weed in the wild. The more casual a situation or location is, the quicker my filter is to unrobe itself.

A friend once told me their grandmother had nineteen children, and I drunkenly quipped:

"Her poor vagina must have looked like an Arby's sandwich."

It killed the table, but it was the kind of joke fueled by the bar and previous drinks — not something I would have said sober and in a professional setting.

One time, I had to present a PowerPoint to my city council, and I implied that their social media was abysmal.

"We can't *all* have an MA in communications." The mayor, who didn't like me, sassily said.

"We could try and have *some* kind of presence." I countered.

There was a suggestion that we have some staff member schedule out posts for the next three months, and I actively snorted. I hope that's on public record somewhere.

My mother, sister, and two nieces went to a tea party at one of those houses that looked either southern or British. It's the type of house that most serial killers own. With younger children in a tea house, one literally experiences the metaphor *bull in the china shop*. There was a small room that was a store where everything was at least minimally forty bucks and made of breakable materials. It was just shelves and shelves of fragile china. My sister and I were steering my nieces like little bulldozers that would otherwise knock into the shelves of china. It was like playing one of those classic 2D video games with the joystick. I get that we were visiting a tea house, but having rooms upon rooms of instantly breakable pieces feels like bad business.

Our server was an older woman who would totally describe herself as excellent. At the time my nieces were 3 and 2, so they were a little rowdy. Not outrageously rowdy, just like the average amount for a healthy child. A child that isn't a little rowdy would be weird.

The tea selection at a tea house is a terrible time if you're indecisive. They have practically every tea in existence — and even rousing flavors that seem too wild for tea. Can you really have chocolate tea? Isn't that watered-down chocolate? Why not just *have* hot chocolate?

"Our tea is good when its made into a golfer." Our waitress explained.

I was shocked that I was not familiar with a golfer. I was a self-described cocktail lover who preferred Long Island Iced Teas, but would be naturally curious about a drink called *The Golfer*. I mused over what it might be. Tea and rum? Tea and vodka?

"Oh, what booze comes with the Golfer?" I asked curiously. Did this tea shop even have a liquor license? We were in Ohio, which I figured was conservative regarding handing out liquor licenses. Our waitress laughed and gave me a look like she was explaining the color red to a twenty-year-old.

"Oh, *I* call it a golfer. But you would know it as half tea, half lemonade."

"So a half-and-half with lemonade?" I confirmed — desiring for us to be on the same page.

"Yes!"

"Gotcha, so an Arnold Palmer."

The waitress soured a little by the name — as if she had dated the real-life Arnold Palmer and did not want the delicious combination of iced tea and lemonade to be referred to in his honor.

Maybe it was a feminist thing? She didn't want the drink to sound masculine? That didn't make sense either — The Golfer sounds more masculine than 'Arnold Palmer,' because I feel like I might walk into a gay bar and meet someone named Arnold Palmer on stage doing drag.

"Hey girls, it's me, Arnold Palmer!" A drag queen would say with jazz hands and zealously-applied makeup.

Weirdly enough, I had another run-in at a tea shower. My friend Joanna hosted a beautiful baby shower with an Alice In Wonderland theme at a tea party restaurant. It was fancy, elegant, beautiful — and any term I would never use to describe myself. Joanna's family had decorated the room with all sorts of beautiful centerpieces.

The lunch was mini sandwiches since we were at a tea parlor. The problem with being a husky man is that mini sandwiches don't fill you up. For ladies, some might have a couple mini sandwiches and become full. Or maybe they would be 'lady-like' and claim they were stuffed on two pieces of bread and five cucumbers. I figured these women would leave and circle the Taco Bell drive-through. I was shoveling sandwiches down my gullet. In my defense, I had double-digit mini sandwiches, but altogether it probably made two sandwiches.

One of Joanna's friends who attended the baby shower had her own baby. Naturally, everyone cooed over the cute child. I'm not one for utilizing the same compliments. All around me, I heard: "Cute baby," "What a cute baby," and "that baby is cute." It just feels forced and unoriginal. I like to make innovative and elevated compliments: "Your baby has the eyebrows of a young Angelina Jolie" or, "I smell a future scholar of business!" It's much more original than the regular complement peddling. At least I can provide a genuine and intriguing compliment.

I hate gender reveals simply because I want to know more about the future child's personality. Instead of revealing biological sex, reveal to me a psychic prediction about whether or not your child will be a bitch or a bastard, smart or dumb, troublesome or polite. A personality reveal would be much more exciting for all involved.

I looked at Joanna's friend's cute baby (although I wasn't going to say cute). Immediately I decided that if no one else would provide original comments, *I* would. I noticed the baby looked slightly tan and said: "I love his tan!"

The whole table paused for a second, and I was worried that maybe I had inferred that the mother was bad for giving her child time in the sun. My friend Billiam, who was sitting next to me, whispered:

"*The child is mixed; the dad is black.*"

I felt my soul depart my body. Having been in a tea house with white people, I had wrongly assumed the child was white with a suntan. I remember clutching Billiam's leg next to me and holding on as if tightening my grip around my friend's thigh would save me from damnation. Thankfully the rest of the tea party continued with no controversial statements from me. It was a reminder that sometimes creative compliments are best left simple and sweet.

The best workplaces for creatives are the ones with fellow no-holds-barred creatives. I teach some classes with a non-profit, and we host quarterly meetings and sessions. Recently we discussed not getting involved if there were physical assaults between students.

"You should try and find ways to de-escalate situations before kids go down on each other," my boss explained, which caused my face to open in shock. I was immediately thinking, 'go down on each other' as the sexual euphemism. My boss had been standing next to me, so everyone's eyes were in the direction of my slightly horrified face visible to the rest of the table.

"You mean *fighting* to go down on each other, right?" I questioned, allowing the room to erupt in laughter. A bit later, we talked about designs, and someone suggested that working backward made the most sense.

"Imagine it's like a recipe." She explained. "Think of it like you've decided to make a pot pie and then figure out the ingredients you'll need."

"A pot pie sounds kinda heavy for summer," I muttered, causing her and the rest of the room to laugh. I love being in these spaces — even if the jokes don't fully land. Ironically, her recipe metaphor was apt due to a recipe challenge we were asking the community to help out with. I immediately let out an "I can provide the recipe of cereal" comment (it wasn't my best joke).

I've learned to finally accept that sometimes I'll need to embrace professionalism when the time is present. But often, I let the mask of professionalism slip, if not disregard it altogether. Recently at my new job, we were talking about an event for families called 'Self-Love Day.' When I read the title the week before, I immediately thought of self-pleasuring. But then I thought, *Matt, you might be too creative, too bright, too perverted, or something because I doubt anyone else thinks this*.

At the department meeting, my boss goes,

"So we want to change the name because it feels... masturbatory."

The entire table chuckled as we bounced around different names.

"We might as well name it the Jack-Off Event," I said under my breath. Immediately I wondered if I had screwed the pooch, only to find a couple people near me chuckling over my joke. Thank goodness this workplace didn't mind my slip of decorum. I've been enjoying my latest forays into the professional world that I'll eventually share. But communicating about it now feels...well, like a *lack* of decorum.

Trying To Have A Social Life

In your early twenties you're pre-disposed to be social. Today is Thursday? No worries, let's have a chill night of bar-crawling and slam tacos like we're baseball pitchers in a batting cage. It's Friday? Funday Friday, time to drink liquor, dress promiscuously, and hit up a low-key party or a bar that has definitely gotten in trouble with the police. It's Tuesday? Well let's still have a night-long dinner and act like we don't have adult responsibilities.

But Saturdays are the Crown Jewel, the belle of the ball that embodied our party social culture. If you weren't doing something on Saturday and you were old enough to actively serve in the army, were you even human? Tell a young twenty-something you're doing nothing on a Saturday and they'll give you a look like you're one of the thousand pound sisters on TLC.

Saturdays involved long pre-games and preparation. One would often feel like a church parishioner who arrived a half-hour before mass simply to pray solo. For the average church goer, this feels like doing more than you needed to. It was like doing a half hour cardio warmup to a two hour cardio workout. My family once got yelled at by a lady in church for whispering before the mass had even begun. She's probably the type of woman who thought priests guilty of touching children were framed by the devil.

Now that I'm pushing into my thirties, I have to know days ahead of time if I'm going out on a Saturday. I can't be told at 3pm on a Saturday that we're going out late *that* night. When I was younger, you simply had to be ready for anything. It was like being enlisted in an army never knowing where you might be deployed. Potentially a basement house party, a dorm room, or a sketchy neighborhood bar that would forget to check for IDs.

Not only would you have to be prepared for anything — the same held true for the parties themselves. My friend Jessica used to host the biggest house parties. There were themes, jungle juice, and a transformed hot box in the garage. One party, I had two drinks and kissed someone who had smoked weed then proceeded to make out with their kitchen toaster. I kept making comments like, "that toaster wants me." That night alone was a perfect night for public service announcements on anti-drug use, anti-underaged drinking, and birth control.

I distinctly remember one night in the dorm room drinking vodka and after two shots found myself "drunk." This was impossible considering I was a two-hundred plus thick boy. Tipsy, *maybe* (although even that feels like more of a stretch than spandex leggings going over a boulder). But me being drunk off of two shots was more unlikely than Bravo picking Cleveland as their next *Real Housewives* franchise. Thankfully, I felt so overcome by those two shots that I left the party before the RA came to write the whole room up.

I remember early on I snuck booze out of my parents' house. My parents weren't drinkers, and so much alcohol was just left downstairs unattended. At the time, I justified that after years of going unused, my parents lost the right to own their booze. I assumed that they would never notice that I had cleared out the mini bottles of wine and unopened eggnog liquor. Years later, I found out that they had noticed, and hadn't cared. After all, who can get that slushed on 8% eggnog liquor, let alone drink any of it? If anything, they were probably happy that I was clearing out their house and home of terrible booze. The booze was so old that it had fermented into a new hybrid of stank. What was supposed to be wine tasted like liquor, and the eggnog liquor had an aftertaste that couldn't be wiped out of your mouth.

When you're underaged, drinking is 50% fun and 50% being on constant alert. You're a gazelle in a world filled with lions who want to write you up, write you a ticket, or shake their head in that 'kids these days' mannerism. Will someone find you with that 5% wine cooler? Will you be shamed? Sometimes it felt like getting caught by the RA was a version of *The Scarlet Letter* — but you'd wear a big D for drunk.

One weekend, my roommate Karly took us down to Ashland University which is located in the middle of an Ohioan cornfield. The trip was overall pretty uneventful — but anything is exciting when it's different from the regular night out. Even a subpar night out at Ashland University provided diversity to our overall party experience. Our perception of Ashland parties was similar to when privileged children do service for the first time and go, "I didn't realize it was this bad!"

The most exciting moment heading into the trip was when Karly's sister told us that she had the perfect match for me. At this point in life I was skeptical of women who believed they had perfect matches for gay men. Sometimes it felt like the *only* thing that mattered was that the match was gay; as if gays were so rare that no other criteria mattered. But other times, it feels like your friends think you're uglier than you are. If you try and match me, a solid 6 or 7, up with a 2, I wonder — maybe the issue is *me*?

Upon our arrival, Karly's sister brought out the match. I was absolutely taken aback. This man was very pretty inside, but was not rocking much in the looks department. It wasn't like I was pro-league baseball and he was minor-league. The situation was that I was minor-league and this guy was on a children's T-ball team that played for fun and didn't keep the score.

When a friend tells you, "I have the perfect match for you," they're staking their trust, skills, abilities, and frankly the entire friendship on the line. That's why I never indulge in playing super matchmaker — too many explosive bombs to have in your hands.

After the matchmaking failure that TLC could have turned into a new programming piece, we prepared for our night out on the town. We discovered that Ashland University's underaged drinking scene was like something out of the 1920's prohibition. Kids snuck through the streets and yards as if they were part of some secret network to smuggle booze. When a house party got word that cops were in the neighborhood, they blacked out the house as if nobody was home. It was a very tense situation — but some of the Ashland kids *loved* the world they lived in which felt Orwellian. And since I actually read Orwell, I feel like I can bring him to the forefront.

You read that right: some kids loved the danger. Talk about some warped privilege of *enjoying* the neighborhood police's constant surveillance and targeting. How do you even manage to party? It's just too stressful, and not worth shuttling around in the dark like some weird historical reenactment so you can drink well vodka in the rundown fraternity house with terrible music in the background.

Speaking of rundown fraternity houses, the house parties that my college house hosted were iconic. They were *always* theme parties. No exceptions. We had a theme party based on *Lost*, the television show where they were stranded on an island. We had a Pumpkin Spice party (we felt like saying "White Girl Party" might be offensive). We had a *Baywatch* theme, two beer Olympics, and even hosted a band who played in our basement. Not only that, but I insisted we had some of the best jungle juice on the block. We just mixed a bunch of liquor with Dollar Tree mixers. What made the experience pleasant was that we had multiple juices. You could pick between a more berry-forward juice versus a peach or plum flavored juice.

When I was under the age of twenty-one, I didn't understand why over twenty-ones regularly didn't want to date, communicate, or otherwise makes plans with those under the age of twenty-one. But the second I turned twenty-one, and was immediately ushered to Hofbrauhaus for liters of Hefewizen, it made sense. It's like you've finally mastered a language and you wished to be accompanied by those with similar vernacular.

I had waited longer than most in my college class to turn legal. And now that I was finally 21 in my senior year, it was time for me to shine.

And shine I did not. I was frequently the DD, simply because I was too cheap to believe in paying fifty dollars for Uber, and probably because I was driving a Trailblazer at the time. I spent too many nights being sober at Dive Bar, a downtown Cleveland bar that pretended to be a dive bar, but was a glamorized heterosexual haven of bad dancing, 90's music remixes, and slightly rude staff.

I'm the cheap friend. I'm fun, I can be ready to clown around and get wild — or even get cultural and introspective — but I'm cheap. I would gladly DD if that meant someone else would buy me a couple drinks for my time.

"Let's go do this expensive thing!" is a phrase I hear — not in those exact terms.

"Are you sure? There's a free bar patio we could sit at."

"Let's go to a fancy restaurant."

"Are you sure? That bar patio has a happy hour with food."

"We can dress up in nice clothes like tuxedos!"

"Well the bar doesn't have a dress code..."

It's no surprise that I travel cheaply. I want that frontier-back-of-the-bus-let's-drive-in-a-gas-efficient-vehicle kind of cheap. When Monica and I went to Detroit, we stayed at the cheapest place we could find dubbed Roberts Riverside Hotel. From the jump that name is fancy. You imagine it's on the riverside and fancy since Robert is a very opulent Caucasian name. Roberts have golf clubs, enjoys ancient ass wine, and have fancy foreign cars. Even saying the name "Robert" is the epitome of class.

Roberts Riverside Hotel is cheap, with mixed reviews, and it's close to downtown. We arrive to find a peculiar parking lot that's filled with random routes and tons of cars. It looked like one of those apocalyptic graveyards of vehicles left abandoned.

After figuring out the parking, we walk in and hotel guests are attacking the staff with complaints about how things are dirty. In the background on television is *Game of Thrones* which weirdly fits the scene. While people die on the television behind us, guests are killing the wait staff in front of us.

I felt badly for the front desk attendant. He's sitting there like Eeyore having an existential crisis as everyone dumps their dirty laundry on him. Literally, the place was so filthy I'm sure there were multiple complaints about the linens. Of course, this guy can't fix your bedroom lights or plumbing issues. Even if he could, he has to listen to another ten people in line complain. I gotta admit, the eighteen dollar resort fee *was* exuberant. If that hotel was a resort, then I'm a goddamn stud. You can't have one ten foot pool and a river view and call that a resort. Okay, they did put lemons in the reception area water but again, not enough to warrant a resort fee.

Monica decided to use her credit card when we checked in, and I would pay my half digitally. Monica's card swiped but was declined, which confused Monica and I but the hotel attendant appeared unfazed as if this was common occurrence. We ran it a few times until Monica discovered that her credit card company had flagged this purchase as a scam! For some reason, Monica's credit card was trying to warn us about what was waiting for us.

Half of the room's lights didn't work, only two outlets worked, there was no microwave, no fridge, there were coffee grounds but no coffeemaker. I guess it was a 'deconstructed coffee' that hipsters like. The bathroom light fixture was off the wall and falling down in a freeform art piece way.

"Sally, how does that falling light fixture make you feel?"

"Well, the thin wires make me feel like society is on its last string."

When you walked into the fitness room, you immediately wanted to run out of the fitness room. That's how bad it was. In a way it did its job! So did that make the fitness room actually good if we are running out of it? There were two broken treadmills and two crusty ellipticals, one which looked like the original prototype of an elliptical and sounded like something straight out of the 18th century. You could churn butter with that elliptical. You can work out and have butter for breakfast. I can't believe gyms aren't investing in dual purpose cardio machines! Take my workout energy and make me contribute to society.

But here's the real travesty. Your boy wanted a nice vodka sprite. It's a perfect resort drink right? Turns out the hotel room didn't come with cups. There was an ice bucket, but no cups. So I had to buy my own cups at the Dollar Tree next door.

While we stayed at the resort, another instance happened which further confirmed this was not a resort. There was 6am construction. Kid you not, we woke up and there was some jackhammer or some loud machine going at it. Another highlight of the trip was when we Ubered from the music festival back to the hotel, and our older conservative woman driver made comments about the festival and the 'sins' happening there. I do not believe she knew we had just been at that festival, but if she had, she would automatically be a top ten audacious bitch of all time.

Being frugal on vacations can backfire (*see the Chastity Shawl essay from earlier*). Sometimes I'm so focused on being cheap that it actually becomes problematic.

My friend Kelsey heard that my other friend Michelle and I were going to Toronto and had frugal spending advice for us.

"As *soon* as you cross the border — go buy some booze." Kelsey informed us like a Jehovah Witness you'd actually want to ring your door. "Because you're on the border, there's no tax on the liquor! It's tax-free liquor right there."

I didn't do any research on Kelsey's statement about the tax-free liquor. Like a cartoon character whose eyes become giant money symbols, I needed no further convincing. Once Michelle and I crossed the border, we got to the nearest store and stocked up on some non Canadian-American taxed liquor and placed it in the backseat.

"Alright — let's go to Toronto!" Michelle said, starting up her car again as we cheered over our savings. However, for some reason the only way out of the convenient store was to cross over to America.

"We have to go through the border again with booze." I whispered. Michelle's hands clenched on the wheel.

"Can you carry booze through the border like this?" Michelle questioned.

I was no borders expert. The only Borders I knew about was the old bookstore that closed down during the post '08 recession.

"Maybe we should just hide the bottle then," I figured, shifting our clothes over the two bottles in the backseat. Michelle suggested putting the bottles in the trunk, but I thought that was a bit conspicuous. After circling the block and crossing the river, we re-entered into Canada.

"Weren't you guys just here?" The Canadian border agent explained. We gave them the sob story of stopping at the convenient store and it exited only to America.

"I see," the Canadian border agent nodded. The story seemed quite believable: American tourists desperate for snacks and beverages stopped at the first stop they saw, only to find it was designated for people leaving the county. I thought maybe we would be fine — but that's when the Canadian border agent asked us to pull up and over to the side.

Michelle and I took a deep breath and complied. Two agents asked us our story and checked the trunk of the car. After inspecting and seeming happy with our story, Michelle and I were allowed through to Canada for the second time in the same hour. As soon as we cleared the border area, Michelle and I squealed with delight like two schoolgirls who had gotten away with slightly mischievous behavior.

"I can't believe we got away with that!" Michelle muttered.

"We almost put the booze in the trunk, can you imagine?"

We contemplated what our punishment would be had we been caught. Maybe banned and banished? I can't imagine it would be anything *that* harsh.

"Is it smuggling when you've actually bought the booze *in* Canada?" I questioned. "If anything, we're back home where this booze belongs!"

The art of the pre-game is something that a cheap man like myself enjoys. For those unfamiliar, the 'pre-game' is to the night out experience as the pre-game practice is to the game. It's a warm up with drinks, some music, and more conversation then when you go out to a bar later and find it impossible to talk.

When the Cleveland Cavaliers won the NBA Championship in 2016, the whole city sparkled with excitement. Even though I wasn't the biggest sports fan — I was a Cleveland fan. I take Cleveland shirts with me when I travel the world as if I'm repping the brand.

"Is that Chanel?" someone on the streets of Paris or London may ask me.

"No, it's Cleveland," I respond with a flip of my long hair (because in this vision I have long lush locks).

The parade took place on a weekday afternoon and my friend group decided to meet at my house before walking to the rapid and shuttling downtown. That was a big day for me — I had tried my first Four Loko. I found it to be swill radiation water and chucked most of it down the garbage disposal.

I was quite tipsy when we arrived downtown where throngs of people were waiting to see the grand spectacle. The corner bar close to where we were posted up had five-dollar Long Islands — so naturally I had three of those in an hour which made the whole trip a twenty-five dollar event. The sun beat down like a dominatrix, and as the parade continued, I continued to soak up booze and sun. That afternoon, I would have a long shower followed by vomit — having been sun-poisoned and booze poisoned at the same time. It was one of the few times when I actually threw up. Probably should have had vodka water at some point.

Most people seek vacation as refuge — they go to Florida or California or some island in the middle of the ocean to delight in tropical paradise. I wonder if people from tropical locations view midwestern forest terrain as *their* version of tropical. Or do people living in tropical places realize to themselves, "ah yes, I do live in the tropics."

And while lapping up their tropical paradise, the average vacationeer probably tries to do much of nothing. They want to relax, and relaxing is doing nothing. Just lying on a beach, or in a chair, with a drink that has a fruit wedge on the rim. I know some people that will take two weeks of their year specifically to go someplace warm and sunny to just unexist for a while.

But I'm not good at relaxing vacations. I've always realized I was an on-the-go vacationer, but it wasn't until a trip to North Carolina in 2021 that made me realize that I can only relax for three days before going stir-crazy. My good friends Alanna and Eric were getting married, and I had been asked to officiate. It was — and I mean this seriously — one of the best honors of my life. Your wedding day is a *huge* deal, so picking a person that's going to act as the minister for the day is at least a semi-huge deal. The plan was to arrive on Tuesday, and leave the following Monday with the wedding on Saturday.

The location was Surf City, North Carolina where tourists ruled for the summer, and the relaxed locals chilled all year long. We had booked in the last week of May before the more expensive June-August dates. After all, I'm not the only one who likes to vacation for a better price. Upon my arrival, I discovered that I would be sharing a room with someone — and we would be sleeping on twin bunk beds that were most definitely designed with children in mind.

I refused. And no — it wasn't one of those stomp around the house and make demands refusals. But it was one of those moments where I just knew myself well enough to know that this was not going to work. Especially when my roommate turned out to be one of those Chatty Cathy types. I love a good discussion, but I view the bedroom as an oasis.

I have a friend, let's call them Nina, who visited her boyfriend's parent's new house which was a very small condo beach property. Nina's boyfriend's sister and partner were also there — which left my friend and her boyfriend to sleep on a terrible air mattress. Upon suggesting that they could go get a hotel purely for sleeping purposes, Nina's boyfriend's mother threw a hissy-fit about how they were ungrateful and implying that she was a bad host. If someone is providing a solution to a situation, it doesn't matter in my opinion. As a host, if someone didn't like the sleeping arrangements, they are more than welcome to shackle up in a hotel.

I found space in an alcove under the stairs. It was the perfect place to set up my mattress pad, and I had an outlet to charge my phone. There was not much else I needed in life. I told Alanna, my friend who invited me on the trip, about my change of plans.

"Are you sure!?" Alanna said, as if I was suggesting I could sleep in the ocean.

I know Alanna felt badly, but I much preferred my hidden alcove underneath the stairs. With the exception of a single spider, I never felt bad about being in the basement.

The first trip, referred to here as *Carolina I*, lead up to the marriage between my friends Alanna and Eric. The days leading up involved no hard plans, and as they slipped by I became increasingly on edge, looking to do something.

"There will be no plans on this trip besides maybe a dinner," someone said when another person in the group asked about plans. I decided to keep my mouth shut moving forward about making hard plans. Instead, I walked the shores and the town area like a specter clinging for social plans. I began to become unhinged after three days of 'relaxing' nothingness.

Recently I spent two days in a row unwinding and doing nothing. I just laid on the couch balancing between different media devices and programs. And then, on the third day, I returned to my full-force energy that needed to do *something*.

Carolina II, which happened in May of 2022, had a few more plans, including a trip to Wilmington. We did a ghost tour that featured outrageous stories of ye old Wilmington, including a few buildings that were currently still haunted.

"They won't even stick around at night in this house," the tour lady exclaimed, turning to the house behind us.

You'd think if that many spirits were so problematic that a business refused to stay past sundown, they'd exorcise the house. But then, it became obvious why one exorcist wouldn't handle this property. The house had been built over the old gallows. You can imagine the hundreds of people who were put to death at the gallows might be...upset with humans.

Downtown Wilmington had plenty of cute places — like an ancient dive bar called Barbary Coast. The place was small and tight, and half of the space was devoted to a single pool table. There was a store with all sorts of gimmicks — including incense called *Booty Call*. I think that's the last scent I'd like if trying to be tranquil with incense.

We were trying to pick a restaurant when I suggested a nearby place that had a good rating. The group agreed, and so we trekked over to the restaurant. We sat down to find that the menu was littered with weird dishes like duck tenders, ostrich burgers, wild boar soup, and Himalayan Yak poutine (could you legally eat that?).

In an act that personally was my hell loop, we scrunched together some tip money and quickly vacated the premises. The group blamed me for the suggestion — which I refused to accept. I had merely tossed it out there because it was close by. None of us checked the menu prior to our arrival which was the real problem. Had one of us investigated, then we probably wouldn't have sat down at a table in the restaurant freaking out over the dishes.

There were some normal dishes, but some people complained that they didn't want to pay fifteen dollars for a burger. I was a bit taken aback at the wallet-clutching. We were on vacation, I know personally I was spending probably fifty-seventy-five bucks a day on food and activities. If there was ever a time to spend a little money, it was on vacation.

The one thing that my friend Alanna wanted during *Carolina II* was an all-group meal. So we all dressed in decently-fine clothes and managed to get a reservation at a steak-house. It was actually our third choice establishment, but finding Thursday night dinner plans in May in a coast Carolina city was an arduous challenge. The restaurant had key lime martinis, which meant I was absolutely sloshed after two of them.

When I was younger, I was given some opportunities to take immersion trips. One trip was to New Orleans. I was under the age of twenty-one, but it was made pretty clear that there would be no drinking or partying on this trip. We did manage to balance our service and volunteerism with trips to Cafe Du Mont — home of the beignet, and Bourbon Street during the daytime which has me quite curious to return during nighttime at some point in my life.

A lot of work had to do with service programs directly connected to the post-aftermath of Hurricane Katrina. The trip happened in 2014, but the hurricane's damage was so deep and scarring. I remember we took a tour in a van and learned so much about the hurricane damage, but also the government corruption and racial injustices that have plagued New Orleans. It is a vibrant city of culture, welcoming and diverse, but a city where the rich and powerful demand their pound of flesh.

One moment that felt sticky was when we volunteered to help sort Mardi Gras beads — I don't know *who* benefited from this service, but we helped sort thousands of beads. Upon further thought, I believed were possibly donating beads back to the different organizations who were part of Mardi Gras. We were encouraged to keep some of the beads as we so desired. Immersion experiences usually involve nice people. So every two minutes someone would say, "oh this bead necklace is *so* you." We probably left with more Mardi Gras necklaces than were sorted.

The second immersion trip I did during college was local. The whole idea was to experience homeless and poverty on a local level. We stayed in sleeping bags at a non-profit, went scrummaging for food, and did various service projects around the community. One night in particular we cooked food using scraps that we had discovered at the West Side Market. The produce vendors unfortunately get rid of some of their product that isn't showable. Bruises, nicks, little issues — and it goes straight into their trash. So we rescued these fruits and vegetables, used spare change to buy rice and beans, and made a little dinner. Nothing will make you more appreciative of the life you have when garbage-picking your dinner.

One of my closest friends Billiam transferred to OSU, so I would find myself going down to Columbus often to see him. Billiam and I actually became close because he was my fraternity little. For those who avoided Greek Life — both dramatically and financially, there was a 'big/little' system designed as an educational and spiritual journey.

When I met Billiam, I thought he was gay. But Billiam at the time kept talking about 'meeting girls.' I'm the kind of person who doesn't have time to speculate on personal sexuality. So I took Billiam at his word and worked to get him hooked up with ladies.

The moment I knew Billiam was 100% gay was during our spring fraternity dance. Our mutual friend Monica grinded up on Billiam during the dance party and Billiam *flipped* out. You would have thought that Monica had stolen Billiam's identity and successfully financially landed a business loan in his name. However, moments later, when a guy grinded up on Billiam, there were no complaints.

"Huh, that's weird," I muttered following the incident. "Billiam's female friend grinded up on him and he was mortified. But a guy, an acquaintance at best, grinded up on Billiam, and he had no problem with him."

It felt like I was doing rocket science when in reality — the math was easier than two plus two.

Billiam would eventually come to terms with his sexuality in Australia, before moving on to OSU. As I like to say, Billiam went down under to find out he wanted to go down under on dudes.

I got trashed on most of these Columbus trips. Billiam is the type of friend that is always ready to go out on the town. I really don't know how he does it — it's like he stores all his energy during the weekdays so he can just exude weekend energy.

Many times I was so drunk that I willingly agreed to get White Castle. My drunk ass would gobble up breakfast sliders at 2am and 'is this chicken?' chicken rings and enjoyed it. I wouldn't say it's a rock bottom — that was exclusively left for moments of vomit and regret.

I've always wondered if there's ever been an issue where a drunk has stammered out: "I love whites...Castle" and for a second people are like okay, they're white trash — thankfully not racist white trash.

Columbus was ripe with stories partially because we would drink and party, but also because Billiam never failed to give us a juicy experience. One time Billiam, our friend Joanna, and Joanna's boyfriend hit the town. Billiam and Joanna shared a friendly kiss and Joanna's boyfriend ruined the rest of the trip with his upset jealousy. Another trip involved us going to the busiest bar in the whole land only to leave in order to get away from a girl who we nicknamed Charcuterie. The nickname for her was the first inspiration for the title of one of my future hits, *Charcuterie*.

Another time we went to a Columbus rooftop bar for happy hour. Upon arrival, we realized it wasn't really a happy hour because the drinks were still 14 bucks each. It was one of those fancy bars where every drink is made with honey, egg whites, ivory shavings, and the zest of a virgin tear. If I'm paying 14 dollars a drink, that drink better make me forget all about my worries and be my personal therapist. I can't even imagine living in LA or New York, those drinks would probably be closer to thirty bucks a pop. The best cocktails in my life have always been in the five to twelve dollar range. After twelve bucks, it feels like the cocktail is trying too hard or is just disappointing due to the price point. There was a happy hour where all the apps were five dollars each, which meant I personally was ordering $20 worth of food. I always feel a little embarrassed when the server comes out with a giant tray of food and it's all for me.

One weekend was devoted to Billiam's own birthday and twenty or so of us went out to an Italian restaurant. The party ended up being so big that we were split into two tables. Thankfully our table was the fun table — apparently the other table was a real drag. The biggest shocker is that twenty people were free to go to a birthday dinner. I have a problem finding twenty contacts in general with whom I would want to have dinner even solo.

Columbus has two main gay bars: Union and Axis (at least, according to my experiences). Union was a bit hipster, a bit less about dancing and more about mingling. Axis could be fairly described as a drug den filled with loud music and louder twinks. I always preferred Union. Union was a bit more relaxed and you could still dance on a platform if you wanted to. I will say — nothing has ever topped the insanity of Akron's own Interbelt Nite Club which, at the time of my singular visit back in 2017, had a public domain stripper pole.

One night at Union, this guy came up almost instantly and said, "look at those calves, you better be dancing tonight." I did that southern 'teehee maybe' tone and instantly found my friends so I could tell them that I was being hit on. Later on, I found him on the dance floor where he was straight and here for his bisexual girlfriend. Getting hit on by a straight guy at the gay bar is like having liver surgery on the day of your annual friends and family beer crawl. It's like being sick on vacation, or going to Buffalo Wild Wings for wings and they're out of wings.

Billiam also has a habit of encouraging us to drink to excess early and quickly. Brunch always has an alcoholic situation and afternoon drinking is part of the day plan. If it's past eight o'clock at night and there's not a drink in your hand, it's a personal affront to Billiam. One trip involved us attending a Margarita festival that was happening in downtown Columbus. The serving samples of the margaritas were quite out-of-control, and we were stumbling out of the park after collecting our drinks.

I adventurously ordered the Pad Thai at a non-Thai restaurant during one drunk dinner. Ordering cultural cuisine at an otherwise Americana restaurant is the Russian roulette of dining. The Pad Thai was served with a soy sauce. Drunk clown Matt thought it would be funny to dramatically toss the soy sauce over my meal like I was a thinner version of Emril. In my attempt to be funny — I spilled most of soy sauce all over my *white* pants. Some might say the biggest problem was ordering a saucy dish when wearing white pants. The soy sauce made it look like I was peeing dark carmine-colored blood. I drunkenly ubered to my friends' place for a costume change — even though my fashion sense was never my strongest quality, being covered in soy sauce never did anyone favors unless you were a dumpling.

I am naturally a cheerleader. Not the kind with pom-poms and the constant demand of letters from the alphabet to spell out subliminal messages. I'm the friend that reassures people on their choices, helps solve their problems, gives streams of compliments, and if needed, shakes someone awake to their issues like how people used to shake babies before we found out that was bad.

The problem is that I often become a confidence booster for other people. But it's exhausting to have a ton of drunk skinnies ask you "how do I look? Do I look fat?" Meanwhile my beached walrus butt continuously goes: "yeah you look amazing, just stunning, really!" I have some friends who could be in a contract with a model agency, be wearing the hottest outfit in their existence, and still feel like their thigh needs to loose an ounce.

It's both awkward and funny when skinny people turn to me, a husky person, and ask if they are fat. Skinny people asking if they themselves are skinny to their larger friends is like asking someone at a funeral if they knew the person who died is dead.

After returning from soy sauce-less pants the night proceeded like the Agatha Christie novel *And Then There Were None*. A couple people got sick, a couple people left. One girl wanted to stay at the bar because there was a football player she was infatuated with. Apparently OSU women were mandated to be on the constant ready for a successful football player to pick them out of the crowd to wife up.

At this point, the remaining members of the group went to a gay bar. We were out with a newly appointed gay man. At that point, he had been been out for two weeks, so a month in gay time. He kept mentioning that people were touching him a little too much. I didn't really have much expertise in that area — all I know is that touching does happen. The only time I'm touched at the club is if someone needs to push past me to get to the bartender.

The following Sunday morning ended with brunch and a book store with 32 rooms. I absolutely loved the bookstore — but the bookstore was a hell-loop for Billiam. While I was saying, "oooh room twenty-four: all these books," Billiam kept saying, "*another* room of books!?"

When I think of the craziest night I've ever had out and about, it's not even a night while I was drunk. My friend Deanna, in the winter of 2019, was celebrating her birthday. When you have a lot of female friends, it feels like you're constantly celebrating something or other. "It's my birthday," "it's my birthday week!", "it's my birthday month!" "it's my half-birthday!" It can be exhausting to handle so many celebrations. Can we just hang out without there being an overarching reason to celebrate? Maybe I just want to smash vodka in my face Cheryl! Writer's Note: Deanna, this is definitely not you, I promise.

My friend Deanna is one of my professional friends who has always and forever will have their shit together. Whereas I string myself along across gigs and opportunities, Deanna has the blessed comfort of one job, the high-rise apartment, and that corporate sheen. My sheen is more like a lumberjack who got lost in the forest for a year and finally returned to civilization. Currently, Deanna has a hot boyfriend, sees the best concerts, and travels more than a train-bound vagabond. Meanwhile I'm single, I see those best concerts in the cheapest sections, and get as much travel as a medieval peasant.

 Deanna's 2019 living situation was a cute 1-bedroom 1-bath downtown apartment studio. It was the type of studio apartment that was probably a nice 1.5-2k Cleveland spot that would easily be 8-10k spot in New York or LA. The studio itself was so white you'd think you were imprisoned in an asylum. But Deanna's taste was HGTV-approved and balanced the landlord's sterileness with some wood features and centerpieces.

 For this night out, there was a whole slew of Deanna's friends who were strangers to me. Thankfully my best friend Monica was here so I wasn't socially at odds. I do think it's fun to blend friend groups — my parents have met most of my closest friends. And I can think of a handful of friends who have become friends due to their association with me. However — not all friends are great at intermingling. You have to be careful — like you're making meth (not that I would know).

 Deanna introduced me to her crush that night — a man so irrelevant in my memory that I'll just name him Gerald. I don't mean that as an insult to all Geralds. Just *this* Gerald. He was one of those stereotypical Caucasian persuasions, the type of man that looked like an impending collection of bad decisions. We've all been on that rollercoaster at least once. Some of us ride that train more than a regular on their favorite public transportation method. The cliche is true, there is something alluring about bad boys, people who don't want us, and people who look so devoid of passion. Like a *Wheel of Fortune* contestant with bad luck, I had spun on all three of those, each time thinking I'd get money when in reality I was landing on bankrupt every time.

 I always feel like I'm on the stage. I'm still debating if it's a personality trait or a small bout of narcissism. So I chatted up with Deanna's friends who were strangers to me. Thankfully, Monica was on my side. It was like having a gun in a bar in Texas, you might just need to pull that surprise out of your pocket. The night swirled with White Claws, Geralds, and light music. But all of that would soon change because of not-her-real-name Jean.

I can't remember how or why Jean got invited. Perhaps she was out on the street — like a social version of an unhoused individual. Jean might say: "help, I have money — just no one to drink this forty with!" And people would walk by and say, "Honey, let's help this person by giving them social plans!" Perhaps Jean was in the apartment hallway and happened to sneak in. A curious neighbor who wanted to probe the medication drawer and sneer at the coffee table book selection. Or maybe Jean was a ghost. Considering the outrageous juvenile behavior that most ghosts appear to command — maybe she was nothing more than a momentary apparition that would haunt our memories with her audacity.

According to Deanna's memory, Jean was a friend of a friend that had tagged along for the evening. But it wasn't one of those friends who you're like: "meet my friend Jean! She's amazing." It was more of a "Jean came along...she's a friend..." There's a major difference when the word 'friend' is distanced from the name of the friend. It's like you're sending out vague warnings that the person you brought along is a piece of shit. Let's run it through another example.

"My friend Lance is amazing at crocheting!" — sounds like you like Lance and he's good at crocheting.

"Lance is okay at crocheting...thanks for allowing me to bring my...friend." Two ellipsis? A refusal to hype up Lance's skills at the crochet? Unsure if Lance should be defined as a friend? I see more red flags in that sentence than an event hosted by the Chinese government propaganda machine!

There are rules to group decorum. Rules that I occasionally disregard lightly. Three rules that are quite universal for strangers are that you shouldn't bombard them with controversial opinions, extremely vulgar jokes, or trauma. I've been known to bend these rules, especially the vulgar joke line. But when these rules are broken, they're broken with purpose. I've successfully read the room and know the rules well enough to know how I can break them.

Jean clearly skipped Etiquette 101, because she immediately began dismantling the social biome like an invasive species.

"Oh, are you eating *these*?" Jean pointed to a bag of veggie chips that was casually being munched on by a few people. Like chipmunks caught eating carrots — the guilty party froze mid crunchery. There were responsive murmurs of 'yes' which made Jean 'tsk' like an old librarian who had discovered people were utilizing the autonomy books for pornographic pleasures.

"You do realize these are heavy on sodium?" Jean asked with the tone that the sodium level was a pipe-bomb waiting to burst. Jean looked at the bag of veggie chips as if someone personal to her had been murdered by that particular bag. Jean went on a small tirade that had key words of 'heart-issues,' 'cholesterol,' 'food industry,' and 'inorganic.' It just seemed rude to gang up on a few people for having veggie straws. It's like Debbie Downer but with an additional bitchy-social-justice-warrior component added in. I don't know if Jean wanted to provide information, or maybe was working as a lobbyist for the potato chip industrial complex. But the whole event was immediately soured and everyone refused to touch the bag of veggie chips out of worry over Jean's retribution.

Moments later, another conversation was interrupted by Jean. I don't know the exact context of the original discussion, but Jean declared proudly that she didn't believe in women's rights. How we had gotten to Jean's opinion was lost history. But Jean's admission that she disagreed with women's rights told me all that I needed to know about Jean.

Jean was the type of woman who didn't have a lot of female friends. She would claim that she got on with men. She preferred to be noticed, even negatively, than not be noticed at all. In a world where she felt empty, she did her best to fill space however she could. I felt like I was playing the role of a psychologist in a spin-off of *The Silence of the Lambs* that featured social crimes.

While the room was slowly deflating like a stress ball that had been squeezed too hard by someone's meaty legs, Jean was divulging some of her own problems. Jean did divulge that she and her boyfriend had gotten into a fight earlier that day. Maybe Jean had yelled at her boyfriend for having a sodium-saturated snicky-snack like veggie chips? I doubt he cared if she was anti-women, most men are.

Unable to enjoy the apartment party, Jean decided to call her paramour and left the party to turn the bathroom into a telephone booth. Jean leaving the party sent a wave of relief through the room that mirrored the moment when a man unbuttons the top button of his pants midway through a buffet. This brief respite shattered as a series of shouts began to escape from Deanna's bathroom. Dee's apartment featured an open living-dining concept, and a separate space for her bedroom in which was the bathroom. You couldn't hide a screaming match within this tight square space.

Turns out, Jean and Jean's Boyfriend got into another fight. The unresolved issues from earlier were now spilling out like the amount of White Claws that we had that night. After all, 2019 was truly White Claw's dominion over the hard seltzer world.

"Fuck you, and fuck your mom too!" was the only line I could make out from her bathroom fight. I wondered — did the fight include his mom? Or was Jean utilizing a standard line you say in anger? Or maybe Jean was actively trying to curb-stomp on a woman's rights like a conservative Supreme Court Justice?

In anger and retaliation to her boyfriend and her boyfriend's mom, Jean slammed her wine glass against the wall of the bathroom. This wasn't a plastic wine glass, or a shoddy glass. A stemmed, proper Crate-and-Barrel wine glass found its way smashed against Dee's bathroom wall. Not sure how that was revenge against the boyfriend who was in Lakewood. I think the reason I don't remember what was said was because all my memory and disbelief went into Jean's temper tantrum.

I have a tendency to dramatize things because I get easily bored and need to be stimulated like some middle school punk. I've jokingly told people that I 'reinvent reality in a creative way.' However, this story has so far been and will remain entirely truthful. Multiple pregame witnesses recall Jean slamming that wine glass against the wall as if the wall was attacking her and Jean had no choice but to act in self-defense. Not only did Jean damage property, but she left the glass on the floor of the bathroom. Let me add that it was a TILED BATHROOM. Unlike flat floors, tiled floors have small grooves and score lines. Cleaning glass from tile? I'd rather move to a new apartment.

If I had been so enraged that I slammed a wine glass against the wall of a friend's bathroom, I would be absolutely embarrassed and be the first person to clean up the mess. You'd think Jean would have came to her senses and taken responsibility. But it was Deanna who ended up cleaning the shrapnel out of her tile floor. She was the host of the party, but also the birthday girl.

Soon we were ready to order Ubers to the first bar of the night. Because there were twelve of us at this point, we divided into three teams for an impromptu *Amazing Race* with ride-share apps. This part always harkens back to 'pick your groups' in grade school or 'pick your teams' in dodgeball. It's a survival situation that even Darwin himself would enjoy witnessing from the corner of the room.

I don't know why Jean was in my Uber team. I think other people successfully paired up quicker and even lied that they were filled up. Thankfully Monica was with me and we watched in horror as Jean made sassy comments to the Uber driver that ranged from his 'slower route' to the bar, his driving habits, and more shocking statements.

The destination was a half-dive-bar meets sport-bar meets pub called Map Room. It actually wasn't that far away — but when most of the group are girls in heels, twenty blocks feels like a hundred. My foursome via the app arrived first even though Jean had declared our Uber drive the most inefficient. As if Jean was trying to prove that rock bottom was a social construct, she got into a fight with the bouncer.

"I need you to take your ID out of your wallet," the bouncer said, firm but polite. Jean had one of those wallet-purse combinations where you could see the ID through a transparent plastic window. But the bouncer wanted to scan the ID or see it from outside the plastic casing.

"Well, can't you see it?" Jean asked, pushing her wallet-purse and the ID closer to the guard as if he had bad eyes. She had pushed the wallet-purse so close to his eyes that she was almost hitting him in the face with it.

"No, I need to hold it." the bodyguard's voice was pretty even, considering he was reiterating instructions to an aggressive woman. Jean sassily took out her card while I did my best to act like I didn't know her. It was hard to pull that off considering we had just climbed out of the same ride-share vehicle together.

We made our way to the back of the bar. A more correct statement would be that Jean stomped to the back of the room. Map Room is designed as a tight rectangle with a long bar. Most of the front had been claimed up by twenty-somethings. The other Uber groups soon arrived, and I found myself double-fisting a gin and tonic and Long Island Tea.

The bar was too peaceful for Jean. Even though Jean had argued with the Uber driver and with the bouncer, she was hungry for more altercation. She was like a debate student who would do anything to win for her preppy private Ivy League school. Everyone has that person in their life who is *always* looking for conflict. Sometimes they find the weirdest things to latch on and argue about. Sometimes they invent it. I'm still not sure how her next battle started.

Unbeknownst to anyone in the group, Jean decided to play conquistador. She had stepped up to a nearby table of people.

"I'm taking this table, we need this table," Jean said to the group who was currently in the process of leaving the table.

Jean didn't need to fight for the table for a few reasons. One, there were plenty of tables. Two, we didn't *need* a table, we were comfortable at the bar. But the final and best reason: the people at the table were *LEAVING*! You could tell a couple people went to the bathroom so the rest of the group was drinking the dregs of their drinks. If Jean really wanted the table, she could have just politely asked for the table. But she purposefully was nasty over it.

I watched in horror as this friend group tried ignoring Jean. But then the anger began to stir between everyone. The inner peacekeeper in me waltzed over with my two drinks. No one else in the group appeared willing or able to handle Jean. I threw Jean under the bus quicker than the speed of light. I didn't know Jean, so I felt no shame in calling her out on her behavior. Sharing an Uber ride to the bar and witnessing a bathroom meltdown barely made us acquaintances. And even if Jean had been a friend, I would have been mortified by her comments and behavior.

By the time I had arrived to intervene, the table of innocent bystanders who were preparing to leave hadn't lobbed personal attacks. But Jean was an artist who had yet to find the right pen stroke and began weaponizing personal insults like an Italian grandmother.

"You're 23 and you need Botox," Jean snapped to one girl. The girl Jean had insulted was a hundred times more beautiful than Jean's very tired early 2000s attire. This poor girl in no way needed Botox. The friend group Jean had attacked were quite close to snapping back at Jean. I don't really recall how the situation deescalated, but fortunately for me I didn't see Jean for the rest of the night. I wonder if she felt personally betrayed that I told her victim that she didn't need Botox.

The group slowly split up as night outs with a ton of people do. Monica met up on a last-second date, leaving me with Deanna. Deanna and I and a couple others moved over to Dive Bar. Dive Bar was a place that *wished* it was a dive bar. Instead, it was what a rich white guy would *describe* as a dive bar had he never been in a true dive establishment.

By this point in the night, I could tell that I was slipping back into sobriety, and I had no desire to try and push myself upward towards tipsy again. In these moments I'm usually drawn to my phone to play games or swipe on Tinder while the drunks around me continue to fly high. But our high flight was immediately canceled when we discovered that Gerald, Dee's low-key romantic situation, ghosted her for *another* woman at Dive Bar. At the time, it was really shocking. But then again, we were at Dive Bar which brings out the trash in people.

Deanna was absolutely gutted — and we walked across Downtown Cleveland as I pulled out every universal truth I could think of. Men are trash, there are other fish in the sea, Gerald was beneath her, etc. We ended up getting large slice of thin pizza that was a bit greasy that becomes legendary when drunk. Dee had a couple tears, but was more so shellshocked like she had seen a demon rather than lost a fuckboy.

"Do you think he would have ghosted you if we hadn't gone to Dive Bar?" I asked, dabbing the pizza of grease as if that was truly going to change the calorie count I needed for this pizza to become healthy.

"I don't know," Dee truthfully answered, doing that internal replay of the night.

We don't often think about how small choices play out. Maybe if Jean hadn't been such a glass-slamming, name-calling (enter word of choice here), she would have made new friends. Maybe if she had separated her anger from her boyfriend and strangers, she would have enjoyed the night out.

But our own choices: of double-fisting a gin and tonic with a Long Island, my friend Monica's decision to end the night with a date, Dee's decision to pursue this (enter another explicative here), going to Map Room, going to Dive Bar, getting pizza...these all made a single strand. And we couldn't have predicated that strand — we just know there will *be* a strand by the end of the night.

That following morning we got a stunning conclusion for what happened to Jean. Apparently her anger had not cooled down, and she decided to visit her boyfriend's house. Apparently the house was locked. So Jean did what any normal person would do: she punched out a window, injuring her hand, and tried kicking down a door. Cops were called, and Jean ended up getting stitches.

We also found out that Jean worked at a TOP BANK IN THE CITY. Let's just say the 'young professional' that she is on LinkedIn was not indicative of who Jean truly was. Months later, I found out that Jean had left Cleveland. I don't know where she is, or what she's doing. But I'm assuming she's angrily strutting about ruining as many people's nights as she can.

All the outrageousness, the binge drinking for conformity, the late nights that involved bad decisions, terrible fast food, and the occasional love interest gone awry, nothing has left me with the same reaction that Jean did. Not-her-real-name Jean would not be toppled easily — and I think Jean herself would appreciate that she ruled all the night outs I've yet to have.

You May Now Be The DJ

When people hear I'm a DJ, their eyes glimmer with excitement. By definition alone, being a DJ sounds like a glamorous job filled with fun, booze, and music. What's there to not like?

I applied to be a DJ on a whim. I knew I had the voice, radio background, and a love for music. A day or so later, On a Sunday when I was writing, I got a call from my soon to be boss and not his real name Shawn.

"I *never* call on a Sunday," Shawn said like he was the Chick-Fil-A of business and viewed it as a non-work day. "But I saw your application and was really impressed. Can you come in for an interview?"

Soon I would walk into a lux office in Brooklyn Heights. The area around the office looked a bit warehouse-grunge. But the interior featured velvets, upholstery, textures, bright, colorful lighting systems, and fancy technology. I sat down with Shawn and his right-hand man, not his real name Juan. At the time I didn't have much of an impression. I knew I could do the work and make good money, and the result seemed fun. I don't remember much from my first wedding with Shawn and Juan. I did a little microphone work and learned about the programs, but otherwise just did a bunch of tear-down and set-up.

I was very chaotic when I first started DJing. I used to be the wedding DJ who would scream during songs, dance with the crowds, and climb speakers and furniture like some Rolling Stones-inspired mess. I'd go out and dance to the "Wobble." I'd go out and socialize with the bridal party. I'd chat it up over a drink with guests. And I'd leave every wedding with a dehydrated, overworked headache. I remember saying to everyone: "well, if I don't leave with a headache, then I haven't done a good job."

I grew out of that young-DJ mind frame and became a bit more focused on mixing tracks and honing my skills as an emcee and host. I don't really remember much about my earlier years as a DJ. Many weddings over the years have blended together, but I remember a few critical memories between 2017-2022.

One of the most insane out-of-the-body moments I've had was in 2018. We were in a downtown Cleveland venue on a beautiful summer night. There was a large number of toasts happening. Usually, you have the best man, the maid of honor, maybe a parent or two, and a prayer. Sometimes the couple will speak for themselves, sometimes it's both sets of parents, and occasionally a random bridal party member or a sibling will also volunteer to give a speech. This wedding had seven members of the bridal party speaking, and I correctly guessed that these were seven longer speeches and not quick admissions of love. But the first speech immediately set the tone: this was not just a series of toasts, it was a roast.

This roast lasted for a half-hour and was one of the longest half-hours I've ever experienced at a wedding. Many jokes were about how the bride was the 'man' of the relationship. More jokes featured the groom's lack of balls, and how the bride had bullied him into marriage. The bride and groom seemed fine with this roast, but I can't believe they agreed that a roast was appropriate given the number of old people who watched on in horror between the balls jokes or various dark and blue-colored humor. Even their officiant joined in on the fun — calling them the 'perfect lesbian couple.' I kept eyeing the room to see the reactions of the guests. Some were throughly enjoying the stand-up material, while a few looked a bit horrified. I specifically remember one old lady who looked like she had been teleported to the future, and did not like what she saw.

My worst wedding of all time was back in either 2018 or 2019. We were out in the middle of Nowhere, Ohio. No cell service and back roads which haven't been maintained since the Civil War. It was the kind of place that I wouldn't be caught dead visiting, although I would probably be found dead if I stayed too long. There were two hundred people cramped in this cute but small barn. None of the guests wanted to listen to instructions, making things like the 'bubble tunnel' and the 'sparkler send-off' nearly impossible. The best man's speech was covered in racist jokes, which caused the tightly-packed barn to groan with indignation. The cherry on top was when a groomsman came up to me.

"I've been a DJ for seven years; you need to be doing more mixing," he ordered a very pissy Matt Hribar. Like most mid-sized mammals and some apex creatures, my anger temperament is a slippery slope that becomes more aggressive on a short circuit.

"Okay," I shrugged. Anyone can do anything for seven years. It didn't mean you were great at something or even that you'd spent a lot of time doing it.

He continued to press me, and finally, I kicked him out of my DJ booth. He was swearing; I was swearing. There were more middle fingers thrown between him and I than an Italian mafia meeting between rival factions. He glared at me the rest of the night and I offered him a smooch which is a heavy offense to a dumb, drunk, straight white man.

"We need to get out of here fast," I told my assistant when we began winding down. "God forbid he tries to fight me…"

Another highlight was when I got to DJ a wedding at the House of Blues. Getting to DJ on the stage of House of Blues is one of those extraordinary little personal accomplishments you don't realize you want until after you finish it.

One time a bride found out the week before the wedding that her soon-to-be husband had bought time with a sex worker. And yes, he had had sex. I wanted to clarify that it wasn't a therapy session or a flirty dinner. The bride told our staff that she would still have the party of her dreams, divorce him six months later, and get half his money. In my head, I wish I had this caliber of intellect. But unfortunately, I think I'd react emotionally and call off the wedding.

"I've been meaning to ask what happened," Juan said with a mystical sigh as if picturing the epilogue in his mind.

Most people think the wedding industry is filled with insatiable brides who demand the world and back. I've not met many Bridezillas, although, on occasion, you run into some Disney-level villains. The funniest constructive complaint I received was when a bride told my boss that I was 'sweaty' when setting up equipment for her July outdoor wedding. There was a fix that I could have provided this bride at the time. I could avoid being sweaty by not setting up equipment or DJing your wedding.

One of the most uncomfortable moments I've ever had at a wedding happened during a groom and mother-of-the-groom dance. The groom's hands were dangerously low, hovering above his mother's derriere. She had pushed herself in instead of leaving room for the Holy Spirit. Her dress had a slit bigger than a tent opening — and I could not help but watch with wide eyes as they gyrated and hipped into each other.

"This is the... *sexiest* groom and the mother of the groom dance I've ever seen," I muttered to my co-pilot Juan.

"Trust me — I've seen dirtier."

The biggest issue I have DJing weddings has to be the equipment set-up and tear down. We're lugging hundreds of pounds into vans and out of vans. Carrying equipment across venues, up and down elevators and stairs — before doing the reverse at the night's end.

Early on, I got into a hissy fit with my boss over a lighting rig. I had done everything I could, and so had my assistant. We had troubleshooted it, and my boss called to imply that I should know exactly what I'm doing on the technology side. We had a big blowout that resulted in the silent treatment for a couple months. We eventually regained focus and my knowledge of technology improved.

None of my mistakes were ever grave, but those appeared to happen to other DJs. Speakers would pop and fuzz, and subwoofers would explode. My favorite story was told second-hand. Two of our videographers flew a drone over a lake when the drone bugged out and began to fall into the lake. The one photographer, Jake, dove into the lake to try and save the drone. He got soaked to the bone, and the only available clothes were my boss' bonus set. My prominent Italian boss was not petite, so Jake looked like a kid trying on his dad's suit for the rest of the shoot. Personally, I would have kept wet clothes on.

The following week, we were at a wedding with Jake, and he was standing near a decorative pond. I immediately shouted out:

"JAKE, WATCH OUT FOR THE LAKE!"

Over the years, loading equipment in and out of the truck at the office has become more accessible. When I started out, it was like rolling boulders in a Sisyphus-like fashion. (Not the sexually transmitted disease, but the Greek God who spent eternity rolling boulders up a hill.) Crates and speakers eventually began being attached to wheels. Wooden coffins of materials turned into safer materials. We even got ramps in 2022 to ease the two-foot jump from the ground to the truck interior.

We usually eat what the guests eat (always the chicken option since it's cheaper). On a rare occasion, we're offered a very weak substitution, think one of those boxed lunches with a soggy sandwich. One wedding featured the most disgusting-looking boxed lunch so I ordered online at a sushi restaurant down the road and left the wedding. If you're not going to try and feed us properly, I feel no guilt in trying to find something decent to shove down my gullet.

Another wedding venue served us turkey sandwiches. When I think of turkey sandwiches, I think tomato, lettuce, mayonnaise, and cheese, preferably Swiss or provolone. Upon inspection, we found that this turkey sandwich came with jalapeño, onions, and cocktail sauce sandwiched on a rock-hard Italian sub roll. It was absolutely revolting, as if the Food Network was in the hotel kitchen with a challenge for the staff: "Open your mystery baskets, chefs! You've been given turkey, jalapeños, cocktail sauce, and a four-day-old Italian sub roll." There must have been some kind of sadist working in the hotel kitchen that day — I have never seen a meal that skanky since.

I was a vegetarian for the first year I DJed, and sometimes the vegetarian dishes were better-looking than the meat meals. There would be decadent vegetable lasagnas, lush fields of harvest, divine pasta, and even a vegetarian pot pie situation that was to die for. However, vegetarian dishes also tended to be the worst dishes of all time. Mushrooms that looked like they crawled off the set of *Stranger Things*. Squash that looked like someone had squashed it with supple derriere cheeks.

Eating meat isn't much better. Hotels especially love serving bland foods — chicken so pink and white that it looks like you're munching on a human arm. The saddest meal I've ever eaten was actually at a prom. It was being held at a country club — and the meat was so bland I felt like I was in one of those science-fiction films where they eat healthy glop instead of food. What made it sad was how *perfectly*-cooked the brisket was. It pulled apart quicker than a middle-school romantic relationship, melted in your mouth like room-temperature butter, and was surprisingly lean. But it tasted like *nothing*. How hard would it be to find some kind of au jus? A pepper roast? *SOMETHING* to give it a lift?

One wedding featured *just* fish dishes. I've always hated seafood, so I just passed and went to eat the opening salad. I can't *believe* that fish was the default dish. I'd take the sad vegetarian meals any day over the fish.

In 2022, I was DJing a wedding with assistant Jetty. Jetty is in their young 20s, slightly nerdy, and somewhat cocky. We were setting up at a gorgeous downtown venue. The owners were two beautiful, middle-aged sociable people. Think of Bonnie and Clyde if they opened an event space and Cylde had a sexy Latin spin.

"I'm going to hook you up with the best drink in the house," Clyde explained with a giant grin. "It's going to be so smooth, do you like tequila?"

When building a new headquarters, does a giant corporation look for a local tax break? Of course I like tequila.

Clyde ran off to the bar to make us a drink. It's always a better time when the establishment is appreciative. Granted, I'm being paid to do a service. But it can be a bit souring when an event space acts like they're the ones paying you. I've had event owners who demanded we pack up our gear by unachievable time results, owners who fed us like dogs, and even event spaces where we were blamed for the event space's limitations.

Clyde returned with a deep brown beverage which confused me. The only deep brown tequila-based liquid I've seen was an Apple Pie Margarita. And given the floating orange slice in the drink, I didn't think tequila was in the drink.

"It's bourbon with orange," Clyde said. Internally I was vomiting — I hated dark liquors like bourbon and whiskey. I could slam back an Apple Royale Shot in a liquor emergency. But even that feels like I'm on the brink of death. But with Clyde being so friendly, I had no choice but to sip on the drink. Clyde watched as if we were meeting his beloved.

"How is it?" Clyde asked.

"DELICIOUS!" I said with full enthusiasm. Considering the drink contained my nemesis, the end result wasn't too bad. It was palpable, and how many times do we go through with slightly uncomfortable things for the people we love or even just like? And I didn't know Clyde from previous experiences. But based on what

I did know, the man had a generous heart, and his homemade whiskey cocktail went down a throat that otherwise would have refused passage.

"We are going to get you the best meals in the house too!" Clyde exclaimed, eager with excitement to share the food with us.

"I can't break that man's heart," Jetty sighed, struggling to get through his cocktail. Like me, Jetty was anti-whiskey.

"No, he's too nice," I said, taking a sip and feeling my throat protest casually. It wasn't a riot, but it was undoubtedly an upset rumble.

Clyde returned later with the best dish in the house, which featured a giant hunk of salmon. Some would have been swimming in the delights of a perfectly-cooked, natural-looking salmon slice. But both Jetty and I hated fish. Jetty later told me that he loved shrimp because 'it tastes like the sauce you dunk it into." To me, it doesn't feel like he likes shrimp. Saying I love shrimp because of the sauce is like saying you like the house because of the land *around* the house. Even if the yard looks great, what's the point if the cottage is untenable? Do you live on the lawn instead?

"Oh no," I whispered when Clyde left. "The best food in the house is...seafood. I hate seafood."

"Well, what are we going to do?" Jetty muttered.

Because I liked Clyde, I ate half the salmon before realizing I couldn't do this to my body. My throat, already coated with whiskey, was buckling as I put the tinny-musky salmon in my mouth. To be fair, it would have been perfect for someone who enjoyed salmon. But I'd instead take the second or third-best dish in the house that had no fish.

Jetty and I smuggled the salmon off the plate into napkins and over to the trash. You would have thought we were trying to covertly plant a bomb. Later on, Clyde returned and asked us how the food was, and we both raved about the food in an Emmy-awarding winning performance . It didn't feel like a lie, the food *was* phenomenal. Our taste pallets were just children unable to drink bourbon and salmon.

I entered 2022 wondering if it was time to slow it down. I had done twenty-eight weddings the previous year and felt like I still hadn't recovered, especially in the September-October period of the season. People in Ohio love having a fall wedding when the leaves turn, and the humid summer air turns into pleasant fall breezes. I do think my outlook was a bit dour, but 2022 proved to be, on record, my worst year for weddings.

When I say 'worst,' I don't refer to *my* work output. I have always retained a high level of pride and determination regarding my work. By worst, I'm referring to the issues, the surprises, the clients, and the general lack of fun. I had rough clients, heavy demands, a lack of tips, and a lot of thankless work.

2022 featured the most boring wedding I've ever done. It started at 3pm on a Saturday, which feels insensitive at worst, and bad planning at best. The ring actually went missing because the best man had dropped it. So countless guests were combing the grassy grounds to find the ring. Thankfully the ring was found but the best man was ridiculed for the rest of the night. For some reason, while I was waiting to start the entrance music, the wedding had just begun. We were fifteen minutes away from the official start when the minister and groom began walking down the aisle. I hadn't been given any indication we were ready to go. This was funky because weddings notoriously start late and never begin early.

I felt horribly because the dance floor was emptier than a craft store at 8pm on a Sunday night. I tried everything — 60s, 70s, disco, old pop, new pop, 90s, R&B, slow songs, Latin songs... but the crowd was stiffer than a gay club at underwear night. There was a moment when a conga line of ten people picked up, but even the conga line felt forced. The room cleared out, the dance floor remained desolate, and the wedded couple were extremely happy with my work.

Another sad wedding was with a lovely couple who chose to do a barn wedding in July. Thankfully it was a more relaxed day because even with it being 80, that barn soaked up more heat than a sponge in a bucket of water. The guests cleared out as soon as dinner was over. The bride came up to me specifically to say, "I'm surprised people left early. But some of my friends said they had to leave early because tomorrow they're going to Cedar Point!"

My mouth dropped further than Pamela Anderson's.

"Are you serious?" That's my go-to when someone tells me something that seems so off-base that it couldn't be real.

"Oh yeah," the bride said with a shake of her head. The barn was located twenty minutes from Cedar Point, so I could see why some people might turn their wedding Saturday night into a Sunday Funday park day. But to say that to the bride? And to leave at 9 PM? I know Cedar Point gets packed, but you can't hold off till 10 PM and act tired or something? Those were some bad friends — and if you're reading this book, be a better liar and use some caffeine to power through the reception or morning after.

While my friends were enjoying their summer Saturdays, I was driving in the middle of an empty Ohio field when a foreboding sense of deja vu overcame me. We were less than two minutes away from arriving at the venue.

"I think I know where we're going," I whispered, hands clutched on the wheel as if I had discovered we were characters in a Jordan Peele horror movie. "And if it is where I think it is, we're about to get to a steep dirt hill."

Sure enough, my prediction became a reality as I powered a Penske truck to the same barn that had been home to the worst wedding I had ever DJed. I could feel the unlistenable crowds and argumentative groomsmen once again.

"Oh my God," I whispered as if in a film where the protagonist realizes his life has been shattered.

We stepped out of the van — although part of me wanted to drive the van up and away. Two men, one younger and one older, stood next to some wooden planks.

"Hi!" I said, pretending to be excited.

"Hello, we're putting the floor together." The older man said.

I smiled, not really sure what to say to that information. We went inside when the old man said, "Well, can we talk with you?"

I was confused, so looked at him and, I'll admit, sassily said: "The floor guy wants to talk with me?"

"Well, I'm the owner," the guy said.

Oomph, talk about a foot in my mouth. Thankfully, I quickly recovered, and we chatted about the event overview. He was lovely but certainly not the best at introducing himself. The onus of introducing himself was on him versus me assuming he was a point of contact. Why not just say, "Hi, I'm the owner?"

The dance floor had yet to be created, so we couldn't set up. We were already tight for time, and this just felt like some poltergeist was making sure I was stressed out. The ceremony soon began, although no one told me about it. The mother of the bride walked up to me:

"Don't I have my own entrance music?"

"We're starting?" Quite often, I become the wedding planner. Part of the job of a DJ is to run the order of events and manage the event overall. But *technically,* it's not my job to run the event.

I played the music for her, and she strolled down the aisle. The rest of the wedding was fine, and the ceremony melted into cocktail hour underneath the barn. We made our way to dinner, where way too many people were trying to fit into the barn. The rest of the night went fine — even without cell phone reception. Finally, it was time to pack up, and I went and got the truck.

We arrive at wedding venues with giant loading-trucks, the kind you would rent out when you move homes. I had initially parked the truck in the front, but the wife of the co-owning couple insisted I park it in the back. She didn't want me to park it in the back to be helpful. She didn't like the truck being an eyesore in the front parking lot.

"I don't know," I told her. "I'd feel safer having the van in the front."

The back parking lot was accessed by a road curved down an embankment into a small lot. I didn't feel comfortable with such a treacherous trip, but there was no convincing her. At the end of the night, I began backing up the truck to try and get around the embankment, only to get the truck stuck.

When I'm in a crisis, I go from 0 to 100 quickly. I'm the kind of person that powers through the pressure but all while my internal body screams and I say things like 'kill me right now,' as if God would hear that and take my life because of it.

We were in the middle of Backwoods, Ohio, with no cell reception and a stuck truck. I immediately pictured us stranded in darkness, unable to call for help. And if we did manage to get a bar of service, would the truck rental company be able to get here quickly? I probably wouldn't be home until five in the morning.

What kept this from being an awful night was that the barn staff helped us push the truck out of the little hole it had fallen into. We swept our gear quickly into the truck and got the hell out of there.

The next wedding had an adorable couple, but time management issues were out the butt. My schedule said that the bridal party introductions started at 6:25pm. But the venue had 6:15pm and the photographers had 6:30pm. I didn't know who we should blame for this mixup — but I assume the bride and groom just messed it up.

It was almost 6:40 PM when the photographers returned with the bride and groom. The bride had thrown up due to the heat and dehydration. No worries! While the bride drank water and ate a peanut butter cookie, the photographers went to set up.

"Are people normally this anxious about being a few minutes late?" The photographer asked me. I gave him a sharp look back.

"Can we just get ready to go?" I countered, a bit aggressively, to which the photographer looked shaken.

I wasn't trying to be overtly rude — but this was not the time for a semantics class. The photographer gave me a little attitude for the rest of the night.

One wedding involved a comment from the couple's parents, who said, "We have been waiting for our kids to get married ever since they were born." I was naturally confused because this had to be an exaggeration. Who gives birth to a child and immediately says:

"Look at this child...I can't wait until they get married. We must ensure they're off to the courthouse as soon as they turn legal!"

Another 2022 wedding was a foray into equipment logistics. Since I work for a company, I take the equipment marked for me. I don't have to cherry-pick anything; I just go there and swoop for supplies.

My assistant Kuru and I were peacefully setting up when Kuru noticed we were missing the microphone for the ceremony. We have two set-ups — the main rig in the reception hall and a miniature kit for the reception.

"I'll have to go get it; we need it," I sighed. I then made the forty-five-minute round-trip journey and returned with the microphone kit.

"Did you get a mic stand?" Kuru questioned, seeing just the microphone kit in my hand.

"A mic stand?" I questioned. "We..."

I instantly knew we didn't have a microphone stand and would need one for the ceremony. I walked down to the van, and once more made the trip. Thankfully Kuru spotted another piece of equipment was missing before I got to the office; otherwise, I might have made three trips that day.

I was striving to please early on when I was a wedding DJ. But five years in, I was growing frustrated with the simplest things. One wedding featured a reception in an outdoor tent and a ceremony space that was a two-minute car ride down the lake.

"Really?" I sighed as if two locations separated by a two-minute drive were five miles away.

This same wedding had a cocktail space outside of the large hot tent. It had some of the worst cheeses I've seen and tasted in my entire life. A good cheese board keeps things simple: cheddar, Swiss, gouda, and a couple pieces of funky cheese. This cheese spread had a purple cheese that tasted like it had been stuffed up in a crevice for a while and a green cheese that made you think of mold and tasted worse than mold. Did being luxurious mean we had to include weird-looking cheeses that people could all fawn over yet not eat since it was disgusting?

The head caterer was trying to be casual and strict, which was a tricky balancing act. She was very nice to me and my assistant DJ but I overheard her moments later:

"I don't know *who* wanted the napkins to look like that." The head caterer pulled on the napkin to rearrange it by a few centimeters. "*This* is how I want them to look! We're not going to have sloppy napkins today!"

The staff mumbled an affirmative and got back to work. The head caterer, who I'll just name Maggie, came over a bit later.

"I know the introductions are slated at 6:30," she began. "But I'm wondering if we can speed this up? The cocktail hour was a two hour long affair anyway..."

I doubted that many guests were annoyed at the extended happy hour. Usually, people were okay with drinks and conversation, especially if there was a good view. Had the cheese selection been better, it would have sealed the guesswork. I could tell that Maggie was just trying to wrap up her responsibilities quickly, which I could relate to. I loved when weddings went a little late — less responsibility for me.

"We can move it up," I said with a nod. I was very flexible with my fellow vendors (specifically vendors who feed me).

"Perfect, we can aim to start around 6:15!" Maggie went on her way with a bit of pep in her step. Moments later, Maggie was once again at our DJ booth.

"Well, don't hate me for this..." The head caterer said with a meek smile. "But we are having a bit of a salad situation. We ran out of spring mix and have to run to the store."

We were in the middle of Where The Hell Are We, Ohio. The nearest grocery store, let alone a place you could get greens, was probably a good fifteen minutes out. When we stopped at a gas station on the way in, they had every chip, candy, dessert, snack, and heavy item you could think of. But there was not a single vegetable or fruit to be found. You could have strawberry licorice or ketchup on your burger — but raw vegetables were a hard no. Anything resembling a dinner salad was non-existent. In fact, I think if you asked for arugula, the counter employees would have thought you were using a slur on them.

The photographers came over, and I can't believe I had to tell them we had to keep to the original schedule and perhaps stall because of the *spring mix.*

"The spring mix is seven minutes out!" Maggie declared as if the pope or president were on route and we had seven minutes to prepare everything for their arrival. I imagined a helicopter slowly dropping down next to the venue. The wind from the propellers flips over the cheese plate (probably for the best). Women clutch their fancy hats while men watch with intrigue over the machinery. The spring mix would disembark quickly from the helicopter. Maggie would thank the man for his time and dedication before immediately putting him to work.

The photographer on site, who was serving a funny lesbian side character in a Netflix original series, loved that joke.

"Can you imagine a plane flying overhead and dropping the spring mix in the lake like a drug bust?" She added.

I let out a bombastic laugh.

"Maggie has someone swim out into the lake to grab spring mix," I smiled. "Handle the package with care. It's the best stuff on the market."

I didn't have the salad that night because it had celery. So I hoped the imported spring mix went well with the guests who ate the salad. The rest of the food was — questionable, to say the least. The kabobs looked like they had used meat stolen from a cryogenic laboratory hosting Walt Disney himself. The sauce was grainy, and I avoided the roasted vegetables. The veggies looked like they had been burned over a dirty stove in a restaurant featured on *Gordon Ramsey's Kitchen Nightmares*.

Moments later, with the spring mix in tow, we lined up the bridal party only to have a board system meltdown. I scrambled at the moment, unplugging, unhooking, moving buttons, shifting inputs — all while the crowd watched with anticipation.

If I had to rank my DJ skills as an RPG character, I'd say my best skills are being a hype man, shaping and controlling the atmosphere, and my natural vocal abilities. I'm good at mixing, and my music knowledge is good, but my engineering side is the weakest. I like to view myself as the talent. And talent is *not* one to mess around with wires and cords.

I clicked something together and the sound finally flushed into the room. The whole hall gave me a round of applause like I had made a tiger jump through a hoop of fire. The rest of the wedding went without a hitch — except towards the end when drunk guests get very entitled.

The sociologist in me notices that the more fun the crowd is and the more eager they are to dance, the more they complain and irk me. I had so many pissy people trying to get their bad requests in. One girl wanted Beyonce's "If I Were A Boy," which is a good song but highly inappropriate for a wedding. It's not even a sad song you'd happily dance to, it's just sad.

People think DJing is as easy as pressing buttons and that part of the job is straightforward. What's not easy is reading the room, reading a crowd, keeping the atmosphere up, and trying to control the vibe. The bride and groom noted they wanted hip-hop and modern but then needed me to play more old songs for the older people. I cut from Bodak Yellow into Come On Eileen into Shout and it weirdly worked. The crowd was so drunk that I could have played me farting over a techno beat, and they would have danced to it.

The couple chose their last song, a cute little EDM-rap track. But when the event was over, we had herds of people surrounding the DJ booth to play some obscure song as the last song. I didn't want to play this song for a few reasons. The primary reason was the venue, which had made it clear that we had a hard out. Playing past the venue's end time never turns out well. The last thing I want is the event venue space yelling at me or neighbors calling the police because loud music happened after 11pm. Second, the couple had picked out their last song. They should have denoted it if they wanted another song as their last song. Weirdly the song that the crowd wanted wasn't on any of the playlists or must-plays. So, where did this song come from? The last reason, the most personal, is that I don't respond well to dickish comments.

Some people think that the DJ is a public domain creature. That a DJ will play whatever song an individual wants. But sometimes, the individual's needs aren't working for the audience. Your bad song request isn't making my mixing board because it's either a putrid song or doesn't fit the wedding or brief I've gotten from the couple. It's like a philosophy trolley problem: do I play "September" by Earth, Wind, and Fire which will win over most of the room? Or do I play "If I Were A Boy" for that *one* person?

Club DJs can easily mix in shitty requests, especially if money is involved. My friend Billiam once gave a DJ twenty bucks to play "Mr. Brightside." The DJ greedily took the money like a snake seeing an egg out in the open. The DJ did play the song, but only for the first two minutes. It felt like we had witnessed a scam, but Billiam was more than happy to hear his song blasted over the room.

"Can you play something from The Supremes?" A lady asked, looking at me like I was a devilish rouge for playing modern music.

"What song by The Supremes?"

"I dunno — just a song by them."

Talk about an easy way for me to roll my eyes. You want me to play a specific artist but offer no ideas or suggestions? It gets worse, though. One time, a slightly tipsy lady made her way to me.

"Can you play something else?"

"*Else*?" I do this thing when someone asks a stupid question where I give them a silly look with direct eye contact. I find that it makes them embarrassed for lauding their stupidity on me.

"Yeah."
"As in?"
"I dunno."
"You don't know?"
"Yeah."
"Just something *else*?"

She finally got the point and slinked off — having provided no genuine impact. The funny thing was that most of the room had been dancing at that point to some old throwbacks. No doubt she wanted modern music to meet that modern mind of hers.

One of my favorite venues in Cleveland to DJ at is Music Box Supper Club. It's a cute music venue on the Cuyahoga River, and part of why I love it is because we can plug directly into their system. No need to carry and push heavy subwoofers and speakers — we just bring a few things, and I can do my usual routine with a little less work.

In the fall of 2022, I found myself at Music Box for a windy day — so windy that the vases holding flowers on the deck fell over and shattered. I wondered — would that be an omen of things to come? As the groom made his vows quietly later on — boats on the river began to honk and blast music below us. I couldn't make out anything from the groom, and more so the bride.

The wedding continued with six toasts that took a half-hour. I recommend that if you have a lot of toasts, make sure their speeches are short. Otherwise, it becomes an open mic night where people practice their jokes. The bride and groom had requested that when the bride's father went to give his last toast — the final and sixth toast, we play the theme from *The Godfather*.

Because of my position on the floor, I had to rely on my assistant to handle the music. It was a straightforward ask: hit play when the bride's father prepares to give his toast. Everything was shuttling along fine when I passed the microphone to the *fifth* speech for the groom's father.

"I've already said almost everything I wanted last night." The groom's father explained. It wasn't like we could go back and read his statements from the night before. Most guests nodded as if they had been invited to the rehearsal dinner.

In the *middle* of his speech, I could hear the stings from *The Godfather*. My ears and eyes snapped up and over to my assistant, who, thankfully, was looking in my direction. The snafu immediately boiled my blood because there was *one* thing I delegated and asked of another, and it went more south than a pile of southern belles heading south down a grand staircase.

When it was time for the music to be played for the actual father of the bride, the music was late and went exuberantly long. I continued to make a causal 'cut the music' slash across my throat. My assistant — either not looking at me, daydreaming, or freestyling the music, did not notice the signal I was giving. It got to the point where I was violently slashing across my neck, eyes wide, and pushing my spiritual energy toward the direction of the DJ booth before my assistant finally noticed and cut the music.

The father of the bride's speech involved a lot of language about his worries that his daughter was going to fall victim to liberalism during her move to college and a lot of potentially *iffy* statements in today's political climate. Sometimes I have to remind myself that I'm being paid — which means smiling and laughing when warranted. Some might feel like an ideological charlatan — but I'm willing to bend like a willow for some cash.

Most cocktail receptions feature a table decked with cheese, charcuterie, and breads. Sometimes — if the couple springs for it — they include fruit and meat. Additional still are dips and spreads like hummus. You know the couple spent money on catering if figs deck out the side of the platter. But there's one aesthetic look I can't stand — when pieces of cheese boards and charcuterie are used to 'decorate' the table. While plates are adorned with meats and cheese, leftover elements sit off the plate like rat turds. It's just a turn-off, and I think it makes the table look picked over and messy. Let the crowds of guests make the charcuterie board dirty!

This wedding featured a guest who I found annoying. But it turns out I was not alone.

"Can you play Lizzo's "Happy Birthday" song for people who have birthdays?" One cousin asked.

"We're only allowed one Lizzo song," I said, pointing to my sheet where the bride and groom had written *only one Lizzo song*.

"Well, you can play a couple." The cousin said poutily.

"We're going to play the one that everyone knows," Juan said, alluding to Lizzo's hit song, *About Damn Time*.

"Which song?" The cousin asked. "Everyone knows *all* of her music."

I believe she meant it as a joke — but her face was a bit too serious for my liking.

"No, they know like three songs," I muttered, trying to be a little dickish. It was not my loveliest moment — but I was not in the mood for this guest's sincere belief that everyone knew every single Lizzo song. We later discovered that the bride's 'one Lizzo song rule' was due to this cousin in particular.

The following week, we DJed a wedding with a few retro songs, but most of the songs the bride and groom wanted were modern. One guest came up early — way before dance time to request a song. It wasn't a bad song, just a song that didn't make sense. Some people think that the DJ operates as a personal jukebox and that we'll just regurgitate their demands over the event flow.

At the end of the night — he arrived with a smirk.

"Even though I preemptively put in my request, I'm upset you couldn't play it."

He spoke in that manly Caucasian politico which is hard to not immediately respond with a rolled eye.

"It just didn't really fit the vibe," I said casually and vaguely, showcasing no empathy.

"You're just like the president — thanks for *all* your hard work," he snorted before walking away, as if playing an obscure 80s song is enough to change America for the better.

Another 2022 wedding featured a friend of the couple who was a professional opera singer. She powered through a stunning "Ave Maria" during the ceremony as a gift for the couple. As impressive as her operatic vocals were, I was a bit jealous that instead of giving the bride and groom a hundred dollars, she could just loan her voice. Nobody ever asks for a novel or a sexy music video for their wedding gift. Trust me, I'd do it.

The worst wedding I DJed in 2022 was a series of minor weird errors. I was loading in with my assistant not-her-real-name Fergie who could barely lift ten pounds due to a bum knee. The load-in involved stairs, and you'd think we were a 1950s comedy the way we were loading into the space. The wedding venue we were at was a giant dome which makes the acoustics bouncy, reverby, and wet. The enormous area made for terrible audio, which was exacerbated by a massive structure that blocked our DJ booth from the rest of the room. The bridal table and ceremony backdrop was made of metal and silk. Our DJ booth was right behind it. I couldn't see anything and therefore had Fergie act like a messenger in ancient wartime who would run between battles to deliver news.

I was not feeling well heading into this wedding. I was four days deep on amoxicillin on the second round of strep back-to-back. Amoxicillin can cause your stomach to bloat and become upset, and I was in the throws of a stomach that felt like a boulder filled with air. I'd rather something happen — whether sitting on a toilet for a half hour or throwing up in the toilet for a half-hour.

To make matters more complicated, the second photographer had woken up sick, so only one photographer was present. Some industry experts later told me that the second shooter being absent wasn't a considerable loss. The couple thinks they're losing out on good photos, but experts tell me a vast majority of the photos used are taken from the lead photographer. With a missing photographer, I knew keeping the bride happy was essential.

Before the ceremony, the priest approached me:

"I think I'm going to not use the microphone; I'm loud, and everyone will hear me."

"That's fine with me," I explained. "I would just run it by the bride and groom."

"I will."

"As long as they approve, that's fine. If anything goes wrong, the onus will be on you!"

The priest laughed as if I was making a joke, and he thanked us and left. I turned to my assistant Fergie.

"He thinks I was joking," I said to Fergie. "I was dead serious. I want it obvious that the fault is on him if he can't be heard."

The ceremony went smoothly, with Fergie acting like a *Lord of the Rings* tower soldier who lights fires to send messages. We were twenty minutes into a cocktail hour when the venue themselves wanted to start bridal party introductions a half hour earlier than scheduled. I was baffled — especially because the appetizers took so long to get out — the microwavable frozen apps had only been out for ten minutes, and the candy table had been decimated due to hungry guests. The venue confirmed this drastic time change with the bride and groom, so we vaulted into introductions.

The three toasts took less than five minutes, putting us forty-five minutes ahead of the expected dinner time. Turned out that the venue, who had pushed for the early start, needed more time to be ready. In fact, it took most of that forty-five minutes we had saved to wait for dinner food. There wasn't a vendor table on the dome floor — instead, we got to eat in the pitch-black darkness behind the stage until, minutes into dinner, we got help finding the mysterious light switch.

The dinner was depressing — cold vegetable lasagna that looked slimier than a conclave of snails. Excruciating boiling chicken that looked like it had been cooked on the surface of the planet Mercury. Cold limp vegetables that whispered, 'how could my life have turned out like this,' as they were loaded onto your plate. Freezing half-mashed potatoes with thick whole potatoes and a secret herb ingredient that gave it a weird Eastern European. Even the bread basket featured rock-hard bread that would be perfect to utilize in a public stoning.

When we returned from dinner, we were immediately accosted by the bride's mother, who wanted us to move a dance up. I tried waiting for the photographer, but the bride's mother was impatient. Thankfully the photographer managed to get some pictures. I started without the photographer being ready due to pressure from the mother so let's hope the photos look good! But this was a great example of when you want things done without the opinion of others.

The bride's mother wasn't done — she approached me moments later.

"I don't mean to be rude, but when you lift your arms up, your stomach becomes slightly exposed, so if you could cover that up."

I was aghast — my face was drawn into shock at her audacity. Thankfully my part-time actor and event host experience kicked in, and I commented on how shocked I was. I promptly said I would address that by ensuring I wore a suit jacket.

First, the bride's mom was no Cindy Crawford in a bathing suit. I would never fat-shame someone (the bride's mother, in this case, *disagreed* with that sentiment). She was on the huskier side of builds herself. If anyone related to a minor wardrobe malfunction, you would assume it would be her. In fact, the bride's mom's outfit looked like a conservative awful 1980s knock-off Dillard's product someone got on a rack in a back storage room where they destroyed clothes that dared to exist in the first place. That back storage room belonged to an abandoned thrift store that hadn't been stepped into since 1992.

Second, can you enjoy your daughter's wedding? Who cares about a little bit of skin when there are bigger fish to fry? Just enjoy the wedding!

Third, we need to stop using 'I don't mean to be mean' when we are trying to be mean. The bride's mom easily could have said that sentiment with a better tone. Let's practice two right here.

"Hey, sweetie, your stomach pops out of your shirt slightly."

"I don't know if you know, but when you raise your arms, your stomach pops up."

I was seething after the mother left with her audacity which was the size of the sum total of a family of twelve's Costco shopping carts. I flicked two twenties towards Fergie and told her that she would be DJing the ten to midnight hours.

After the first dances, we were scheduled for a dollar dance. My notes said the DJ should explicitly announce the dance and start leading. Naturally — that was wrong because Grandma wanted to speak for a few minutes about what a dollar dance was. None of this was on my itinerary and was news to me. I get very pissy about these details because I should have been notified beforehand. Just let me know at some point in the night that you want grandma to talk. Otherwise, I'm just going to assume we are moving along as scheduled.

Grandma, who couldn't hold or speak into a microphone to save a shrimp from a cocktail tray, led us into the polka. At this point, an old man hobbled up to the side of the stage. I went over to talk with him, thinking he would make a terrible request.

"The sound quality sucks in here," the old man grumbled.

"Well, I think it's the space."

"Can you do something about it?"

I wish I had the power to just automatically snap my fingers and create soundproofing. But alas, as supernatural and scary as I might look, I am pretty human.

"This venue hall is a large dome, a large room...not a good space for sound."

"Can you *try* something?"

I felt like the scenario where a customer asks for a product, is told they're out, and the customer asks if they can check the back. As if by reviewing the back, angels would conduct a magical delivery of the customer's desires.

"Yes — we heard she wanted a *red-colored* boot. Here you go!" The angels say in a flurry of pretty sparkles. Out of nowhere, red boots save the day for the retail employee and the bitch-ass customer. These days I imagine angels the way Revolutions describes them as giant puffy balls covered with eyes. Imagine one of those giving you miraculous customer service.

To appease the old man and play petty for myself, I went behind the speakers, subwoofers, and main mixing board and acted like I was examining and turning various knobs. It's like when you have to fake devour the plastic food a young child serves you.

"Oh, this is delicious!" A parent might say as they press the plastic potato to their lips.

"Ah — !" A fictional version of me exclaimed with a chipper smile and a Santa's elf-demeanor. "I had the shitty audio button turned on! It's turned off now — and the sound quality will be perfect!"

I returned to the old man with a slight frown that an emotionally astute person would have read as the correct petty smile disguised as a frown.

"I've done what I can. Hope that helps."

I did not do what I could because there was nothing to do. The old man hobbled off, talking about the audio quality, and I internally cheered. I might not be allowed to be rude to the bride's mother, but that didn't mean I had to give pristine service to a random guest. The dollar dance was cut short. It was supposed to last a while, but I guess everyone was cashless and forgot their Venmo at home.

I played things off their extensive must-play list; I played classics that got everyone on the floor. I played line dances, retro, 90s, and modern, yet the floor could not catch fire. I turned the keys over to Fergie, who played every sizzling dance track, hip-hop number, and pop music to which anyone with a tingle in their limb would dance to. I was behind the stage, working on personal projects. Around 11:15, Fergie came to me.

"Everyone's gone."

"Really?" I didn't believe she was accurate — the event went on till midnight.

"The bride left; there's like two people left."

I immediately stood up to find two lone younger-looking adults slow-dancing to a song that was undoubtedly not a slow-dance number. The only other humans left were the wait staff tearing everything down. I approached the event coordinator to wonder why everyone was gone.

"They thought it ended at 11." The event coordinator explained. "In the contract, they get six hours, so they did homemade math and thought it ended at 11. But we agreed to go to midnight to give them that free hour."

Another miscommunication to add to the pile that night. But this time, it was miscommunication I appreciated and benefitted from. I quickly began pulling the plugs. At that point, I had four more weddings in 2022 — could I truly make it out alive?

The following Saturday, I was pretty happy. The last few weeks, I had woken up feeling overworked and disinterested. But realizing the year was coming to a close, and that I could count the remaining weddings on one hand, made me, at best, neutral.

The wedding was excellent, with plenty of dancers. The only funny moment came when we waited in the buffet line for food. The venue was an Irish place that served tasteless chicken, overstewed beef, broccoli that looked tortured, and mashed potatoes that felt too wet. Typical Irish American fare.

"I apologize for the wait on the potatoes," the caterer said with a sigh. "They'll be out shortly."

"It's like The Great Potato famine over here," I joked.

"Oh my gosh!" A girl in front of me said. "Too soon!"

"No, it's not," I said, feeling like I had to recover from such an accusation. Was it really too soon? After one hundred years, you can make historical jokes based on historical references, right?

With three weddings left in 2022, my maniac desperation to get through wedding season became more evident. For each wedding I do through the company, I usually get a call from Juan the Tuesday or Wednesday before to talk about the upcoming wedding.

"I just want you to know that the bride told me her mother might be overbearing."

Rare as it was for me personally, an overbearing bride and groom felt within their right to be so. But an overbearing parent was *always* worse. To guarantee that their child has the best day of their life, they create original drama that stresses out vendors, coordinators, and their own children. It feels like a unique hell-loop to be the parent originating stress over your child during their wedding.

One of the things that the bride's mother was particular about was having *two* microphones — one for the officiant and one for the reader.

"I just can't see it as a one-microphone system," the bride's mother had said.

I could see it as a one-microphone system considering I had done audio for a hundred wedding ceremonies, and it had always been one microphone. However, we showed up and made a two-microphone system only to find out that there was no reading, and it was just the officiant, and thus, we only needed one microphone. The bride's mother remained on her best behavior, which had me wondering if the bride had said something earlier...

With two weddings left in 2022, you would assume my hellish year would curtail with a whimper. But instead, one of the largest fuck-ups that has ever happened on my watch went down, and genuinely I was not at fault. Most weddings have a processional song, a bridal march, and a recessional song. However, this wedding had a single song for both the processional and bridal march. It was weird but nothing abnormal to the point where I would question it.

The ceremony was finally ready to go twenty minutes later than planned. The event coordinator, in her haste, asked me to play the song and get started, only to tell me to delay by looping the song. The same orchestra song was looped twice before we finally had the show on the road. Finally, everyone and their mother had gone down the aisle, and we were waiting for the bride. I just stood still since the same music was supposed to play for the bride.

The event coordinator gave me another thumbs-up, which confused me. I made some hand motions that probably looked like wretched sign language. Finally, after the confusion peaked to a boil, we met on the sidelines.

"Where's the bridal march?" The coordinator asked.

"It's the same song."

"No, there's a different song."

"So I should play the recessional?" I asked in confusion.

"Yeah," the event coordinator asked.

So I ended up playing the recessional song instead of the bridal march. Immediately something felt off — and I wasn't sure why. While the ceremony was underway, I convened with the event coordinator.

"I know she wanted the bridal march theme," the event coordinator told me.

"That's not what I have," I muttered, not upset with the event coordinator but with the lack of logistics from my company.

I called my boss, who blamed the bride and the event coordinator for not communicating. The event coordinator blamed my boss for not sharing. I could feel my anxiety rising again. Earlier in the day, I had helped two friends in a pinch by officiating their wedding, so I was already in a discombobulated state.

Due to the pictures the bride wanted, the reception started a half-hour late. We switched some things around on the time schedule. Things finally seemed to be cooling down until a girl approached the booth.

Everyone yells their requests over the booth. Loud music blares, and they're too lazy to walk the extra seven steps to talk to me on the side. I've lately become impatient and have asked people to circle around because I can't hear them. The beauty is that some people think that my sign language-Esque motion is telling them to go away. Unintended benefits are beautiful.

One girl held a TikTok to my ear and asked if I could play the song.

"I need a song title and artist," I said bitterly.

"I'll go take a look!"

Another girl pulled up a YouTube song and claimed the groomsmen would do a surprise dance. Playing off YouTube is tricky because you must silence the video and its ad before it blares off the speakers. It's an athletic, artistic maneuver of buttons and timing. The groomsmen did have a half-baked dance. The same girl demanded Latin multiple times, and another man requested The Monster Mash.

"I'm going to have to run that by the bride and groom." I said in response.

"I already mentioned it; they agreed!"

Since it was a small wedding, I decided to roll with it, all things considered, and it went over well.

After the wedding, I went home and grabbed a few hours of sleep before post-wedding morning brunch with the friends I had married the afternoon before. While enjoying brunch, I realized I had left their marriage license in the truck I had rented the night before for the other wedding. Horrified — I left brunch early to drive to the truck rental place to grab their marriage license. Thankfully I arrived fifteen minutes before they closed. At this point, I was glad that I had one remaining wedding that year.

The last weekend of wedding DJing for 2022 was a mess for almost everyone.

One DJ, I'll name Richard, got into a few tiffs with the event coordinator. He wrote a Facebook status saying, "Ladies, never hire your friend to be an 'event coordinator.'" Apparently Richard had friends at the wedding and someone ratted him out to the event coordinator herself. She ended up calling our boss and making a stink. But considering it was Richard's personal Facebook page, and that it wasn't technically calling her out, my boss didn't care at all. Lessons to takeaway: don't post things day of, never trust your friends enough to assume they won't rat you out, and if the glass slipper fits...

Meanwhile boss Shawn and his assistant Albert had a run in with another event coordinator. They had been told earlier by a server to go in one location. Lo and behold the event coordinator arrived screaming how they had to move it now.

"I kept telling her she was not allowed to talk to us like that," Shawn muttered. "So then after some yelling, we did finally move. But can you believe that?"

"I don't know *why* you would you would believe the server over an event coordinator," the event coordinator had appeared snarled.

"She emasculated the server!" Shawn said.

"I dunno about emasculated, more of a power and status move if anything..." I cooed.

But while others dealt with the regular onslaught of inefficiency, difficult and general toxicity, my last weekend was a beautiful, fun ceremony where I raffled off gift cards to attendees and played fun jams throughout the night. It was a great way to end a questionable year with a reminder of why I'm an entertainer in the first place.

That Flower Smells Rotten

There are two styles of disc jockeying: club DJing and event DJing.

Club DJs match drum beats, spin weird and random songs, and usually play their own produced music for their fans. It doesn't matter how bad their music is — they just do it anyway. It's their privileged right as someone who is otherwise providing good entertainment. Some club DJs might play thirty seconds of a song before being called to switch songs. You might see them at a nightclub surrounded by a bunch of middle-to-rich class youngins who are slamming drinks back quicker than the music switches.

Event DJs are more atmospheric. For weddings, you're constantly trying to get people on the dance floor while appeasing the bride and groom. It's a bit more stressful — after all, a good DJ enhances the wedding. While a lousy DJ can ruin a wedding. Most of the other events are casual. I love DJing cruises because most people are relaxing to the music and not dancing. Sure, if people start dancing, that's great. But I don't feel pressured to turn up the dancing on a cruise. Sometimes dozens will dance on the boat's small tight dance floor, shaking the ship so hard you'd think we hit something in the lake. It's even more relaxing to DJ during a lunch cruise. Grandma Jean got on the boat for a relaxing lunch cruise, so you can't play Cardi B's "WAP" through the subwoofers. She wants to hear some Motown casually in the background while she eats bland chicken with watered-down gravy and coos over the lake.

Once in a while, I get to do an event that's not a wedding. Proms aren't too bad, although the staff administration must demand that the DJ plays clean music. The clean versions don't seem to work, especially when there's a song where every other word is explicit or the innuendos are clear as Vaseline. You might not hear it because the lyrics are poems or one single word is bleeped out, but Principal Smith is dancing to a song about fellatio.

    This one prom had students clamoring for a single song that did not have a clean version. I felt like a religious extremist trying to ruin everyone's night. Most of my anxiety isn't about whether I know the music. I don't really care about *learning* about what the kids are listening to. The pressure is more connected to not knowing what to play. That's why I prefer schools that give me giant music lists ahead of time.

    The gigs I can DJ in my sleep are 5Ks, new store openings, and charity benefits. Events where you can play anything and nobody notices or cares. One of my favorite events was a charity fundraiser party-dinner benefit. English needs a word to summarize the compilation of that event description. During this event, I cued up songs on an automatic playlist which made them happy and impressed. The best part came later when I was asked to emcee the raffle and was able to crack some jokes and turn the party into a comedy.

    In early 2022, I was asked to DJ an anniversary party. I figured it would be a fun time, easy work, and low maintenance. This was my standard life approach to friends, relationships, and passions. Because it wasn't a full-on gig, I had to load two speakers, two mixing boards, a cable bin, and various other musical sundries into my tiny but effective Mitsubishi Mirage. It was like trying to fit a cucumber in a toilet paper cardboard roll. It managed to fit, but some major busting was happening at the seams. A few times on the drive to and back, I questioned the safety of having music equipment pressing against me and the car's gear shift.

    I precariously drove a half-hour to a small township on the east side of Cleveland. The party was happening at an *historic* town hall. I love history but disagree with those who label anything that's been around for a century as historic. Especially people who pick out historic venues for their events and want you to know it's historic. It reminds me of Ohio State University students who religiously scream: "it's THE Ohio State University."

Certain historians might be shocked at my seemingly lack of respect for historic buildings.

"But this building was established in 1814!" They might bluster.

Cool, but it's not like Abraham Lincoln had anonymous gay sex in the historic building? Did something significant happen here? No — it's just wood and stone that's lasted for two hundred years? Just a bunch of random folks filing their permits and taxes on this city property, right?

I enter the venue to scout out the location and meet the couple. It was their fiftieth anniversary and they were around 70 years old. The couple, Cindy and Brian, were already dressed for the party while shuffling things around the space. Cindy looked like the type who was probably the popular girl in school, and Brian looked like the type who enjoyed a cigar night until his wife called to tell him to get back home. I had an acceptable initial reaction of them.

"Which table do you want me to set up on?" I asked. This was the question that ultimately led to the downfall of this entire story — after all, why would a DJ arriving at an event venue need a table?

Cindy and Brian looked shell-shocked, as if I had spit on their child. They asked me why I didn't have a table. The answer was simple: my company didn't give me a table. The venue provides a table for the DJ 99% of the time. Part of the contract my boss provides for clients states that venues are to supply a table unless requested. And if you knew you wouldn't have a table, why not ask? I don't think I could fit a table in my car, but I could have tried.

What had started as a 'cute' discussion about the table had devolved into Nancy Drew and the Missing Table. The answer was quite simple: the missing table was Cindy and Brian's fault. This wasn't a psychological bonfire chat where multiple answers could be accurate. I was clearly in the right, and the customer was wrong. I was not going to roll over and say, "oops, we messed up!" I did exactly as I was told.

This discussion about the missing table got to a point where I awkwardly told them I didn't need a table. To say I didn't need a table was like saying that a shark didn't need seawater. How could I DJ without a table? DJ on the floor? With a slight sigh, Cindy returned home to fetch me the table. Cindy assured me she would let the dog out one last time anyway — so the trip was not just purely for the table.

The rest of the night appeared to have progressed fine. Brian and Cindy's anniversary party featured ancient guests who were old and had gone to high school probably during one of the wars in the 1950s and 60s. So I played a lot of older music. I ran into a few tech issues but, thankfully, had developed loopholes to get over the problems. The food was pristine and I played all the music they wanted. Brian and Cindy had given me a sheet of a hundred songs that I slowly powered through. I prefer when I get so many tracks because it puts the onus on the party organizers.

"Well, why did no one dance at my event?"
"The hundred songs you chose sucked."
"Well then why did you play them?"
"Because you told me to play those songs?"

The old people who had attended slowly left (as in walked slowly and not all at once). It was time to wrap it up for the evening. I tore down and vanished quickly and made sure to hand back their table. I was thankful and gave my pleasant 'you're a client' sugary appreciation as I hopped into my storage unit of a car.

A couple of days later, my boss hit me up because Cindy and Brain had some 'feedback.' I am known for my overzealous interest in critical feedback. I had a fellow actor who once told me that he had never met an artist so demanding of constructive criticism. But Cindy and Brian's fuss blew me away.

They were mad that I didn't have a table. Upon investigation, my boss told me they had *confirmed* two days before that Cindy and Brian *would provide a table*. Brian had claimed over the phone that "the venue has tons of tables." He echoed confidence like Oprah: *You* can have a table, and *you* can have a table! The fact remains that it's *not* my job to bring a table.

The second claim was that I didn't play the music they wanted. But since they provided a list of a hundred songs they liked, *I only played* the music *they* wanted. If they didn't like the music selection, then that was a slam against their personal taste. It's like asking the chef to whip up Caprese and chicken parmigiana and then complain you didn't want Italian food.

 The third claim was probably the most confusing. Cindy and Brain added that they were disappointed I didn't talk more about the music. It sounded like they wanted more talking during the songs? The way I pictured this feedback was that they wanted me to act like I was on a live radio show?

 "DJ Matt Hribar here — up next is a classic song by Eurythmics. It peaked at #4 on the Billboard Hot 100. You're dancing at a live anniversary for Cindy and Brian, who were probably forty when this song came out!"

 Even though that request is ridiculous, it's a request I could have executed had I been *told* to do it. When I DJ music, I try and keep my voice to a minimum. People usually come for the event, the food, and the music. They don't want to hear a loud, obnoxious guy hog the microphone for the entire night.

 What's more frustrating are these secret expectations that get pulled out late in the game. It's like painting a bedroom for your grandparents, who then complain that they wish you had painted just *one* wall instead of the whole room. Or someone two years into a relationship saying, "I know I agreed with you earlier that we wouldn't have kids — but I have *always* wanted kids and was hoping I would eventually change your mind!"

 Had Brian and Cindy asked for a weird request, I would have done my best to meet that request. I work in a client-facing business, so naturally, I always go out of my way for clients. I've had clients ask for songs that I knew would clear a dance floor quicker than a nerve gas bomb. I've played extended versions of songs for clients where even the radio edition felt too long. I would have talked over the music if they had clarified it beforehand. Even though all their guests would have been internally thinking, '*can this guy shut up and let me dance in peace?*'

 As much as Cindy and Brian's review was harsh nonsense, it spun me out more drastically than that 2009 British PSA where three teenagers slam into a car at 25mph and all die. Cindy and Brian had opened up a can of worms by crashing into my hypothetical car of teenagers. This caused me to reassess and question my skills. Had I peaked? Was I dialing it in? Was I no longer a good disc jockey for the average Joe and just masquerading with no skills? My imposter syndrome was a big bad wolf kicking down the straw hut to devour my swine.

The next time I DJed wiped out my anxieties because it showed me that *I* was *not* the problem. It was like a Maury parental DNA test result. "Matt, you are a good DJ!" This news caused me to run around the Maury set with glee.

Cindy and Brain were just a weird old couple that seemed hellbent on being critical. They enjoyed nitpicking and, I assume, had nothing better than to look for little cracks and holes like an anteater at an ant picnic. The good news? I wasn't going to see Cindy and Brian again and I assumed they'd pick someone else if they needed a future DJ.

Dear reader, this narrative would be a quick paragraph in the previous essay if that were the case. But a month and a half later, after Cindy and Brian's review, my assistant Josh and I arrived at the Glidden House. The Glidden House was another *historic* venue in Cleveland where the Glidden family had once lived. As we began to unload, I noticed that five people were simultaneously unloading flowers. My original thought was how could a wedding for one-hundred attendees need a whole team of florists.

Josh and I went to work unloading the stacks of equipment. I was in the back of the truck when I heard a 'Matt' come out of an older woman's mouth. Befuddled — I turned and looked on with curiosity.

"Do you remember me?" She asked. Initially I didn't, because I do not have a solid memory. My memory is like a gaseous matter hanging out in an empty cavern. Sometimes the gas remembers solid information but most of the time, it's just whimsically whisking away around itself like a wind tunnel. Later that *same night*, I ran into a couple who had taken my beer tour several months before. They knew me — but I wouldn't have recognized them until they had tipsily introduced themselves to me and put in a request for an obscure 90s song. They had tipped me good money back on tour — so you best believe they got their obscure music. She was so drunk that she was tripping over her husband by the end of the evening.

"You DJed our anniversary dinner!" Cindy then added, which was like unlocking a floodgate. I felt like one of those subjects where therapists can get them to remember all sorts of details and stories otherwise locked away. Upon Cindy's re-introduction, I regained memory of their stupid review and went to collect myself. The inner Libra in me smiled and said hello. Cindy made a foolish comment:

"Oh, are *you* DJing the wedding?" Had I been bold or quicker on my feet, I might have said, "no, we're actually DJing for the valet." What did she think I was doing there with speakers and subwoofers?

Cindy soon departed, as I'm sure her four assistants improperly placed too many flowers within the venue. As soon as Cindy was out of earshot, I filled Josh in on their anniversary dance fiasco. I'm a living version of the scene in *Bye Bye Birdie,* where they all call each other on the telephone to gossip.

Even when recounting the story to assistant Josh, I noted that maybe Cindy and Brian weren't bad people. Conceivably they had just shown a wrong side, a small rotten side, with me. Perchance they were having a stressful day setting up their party? Could they *think* they had communicated their expectations correctly? They were old enough to be getting social security. Maybe they had a memory 'oopsie-daisy?' Who was I to judge? To quote one of Cleveland's judges who used to monitor judges, "who am I to judge judges?" I believed in the message, although that judge was actually in charge of the judges. So he looks like an ass compared to how I look like Mother Mary.

It wasn't just Cindy who was there with flowers. Brian was her assistant, dressed as if he was picnicking with the Kennedy family on a grassy knoll. He was certainly not dressed for the hands-on work of floristry. I don't really 'boss' around people who work with me, but I immediately commissioned Josh to run some intelligence. Josh listened in and found outthat Cindy ran the florist company from her basement, which didn't seem like a great place to store flowers.

"I don't think it's you." Josh pointed out early on. "They're definitely weird."

The first thing I noticed about Cindy and Brian's florist company was how many boxes, bags, and things they had. Their stock was too much for a small wedding and their final exhibition. It was like being commissioned to paint your grandparent's bedroom that new shade of red and bringing five buckets, twenty brushes, and three ladders. Was there no way to streamline that process?

Josh and I finished our entire DJ set-up in less than two hours, while it took five old people *four* hours to put up some centerpiece flower designs and finish the bouquets. Couldn't the floral arrangements been handled last night? Especially if you're going to take the time of a *Lord of the Rings* director's cut movie to set up on the day of?

Cindy and her henchmen were so behind on the bouquets. A few bridesmaids came over to inquire if the bouquets were ready since the ceremony was a half-hour away. Cindy was unhappy with their demands and got to work doing the bouquets. She stifled some sassy expletives under her breath as she struggled to tie a few flowers into a bouquet. I know flowers aren't forever — just Cindy's attitude is — but her time management was more atrocious than yogurt that's been pushed back to the fridge and then abandoned for a few month.

I figured my comeuppance would occur at some point, but I was curious how it would arrive. Like Rihanna at a fashion party, it arrived in a blaze of glory that I would savor. The Glidden House had a decently sized rectangle-shaped storage room in which I had put some boxes and gear. Out of laziness, I decided to keep our equipment close to the door. We weren't blocking anything — and there were a few things in the back of the rectangle. But why bother taking the extra five minutes to push and rearrange the back half of the closet? We only needed the space for the day. I wasn't going to Marie Kondo some venue's closet for efficiency. Also, I didn't work for the hotel, so I wasn't going to organize a company's closet.

I used the rectangular closet space to change from my dirty setting-up DJ clothes into my fancy wedding clothes. Midway through — half-bare and all — Cindy walked in on me. I did one of those sing-songy "I'm changing!" yells. Cindy left to probably go make some last-minute bouquets. Moments later, Brian knocked on the door and since I was done, I opened the door. He stood there looking like he was ready to spew Boomer attitude. He was also the first person who, for me, ruined the aesthetic of a white suit.

"Oh, is this the *storage* room?" Brian asked as if he had walked into a blank space instead of a room filled with storage. I couldn't tell if he was hinting that I shouldn't be changing in a closed-off closet room.

"Yes," I said, void of emotion. I was standing in front of Brian which obscured a proper view of the room. From where Brian stood, the room looked small and full of things. He couldn't see the free space beyond the pile of equipment.

"It's pretty full," Brian said, looking around the closet. "Doesn't seem like there's any place to put our things...."

"Oh, that sucks," I responded before leaving the room, closing the door behind me and trying to keep my shit-eating grin under wraps as Brian looked around for alternative storage situations.

My revenge was complete. Had I told Brian about the available space, they would have easily been able to put their things in the storage room. It probably would have involved work out of me — and had they been nice, I would have been willing to be less lazy. But instead, they had to put things in God knows where. Due to space issues, they *left* an actual *cart* on the *wedding venue's floor*. This happens when you treat people poorly — you don't have storage space for your boxes, bags, and totes.

The florists were still building decor even though the wedding was minutes away from starting. The floral arrangements were less stunning than you'd assume, given the time allotment. A bunch of white flowers in a vase that looked pretty but wouldn't win awards for complexity. Usually, I hear a comment from the mother of the bride or groom about the flowers. But like the flowers, *mum* is the word.

The ceremony was lovely, although the wedding featured many drunk non-listeners. The photographers had tribulations gathering those involved in group shots which caused the wedding to run an hour late. While we waited for the bride to bustle herself, I got a tidbit from Emma, a photographer.

"The bride and the bridal party are upset that the florist is here," photographer Emma told me. I immediately wanted to collect and examine the evidence to *j'accuse* Cindy and Brian. I'm a broken detective receiving foggy clues to solve a case.

"What?" I commented. "But isn't the florist supposed to set up the flowers? Why would the bride and bridal party be upset with the florist?"

Emma didn't know — which left me confused. Maybe they wanted someone other than Cindy to be present making the flowers? But that seemed stupid.

I returned to the DJ booth to see assistant Josh eyeing me with fervor.

"Cindy asked me where we are eating," Josh explained.

"She asked *what*?" You could sense the tension coming off of my body. "Is Cindy eating with us?"

I would rather eat with a rabid raccoon. I would have less of a chance of being attacked if I was with the raccoon. Especially if good food was positioned between the raccoon and me.

Moments later, having changed, Cindy appeared in a black dress. I know black dresses are classy, but they feel a tad morbid at weddings.

"Oh my gosh," I whispered to Josh. "I think she's *staying* to eat with *us*!"

I was not looking forward to dinner with Cindy and Brian. I was blessed that I was a fast eater — this was the first positive feature of my fast-eating technique. I waved over the Glidden House event coordinator.

"Do florists usually stick around to eat?" I questioned.

"Sometimes..." The event coordinator mused. This threw me off because I had DJed one hundred weddings and a florist had *never* stuck around for dinner.

"Well, the florist...I think she's sticking around? Does she have a vendor meal?"

At that sentence, the Glidden House event coordinator finally caught up with my level of horrified. She appeared startled, as if eating dinner with a rabid raccoon.

"No, I don't have a meal for her!"

"She's here *with* her husband," I muttered, my eyes looking at Brian, who was still wearing his B-list golfer uniform. I'm not usually a snitch, but there are some people I will absolutely narc on with delight. The event coordinator looked so confused, so I reassured her that maybe it was a fluke. But then I noticed a glass of red wine in Cindy's hand. Cindy was walking around the venue as if she owned the place. She had been a dancer and stood in a pose that reeked of pretentious posture.

"She's *drinking wine*," I told Josh as if she was praying to Satan in public. "Can you believe it?"

"She's staying." Josh nodded vigorously. He was my Gretchen Weiners to my Regina George, my Darth Vader to my Emperor Palpatine.

As if God was personally watching out for me, the vendor's table was set for Photographers Emma, Kim, assistant Josh, and me. From our seated position, we could see Cindy grabbing another glass of red. Was she a florist turned wedding crasher?

Thankfully Beth, the Matron of Honor, walked close, so I pulled her over and asked for details on the florist. Beth's face lit up, which indicated significant gossip was about to pour down our gullets like worms from momma bird to her babies.

"Well, the florist *invited herself* to the wedding," Beth explained. "Cindy texted Cassie and said she and her husband were going to stay downtown the night of the wedding."

Cassie was the bride and a lovely woman.

"Who *texts* that to a bride?!" I remember gasping out loud as if we were in a Jane Austen novel, clutching our pearls whilst sitting in the parlor. I knew for a FACT that Cindy and Brian lived a half-hour from downtown. They did *not* need to spend the night downtown. It wasn't like they were flying in from Boston to set up their average flowers. Secondly, why are you asking the bride to be your hotel Yelp review? The bride isn't the Downtown Cleveland tourism board who can whip up hotel recommendations like a concierge. Just find a hotel, Cindy.

"So Cassie showed me the texts and felt like the florist was asking to come to the wedding," Beth continued.

I would have texted Cindy back with a, "I'm not sure about the hotels around here." The one time in my life where I could execute good minimalism.

"So Cassie invited the florist and her husband to the wedding, and they were *so* honored to be invited," Beth filled us in, placing a sassy emphasis on the word 'so.' In the background of my vision, I could see Cindy filling up her glass of red wine. Moments later, assistant Josh would press Cindy about how she managed to get an invite.

"Well, I know she had a couple of COVID cancellations, so I figured I could ask." Cindy's confession was of top-tier Bond villain excellence. Utilizing sick dinner guests to sink your claws into an invite? Half the villains we see in stories are subpar in manipulation compared to Cindy.

"Wow, that's crazy," Josh responded to Cindy (or something of that magnitude).

"Brian feels a bit out of place," Cindy explained. Brian was experiencing a normal reaction to inviting your way into a wedding. The fact that Cindy felt nothing made me theorize she might be immune to emotion in that sociopathic tendency.

I left to use the restroom soon after eating dinner. The chicken was a bit balmy that evening, and my stomach become wonky by mediocre food. When I returned, my assistant Josh looked like he had discovered the location of the Declaration of Independence.

"You missed it!" Josh exclaimed. "I got into a *fight* with Cindy."

Like a cat who calmly jumps a ten-foot distance, I sat in my chair as if I had discovered the lost city of Atlantis.

"So Cindy comes up to me and starts massaging my shoulder *sexually*," Josh explained, using his shoulder as an example. It was that weird 'grab the skin, pinch the skin, set down the skin, repeat' motion which was more sensuous than the average shoulder grab. Josh looked like a young man who would be an easy mark to sensual older women.

"It must be the red wine." I cajoled. "Red wine instantly makes people horny."

I had just invited the image of Cindy and Brian 'getting it on,' which caused the vendor table to shudder.

"So what happened next?" My standard soft baritone was squeaky with excitement.

"Cindy told me everything's running behind, and it's so late."

Didn't take a detective with twenty years on the force to notice that.

"Cindy told me I should get the show on the road," Josh explained. "She told me to get you to start playing dance music."

Cindy's demands for me to just start playing music out of her impatience was not going to happen. Weddings do not go by the schedule of a guest, or a hijacking florist who is a guest. Wedding schedules are dictated by the bride and groom. If the bride and groom need five or fifteen minutes extra before we start dancing, they're getting that time.

Sometimes time issues happen outside of the bride and groom's control. Earlier in the night, we began to introduce the bridal party. We were going to make toasts only to find several missing bridal party members who had left to put their children to sleep. Had they never been to a wedding before? We waited around ten minutes or so for the bridal party to return. I wasn't going to judge them at the time, but who was watching young children in that hotel room!? What if they electrocuted themselves in the bathroom and put porn on the television? Worse yet, what if they ate all the expensive candy in the mini-fridge?

While Cindy was fingering Josh's shoulders, half the dining room had yet to be served with food. The Glidden House's kitchen staff refused to serve food while people were walking around. I had made *five* announcements asking people to *sit down*, but it had been like herding manatees into reciting Shakespeare. I know this was out of my control because the attendees had already proven to be terrible listeners.

Cindy wanted us to start the dancing even with half the attendees still waiting for overcooked plain chicken. Granted — maybe she had a *point* considering what food awaited the guests.

"Well, I snapped back to her to get out of here," Josh said.

"You *sassed* Cindy?"

"I did! Cindy moved towards the door after assaulting my shoulders and said, 'Did you sass me?' And I said, 'Get out of here,' so she tumbled out of the room."

I could not believe I had missed it. I used to have terrible FOMO that melted away as my age increased. I rarely feel the need to be at certain moments or events. I wish I had remained abode to witness how that exchange went down. I rarely, if ever, have regrets. But missing this fight is a regret.

"Cindy kept talking about how they have to tear down the flowers too," photographer Emma chirped in. "She keeps saying they'll be here till two in the morning."

"What is there to tear down?" I questioned. "It's flower bouquets? Don't guests take them to go, or the hall throws them away? The wedding ends at 11. I doubt it would take till two in the morning to clean up flower *bouquets*." Also — she's having a whole bottle of red wine. Why is she imbibing so much wine if she plans on working tonight? She's drinking wine like a royal figure on *Game of Thrones*.

We soon returned to the main room and eventually were ready to vault into some first dances. I noticed where Cindy and Brian were seated and discovered they were at a random back table, sitting next to a young-looking couple and a middle-aged couple. It was the type of wedding table where you could tell the bride and groom didn't have a theme for the table. It was a 'welp, I guess we'll just put them there' table. First dances began, and when I looked to the floor, Cindy was present front and center to take footage and pictures.

She was arguably one of the most noticeable strangers at the event and dared to push her way to the front to grab photos. And why would she even want those photos? It's one thing to get pictures of your flowers and maybe the bride holding your bouquets. But their romantic first dance? Who wants that in their phone storage?

Finally, Professional Dancer Cindy's moment was here. I spun from *I Wanna Dance With Somebody* into *Dancing Queen*: the perfect vintage duo that all ages love. Cindy dragged her husband by the arm to the dance floor so they could join in the fun. Cindy and Brain danced right in front of me. Whether she was hard of hearing or simply wanted me to watch was a 'judge for yourself' type situation.

As I looked down to prepare the next song, I looked up to see an old, wrinkled, bejangled hand reaching up from the floor. In a drunken dancing daze, Cindy had toppled to the floor and was serving movie-dramatic levels of 'pick me up.' Brian reached down and pulled her up by her arms — which was the *worst* way to help someone up. Especially for someone as old as Cindy; I expected her arms to pop off like a Barbie doll.

After being helped to her feet, Cindy walked off the dance floor. She didn't walk; it was more like a baseball player who had been hit in the leg with a baseball hobble. The two sat down like the first contestants evicted from Dancing With The Stars. Cindy, in particular, had disheveled hair and schmeared lipstick. At some point they left the wedding, probably because Cindy was drunk and injured.

Cindy and Brian did not return to tear down their floral scapes. They were not 'working till 2 am.' Their floral arrangements were taken by guests or thrown away. And while I can't say I missed them, I was blown away by their epic audacious Caucasian boldness. There was no anger in me. I had gotten my just desserts with the storage situation, and they had left me with pages of material. Cindy and Brian, whether you're currently causing devastation via dysfunction or preparing to leave a scathing review to someone properly doing their job, I thank you. Thank you for proving that even on my worst day, I could not rack up such a collection of faux pas that you displayed.

Thank You For Your Service

When I arrived at Richmond, Virginia, one rainy Monday evening, I wasn't visiting for the views. I was here to see a good friend who had recently moved to Virginia. On my way to North Carolina, Richmond made a perfect pit stop and an opportunity to catch up with Emily Mangan. I pulled up in a transitioning neighborhood (transitioning being the white people's definition of gentrification) and parked my car on the side of the road. With blanket, pillow, and bag in hand — I was ushered inside by Emily.

Emily is a mix of archetypes. She is the sexy librarian who is helpful with your research but also down for a craft beer. Emily is a witty comedian with a sharp tongue. She is a warrior for people with a heart too big for her body. Someone both decisive and calculative while surrendering to the chaos that whips up like a hurricane around her (I would like to believe I helped her get better with hurricane preparation, given that I'm a constant spinning typhoon of inescapable water).

We crossed town to get some Mexican cuisine in Emily's Prius, a car that held many memories from trips to the beach, excursions for food, and an escape from pressing matters. Emily's younger brother Patrick was joining us.

"Working on some new music?" Emily asked as she carefully turned down side streets. The aux cord was passed quicker than cocaine in a 1980s bathroom, and I played some demos. Certain friends have limited patience with my ability to rattle on about my projects and stories, books and albums, media, and art. Emily has always shown patience while I explain my upcoming concept album or which story I want to construct next.

After eating a burrito the size of my head, we moved on to a grocery store called Farm Fresh. Like any other grocery store, it was designed to harbor everything you'd expect. But I walked around like an Amish on rumspringa witnessing technology for the first time.

"They have *vanilla melon hard seltzer*!" I gasped with the excitement of a single mother who realized they were getting a free night to themselves.

"That looks disgusting," Emily said, eyeing the vanilla melon hard seltzer the way the father character must have done to the runt of the litter in *Charlotte's Web*. Meanwhile, I was Charlotte herself — but substitute piglet Wilber for sugary booze.

We had come to Farm Fresh for ice cream. What sounded like an easy task, turned into an indecision of struggles over the flavor. Patrick lingered in the background, throwing out suggestions that neither Emily nor I seemed to appreciate at the time. It felt like we were parents — and letting your child pick the communal ice cream flavor would be bad parenting. We settled on S'mores, hoping the texture and flavor elements would be intriguing. Anything was better than basic vanilla in my book.

The cashier was lovely, and when I told her I was from Cleveland, she looked taken aback as if I had flown in from Sweden or Malaysia.

"Well, aren't Clevelanders quite nice!" The cashier said with a smile. These moments were the kind that made Emily roll her eyes with the full force of a Genghis Khan army division. Emily wasn't rolling her eyes at the cashier but at my natural charm with strangers.

Ice cream in hand, we returned to Emily and Patrick's shared house.

"We keep our dining room as an art space, music listening, 3D-printing room," Emily explained.

"So it's perfect for a night," I said, helping them set up the mattress. Their kitchen was filled with snacks.

"We're a Costco family," Emily said.

"You guys have enough snacks to feed three after-church functions." I smiled. Emily's schedule was rough right now — she was balancing a few opportunities like a seal might balance three latex balls on its nose. Like a seal in the water, Emily was graceful even under pressure. I could see light tiredness in her eyes — but she kept a warm smile my entire stay as if pushing through the pain of her work to be the best host she could be.

"I'm excited to interview you," I said, turning on a recording device while returning to my melting S'mores ice cream. At this point, we felt confident that S'mores had been the right call.

When I graduated college in 2016, I hit a brutal, dark patch in my life. I had graduated college, left behind the title of 'student,' and was now expected to just run into the adult professional sphere fully polished. I felt half-baked — like a cookie that missed out on crucial pre-oven elements of my bake or even needed more time in the oven. I was supposed to be a tough cookie; instead, I was a pile of mushed dough masquerading as a circle of cooked cookie.

This time was difficult because I was banking on an opportunity that ended up being taken away. It wasn't my fault — no drunk Instagram posts or inappropriate behavior. They had ended up reworking the department, and the job given to me had vanished. It was like giving a magician a twenty-dollar bill for his trick, only for the magician to run down the street.

I wrote one of my favorite stories to date in this dark time, so it wasn't all bad. In fact — maybe it proved that I needed more rough times so I could create better stories. I had thankfully gotten some part-time work at a few places, one being the radio station on their events team. But I was still looking for something new when my mother found an opportunity back at my high school. They were looking for recent college graduates who would be interested in doing a year of service.

When I applied and interviewed, I remember talking about how service and action had always been important to me. I didn't say this at the time — but I did it because it was doing *something*. I knew I needed some kind of action, and at the time, I didn't really realize what I needed. But there wasn't a call from God or a higher purpose asking me to do this. It would just be something to do and hopefully enjoy.

From the jump, the experience was much more atypical for everyone involved. There were usually three to four volunteers serving the high school every year. That year only yielded one recruit: me. This became problematic. There was no way that I could do the work of four volunteers. And yet — as much as I tried to do, I felt like I was disappointing people because I wasn't bringing in the total yield of four human beings. It was as if they expected the farm to produce as much milk with one cow — when in reality, you can milk that one cow as much as you want, and you'll still end up with the same amount of yielded milk.

The school also received a Jesuit Service Volunteer. The programs set up young post-college graduates with volunteering opportunities across the country. Emily Mangan was one of seven Jesuit Volunteers in Cleveland, and she had been chosen to work for the service programs of my alma mater. The seven volunteers lived in a cute house, cooked and cleaned together, and bonded immensely. How could you not when you were doing such an interesting, cutting-edge program and living simply together?

I was allowed to stay in a large house on campus, which I declined. I had lodging going into the program and I had zero desires to live in a four-story house alone. That sounds like the beginning of a serial killer Blumhouse production. It was a beautiful house — much more ornate than even the house I bought and live in now. But at the time, living alone in such a giant space was not going to happen on my watch. Some people were confused, maybe even upset, that I wasn't using the house. Emily meanwhile enjoyed the benefits of my absence.

"Thank you for the keys — we used them to go over and watch The Bachelor and CAVS games. And our house didn't have A/C, so we also used it for the A/C."

My first official question during our impromptu interview with ice cream was Emily's first reaction to meeting me. I told her the truth.

"Emily, I instantly thought you wouldn't like me."

Both Emily and I laugh over that ridiculous sentiment that became untrue. I know I refuse to get drinks with, let alone host, people I dislike. No way would Emily host someone overnight on a Monday night if she couldn't stand them.

"From the jump — I'm very loud, no filter, obnoxious," I explained my rationale. "But you looked mannered and ordered and a little serious."

"I remember your Easter-egg-colored shirt and your Christmas-colored tie." Emily joked that I was notorious for blending destructive patterns out of laziness and deeming them fashionable. "It was like a half-untucked shirt — and your *shoes*!"

Back then, I wore shoes until they practically disintegrated into ash.

"You looked like you rolled out of bed or something!"

"I will admit — to this *day*, I have issues with that. I just always have to *go*. So, I remember jumping pretty quickly into the work. But how long did it take for us to be friends?"

"I think it was quick. We figured out early that it was just you and me. There were supposed to be six other people. And we were stuck with each other.

"At times, I just didn't think you were a real person." Emily continued. "I thought to myself — *this guy is unbelievable*."

Both my ego and my storyteller mindset asked Emily for detail.

"I don't know — you're just *indescribable*!" Emily's voice feels full of disbelief. "You were non-stop all the time. It's unmatched."

"I remember us doing a lot of walking."

"We would just leave our jobs and walk around." Emily cackled.

"We would leave for lunch, and it was 10am."

"We'd come back around 4pm."

Emily and I have an outstanding rapport — in case you're not feeling it.

"I quickly began testing the water to see what I could *say*. I think we were experiencing issues — not with each other, but with the work, organization, and peers. So I kinda just decided to confide in you about these issues — hoping you felt the same way."

"I don't know when we started bitching about our lives, but it was pretty early on. We both saw through the bullshit *immediately*. We would just look to each other and say, 'can you *believe* that?'"

Emily and I believe that service has nothing to do with oneself. The acts you do might make you feel good, but they are *more* than just your actions. It's about the community, the world around you, the social problems and ills that affect our community, and the more incredible world. But sometimes, we would run into people that loved to pat each other on the back for doing the bare minimum — or people who failed to understand there was more than just their one hour of volunteerism.

People misread this story. They are apt to reference the starfish story of the kid throwing starfishes back into the ocean.

"But the starfish got back in the ocean because of him."

The stress in that sentence should be how the starfish got back into the ocean. Not about someone's involvement or motions.

"Sometimes I felt like people around us were a bit *self-serving*." I pointed it out to Emily.

"Some high-schoolers we worked with were looking for a college essay." Emily nodded.

Every week, there would be a club for students and personnel to meet and discuss service opportunities. It was one of the most painful things that Emily and I had to experience due to the amount of 'look at me' that would plague the meetings. Each meeting started with a prayer. Instead of saying it together as a group, the prayer was started and passed off to whomever felt *called* to say the next line. It was like prayer improv, except you know the lines. People hesitantly participated due to fear of being interpreted as someone who greedily grabbed a line of prayer. So it would take two minutes to power through eight lines of prayer. During this time, everyone would awkwardly look around to see who would go next. It was the ultimate game of chicken yet with God's grace.

"We were really good at avoiding masses and pep rallies." I pointed out.

"We would roll in around 10am, dick around, and pretend to type up emails," Emily said, recapping our daily existence. "Then we would say, 'we're off to a meeting,' when instead we would workout at the gym for an hour or two. Then we would do lunch —usually just scrounging off free leftovers in the teacher's lounge, and then finally, we would be back an hour before teaching our classes, and our coworkers would be like, 'where have you been?' And we'd just say 'workin'.'"

"I think I played some loud music. And got in trouble for playing music loudly at my desk." In my defense, the presence of music helps memory.

"Your desk was just *blah*," Emily said, her hands and mouth open to visually communicate how messy my desk was. There were a couple of different emails sent out about keeping the desks presentable. It was in a vague script — but we all know who was being referred to in that group email.

A big chunk of our job was running after-school programs that ran from 3:30pm or so to almost 5:30pm. Emily was in charge of a Violin club for 3rd through 8th graders and an adventure club geared towards 6th-8th graders. I meanwhile wrangled up the younger kids for Homework Club and Lego Robotics.

Homework Club revolved around finishing homework and then having fun after the homework was done. Most of the kids didn't have homework so instead they would play board and computer games with the high school volunteers. The program ran itself.

I was highly incapable of doing Robotics — it was like asking a cat to share its knowledge of dog culture. The first semester involved taking Lego Robotics from the early 2000s and programming them to do things. It was a mess — partially because I didn't know the lego robotics program, robotics, Legos, or really anything in the laboratory science field. Thankfully, a physics teacher on staff helped with the class, and the high school volunteers tended to be super nerdy and knowledgeable. Emily felt the same way about the Violin Club especially since some of the young kids had joined the club because of their parents and not because they believed they had a future in the orchestra.

We were supposed to do a whole robotics tournament, but it got snowed out — the living antithesis to the idiom, 'much to my chagrin.' I liked working with the kids, but they weren't that invested in the competition. It wasn't like we had a shot at winning; we would be competing against highly qualified school teams working in class. Meanwhile, we met once a week for twelve weeks after school.

"The second semester of Robotics was much more fun because we just did fun science experiments," I remember. "Who could build the tallest tower without crashing? Who could successfully build a bridge between two desks? It was educational but much more relaxed. There was science, but I didn't need to overdo the science elements of it."

It felt like I was hosting my own reality television program with the different competitions and activities we would do.

On Wednesdays, Emily and I hosted Bigs and Littles. The program paired younger kids with a high-school 'big.' We then would do activities, trips, and games with the partnerships.

"Do you remember when we hosted a Cotillion?" Emily asked.

Oh boy — did I remember it! But I wanted Emily to run through it for me.

"We were appalled by their manners," Emily said in the set-up. "So we wanted to try and inspire them. We brought in ties and had everyone wear them. We had plates and plasticware and some light bites. We were trying to do table manners and place settings. And it was so windy that day... all the plastic and paper flew over the yard. I don't think we got to the point of the event because we had to ensure we weren't littering."

"Another event was when we did a West 25th Scavenger Hunt," I recalled. "This was back when I thought it was a good idea to bring young children and high school volunteers to Cleveland's busy restaurant and retail district down the street from our office. In a moment of panic, I was worried I had lost two of my students, who were quickly found. I had never experienced such adrenaline. It was a true moment of horror in my life.

"I was flipping out — you could hear me running up and down the street. Well, you probably always can hear me — but still! I probably shouldn't have relied as much on the high-school volunteers. Sometimes they came in clutch, but sometimes it felt like they were useless."

"Sometimes the high schoolers were just as bad as the kids." Emily pointed out.

Besides after-school programs, Emily and I were also part of the team that led two of the school's larger service endeavors. Emily worked on a team that would go out on Sundays year-round to provide food and resources for the unhoused community. They built relationships and would go down the streets of Cleveland to serve a hot meal and catch up with the connections.

"I will never forget when we sat in the kitchen peeling carrots for carrot soup. We had twenty pounds of carrots and needed to figure out what to do. It was actually delicious, but it took us hours."

I helped the service organization that provided pallbearers to those who needed it for their funeral services. It was a very touching mission; the work was some of the most complex emotional work I've ever had to do. There's a certain set of emotions when you're amongst ten people at a service for someone who has passed. It's a real call to your own mortality. And you're wondering *why are there no others here?*

When I brought up those memories of being a pallbearer to Emily — she immediately made a connection to a character that rang a chord of memories through me.

"We have to talk about Smitty."

Smitty was quite the character. He had one of the most devious little smiles I have ever seen on a person. He was a large man, too — over six feet tall with white hair. But he had a smile that looked like it belonged on a troublesome deviant little southern girl named Jezebel. Smitty had the same thing for lunch everyday: a baloney sandwich and a diet soda. It was the kind of diet that felt straight out of post-World War II America. He would sit in the front lobby with his meal — another thing that puzzled me because we did have an exemplary kitchen area. Smitty, unfortunately, stopped being a volunteer towards the end of our year sentence.

"Didn't he run over too many curbs with the van?"

The large vans were not sturdy enough to take direct hits from curbs.

"I might be making this up, but he got into an accident or two, right? I know he didn't run anyone over — but some not-so-pretty things happened."

Emily confirmed that Smitty had racked up too many problems behind the wheel and was no longer allowed to drive high schoolers.

"All I remember about him is that smile. It was a capital C rotated to the side."

One of our favorite stories, I'll call 'The Ballad of Shay,' is about a woman we helped over our year.

"I helped buy her a train ticket to Nashville to get her away from an abusive situation with a boyfriend," Emily recalls. "And there was a baby involved, I think too. So the program spent a lot of money to get her that ticket. We helped her get out of Dodge. I dropped her off at the bus station. A couple of days later, you and I were in my office, and a coworker told us that Shay was coming to see me! And then yes — there was a lesbian plot twist post-Nashville."

The verdict is either Shay got to Nashville, said something to the equivalent of 'hell no,' circled the train station, and came back to Cleveland, or never boarded the train to begin with.

Another ballad was Regina. She had a powerful personality and had some untreated mental health issues. She would constantly tell people that they were soldiers of God — or the opposite. I witnessed her speak to a few people, and she sensed evil in them. She was opinionated about her faith and the world around her. Considering her life circumstances, her opinions were the only things that she could control. Regina got into a fight with someone in the office, repeatedly saying that they gave off bad energy.

Regina's neighbor actually tried to set her house on fire. They threw a Molotov Cocktail through her horse because they didn't want her living there. She was squatting — and was also a hoarder and would bring in buckets of things from her daily travels around the neighborhood. During the fire — at the age of 65 — she jumped out of the second-story window to avoid the flames. Emily visited Regina in the hospital to find out that her dog and cat had both passed away.

"What about Stanford?" Emily's smile turned into a sidewise C like Smitty.

Stanford was another unhoused individual we worked with a lot. He would constantly visit — with a little limp and confidence that powered through his stutter. Stanford would walk into the office and immediately start demanding things. He would need clothes, products, and food, and we would, of course, rush to meet his needs, often at a personal inconvenience. You would be knee-deep in quicksand, and Stanford would stress how much he needed a baseball cap.

"I need a size nine brand new black shoes." Stanford would strongly request.

"We gave you a pair last month." Emily would respond.

My favorite Stanford story was when he asked Emily for something but was not happy that the item was the color he wanted. Sometimes it felt like Stanford was double-dipping.

"He would barge in and then leave after he had put in his request." Emily pointed out. "One time, he asked for a radio."

Most of our work during the week was directly with younger students.

"The family I think about the most is the Smith family." Emily veered. "Four kids in one family with drunk parents...."

This was a harsh reality for some of our students. Some would get picked up extremely late by irresponsible parents who, in a way, considered their children afterthoughts.

"What about the two brothers — the Mellando Brothers?"

We weren't sure about their names at first, but our memory worked in our favor that night. The older brother was Brian and the younger brother was Justin. The older brother was well-behaved, but the younger brother lacked social awareness.

"They had just gone to the doctor's that day," Emily said concerning one day in particular with Brian and Justin. "The doctor had told Brian that he was overweight and needed to be careful of what he ate so as not to get diabetes. And you know they had Wendy's every day."

Across the street was *the* iconic Wendy's. Hordes of young men from the school and various community characters always kept Wendy's flush with cash. I'm sure Wendy's was constantly turning over kitchen appliances to keep up with the order demands.

"They weren't supposed to eat Wendy's anymore. Apparently, Brian did visit Wendy's sneakily. Brian came into my office one time, and Justin arrived and immediately asked Brian if he had partaken in Wendy's. Brian denied the accusation twice over, which caused Justin to scream, '*I SMELL IT ON YOU*!' which caused Brian to confess that he had indeed enjoyed Wendy's."

"My favorite Justin story was how he was really misbehaving, so I had to revoke his popsicle privileges." I sighed. "I'm a terrible disciplinarian — but he was so out of control and unmanageable that day. And upon finding out he wouldn't get a popsicle, he had a *meltdown*. It probably would have been easier to give him the popsicle at that point...."

Many things were asked of Emily and me that we were unequipped or underprepared to handle. The largest challenge by far was asking Emily and I to be the spiritual counselors to high school volunteers.

"I think I lead one single reflection," Emily confessed. "I didn't even touch on it."

"I would make it quick — quick prayer, in and out. It just felt grandiose to what we were doing."

"One moment I will never forget — and I think about it because you deny it — is when you called a high school volunteer a *crackwhore*!"

"Run me through this because I have no memory, but I don't think I would push that line!" I gasped. These days I would certainly know better than to use the term in the first place.

"I wasn't there," Emily prefaced. "Your team arrived downstairs from the reflection space, and one of the students, Meg, said that you called her a crackwhore! And you said, 'No, I said *like* a crackwhore."

"So many problems here," I said with a laugh. "I shouldn't be using the term ever in the first place. But then, why would she be defined *like* a crackwhore to begin with? I wish I knew the context behind that."

"Moments like that made me think you were unreal," Emily said to me.

One of the benefits of our free labor for the year was professional development. It was designed as a way for Emily and me to discover more about the world of professionalism, create contacts and networks, and eventually leave the nest of volunteerism for the real world.

"More often than not, it was canceled, or we went to a coffee shop and chatted for ten minutes about what was going on," Emily recalled. "It was so dumb."

"That was the biggest disappointment for me. The whole idea for this role was that there would be advisement with my career. I liked working with people, and I loved the service. But I didn't get professional help or those promises."

One of the professional development sessions that frustrated me the most was when we did one of those 'your personality is this color' tests. I'm the type of person who loves quizzes — give me my astrology of the day, my Myers-Briggs, my temperament tests, and career tests all day.

Going into this test, I was excited, and I loved finding out that I was orange. What I didn't like was how it felt like being orange was a bad thing — the descriptors surrounding the word felt negative — 'loud,' 'boisterous,' the kinds of things you say passively aggressive to someone who you're trying to get along with but has you at your wit's end. Emily got the color blue — which had words like calm, serene, and graceful. When you stack up our colors against each other, I look like a real character.

Emily confidently feels like I overanalyzed those test results.

"I remember you *flipping* out about being orange." Emily laughed. "You would not let those descriptors go."

"The words they used to describe orange were so terrible —."

"They were not that bad!" Emily doubled down with a cat's grin. "But you wouldn't hear otherwise. And its *fucking* colors!"

I have a habit of sometimes beating a personal issue to death so others can see how 'in the right' I am. I used to be very defensive — and I sometimes still showcase that defense by playing an aggressive offense.

My favorite session of professional development involved using Strength Finder, a psychological assessment of one's strengths. I thought creativity or communication would be my biggest strengths but they were merely on the top five. My biggest strength was ideation. At first, I thought that was a lame strength until later that week, I realized that I was full of too many ideas. The psychological assessment came out to be accurate. Emily's number one strength was empathy.

"Another core memory of our year of service was constantly going over to the faculty lounge to get coffee, tea, cereal, and other delicacies." I said in a dream haze of remembrance over free food.

"Jungle Java — the worst coffee ever." Emily followed up. "And anytime they had chocolate Chex cereal... we would be there *all the time.* I've never had chocolate Chex outside of that school."

It was awkward sometimes to go into the faculty lounge because I would often be confused for a student. Sometimes I'd enter the faculty lounge to the stairs and walk into a faculty member who didn't know me. I was rocking a bold beard and looked a tad older, so it was shocking that people would mess that up.

We were doing our year of service when Trump was elected into office. The Wednesday after Election Day 2016, Emily and I were leading our program, Bigs and Littles. We decided to take everyone to the nearby beach. It was a terribly windy and grey day as if Mother Nature was protesting the situation. Emily was quite depressed and I was shell-shocked, if anything.

"Nobody wanted to be at the beach." Emily mused.

"It was the worst beach trip we have ever had."

"It was a metaphor for what was coming."

Another sad moment was when we did a prayer service at Potter's Field. It's off the map — although I remember precisely how you would get to it. The city dumps the ashes of all the people who cannot afford to pay for their own burial services — either all alone or otherwise no one in their family can pay. Visitors are not typically allowed — the idea being that people can't 'cheap' out on the burial costs and still visit their loved ones. It's a stark thought process and a starker place. There's nothing denoting its location — it is just *a place.*

"I think about Potter's Field often," Emily said when I brought it up. "Thousands of people. No gravestones, proper grave, no family that can afford their burial, homeless people...."

The discussion felt like a tangle of strings we continued to dance through. We would momentarily grab a few bunched strings, react emotionally, move forward, and slowly lose old strings for new strings. To an outsider, it probably sounded like a collection of mumbles — but to us, the direction of our conversation made perfect sense.

"Let's talk about Jesuit Dinners." Emily mused, staring at me intently. I was invited to the Jesuit house for dinner every Tuesday and Thursday. Usually, there would be three or four volunteers who would go around. There were between eight and twelve Jesuits — and a few of them really liked me. Most of them were older, a bit more stodgy, and not fans of mine. I felt like the awkward grandson of grandparents who felt obligated to see their grandson then really enjoy the company.

"They had the best food." Emily sighed, dreaming of the food cooked not by Jesuits but by a maid.

"I had mixed feelings about those dinner. My existence, in general, always felt like a tightrope based on my demographics."

"They had some old men who were stuck in their ways." Emily chirped

"At the time, I was fine with it, but it really was a bit brave to continue to put myself in that place."

I don't deserve a gold medal, but there is something to be said about placing yourself in slightly unfavorable places. No one was ever really mean to me — but there were things left unsaid that, if told, would certainly cast a dourness over those meals.

"You would push it so much with those older men. Some of the things you would say...." Emily pretended to clutch her fake pearl strand necklace. "My favorite joke you cracked in that house of Jesuits was when you suggested they get a dog and name it Emmanuel so they could say, 'O come, O come Emmanuel.' It was so funny. That's the thing — you would always make us laugh."

Emily's compliment reminded me of the time we had a 'job review.' Emily doesn't recall hers, but I remember the one note I received. I was told that my emotions dictated the emotions around me. If Matt Hribar is happy — then everyone is happy. And if I'm not, then nobody is. It felt a bit accurate but also a bit uncalled for.

"I've always been in...touch with my feelings. I wouldn't say I've always been in control. I've always known how I'm feeling and why. And I'm not going to pretend to experience a different reality for someone's comfort. I don't want to upset people because I'm upset — I just live life transparently."

Emily's favorite moments appear drafted from *The Office* or *Parks and Recreation*.

"We had a bet." Emily's face always lit up when an outrageous story was on the horizon. "You would talk non-stop about how you wanted to do stand-up comedy, so I finally said you just need to do it. And we made a bet that you had five months to do stand-up. So because you lost, you had to make a vow of silence — a whole week of you being silent."

"And I remember sticking to it!"

"You *stuck* to it, which was annoying because you can't come to work and not speak."

"I had a writing board!"

"We were literally at a staff meeting with five people. There was no hiding, and our boss turned to you and couldn't believe you were sticking to it. You lasted for two days which was just way too long!"

"I don't see a problem — I lost a bet!"

"Yeah, between you and me. You wouldn't talk to *anyone*!"

"It speaks to my character — I try and live up to my bets and promises." I joked. "I think finally you were like, 'please, talk!' But I didn't want to give up and let you win."

One of the most horrific moments for Emily was when we reenacted the washing of the feet. For those unfamiliar, Jesus himself washed and kissed people's feet — for that alone, I would label him a martyr.

"I had to wash and kiss the most disgusting pair of feet I have ever seen," Emily gagged over the recollection.

As much as Emily and I may have started drama — or at least maybe it was the irk to some people who desired more conventional things — we were far from the biggest scandal. After our time, a married staff member was fired for having an extra-marital affair with another employee.

In the fall, it was just Emily and me. But in the spring, we were joined that semester by a Jesuit novitiate — Billy. Billy, a budding Jesuit, loved nuns and reading and somehow was the perfect blend of Emily and me with more commitment behind his faith. He was pleasant, sweet, and funny — someone you could socialize and philosophize with.

Another character was Thomas — another budding Jesuit who unfortunately would not be chosen to participate in the program. He had what I call an 'Eeyore Tone' — you know, the people who, even in their happiest moments, feel sad due to the tone of their voice. It's not precisely a Debbie Downer — but it's shades away from it.

We got to a point in the night where our recollection began to dim like two mighty lights powering a stadium of memories. We called it, worrying about overheating our little adult lives. Even then, I knew there were dozens of little stories, of characters, moments where we began to recognize that we were post-college adults.

So many of these stories featured times when we felt underprepared, underutilized, and thrown into things that we had no knowledge of or control over. It felt like, if anything, a fast track into adulthood. Our frustration with what was happening was just the top of a glacier of systematic societal problems, corporate frustrations, adult relationships, and human error.

It might seem like we stood on top of giant podiums lauding how excellent we were — but both of us suffer from shades of imposter syndrome. How do we fit into this modern world? Are we capable of doing the jobs we have been tasked with, capable of handling our dreams and executing them? Some of our peers have skyrocketed onto scenes that we are barely gripping onto — even if others think we've made it.

The following morning — I helped pack the blown-up mattress, enjoyed a cup of coffee, and watched as Emily put together her professional work ensemble. While Emily could rock the pantsuit for the masses — I always loved her best in florals, cardigans, and older pieces of clothing with character that measured a mile long.

"I'll see you soon," I said while throwing suitcases and blankets in my trunk like a killer hoisting bodies. We have the kind of friendship where we might go a couple of months without speaking or maybe a year without seeing each other. But to say it's like 'riding a bike' understates our experience. Is it trauma bonding — perhaps trauma with a lowercase t — or maybe platonic soulmates in action? Is it because opposites attract and balance each other? The country frog appreciates the loud boisterousness of a city dog, while the city dog takes in more life around itself, like the country frog?

"See you soon," Emily said — climbing into her vehicle to head an hour into work. I meanwhile had four hours to go till North Carolina — and part of me was hankering for a breakfast biscuit.

Audioaddict

I've met the occasional person who doesn't like music, which always horrifies me.

"What do you mean?" I question with the veracity of a sanctified, bona fide believer meeting their biggest nonbeliever *ever*. It's time for me to bring out the convincing material to try and change their mind.

The answers cross a gamut of how they just don't have the energy, inclination, or time to expand their musical horizons. They let radio stations dictate their music — and sometimes don't even react to the music they hear.

"I'm just not a person who *resonates* with music," these particular people say as if music is impossible to connect with. It must be a sad existence to find yourself not enjoying audio. Often these haters of music aren't listening to podcasts and audiobooks either — they just have no desire to tickle their ears.

And what do you say to these non-sound believers?

"Have you tried cleaning your ears? Have you tried unclogging the emotions in your heart? Have you tried being human lately?"

When I meet people who say they hate reading, that situation feels easier to parse through. Have you found the correct genre? Maybe you haven't discovered authors you like more than others? Has forced reading in school given you soft trauma? At least people are a bit more honest with reading. Some just don't like to read words, words like this essay. They think it's boring or they aren't charmed by my robust vernacular. Reading feels like work — not a relaxing pastime or a place where they can board the imagination train.

Even those who don't watch much television get a pass here. These days I hate how often I find myself glued to my television, iPad, or iPhone streaming shows on repeat. I refuse to get a second television because it feels gratuitous as a single man living alone. If I want to watch tv — I do it in the living room. My bedroom is a place to relax, sleep and constantly shift piles of clothes around.

Music has always been an essential part of my life. My mother had a giant CD collection, and I'd gotten familiar with artists like Madonna, Kate Bush, and Tori Amos at an early age. I knew about *Running Up That Hill* before the whole world did. I was also known for singing along loudly to music. It took till college for that part of my identity to be scrubbed to the conformity of not singing along to one's iPod. I must have thought that a music producer would jump out of a bush and sign me to a major label.

My grade school didn't have much of a choir — but we did have singing practice where we would practice the music for the school mass *before* the school mass. Think of it as football practice before the big Friday game. But instead of throwing footballs, we would make sure we knew what songs we would be singing. Even at a young age, it felt like a waste of time.

I recently saw my classmate Bridget who told me she only got one demerit because the girl next to her during singing practice kept talking to her. Mrs. Zingales — one of the most excellent teachers at the school, reacted very poorly to these hushed whispers and wrote them up.

"I'm genuinely shocked," I told Bridget after hearing her story. "The only memories I have of Mrs. Zingales is that she always had those sour cherry candies that she would hand out to students who did well."

In pre-COVID times — Mrs. Zingales would have buckets of sour cherries that students would compete for, like seagulls with a brown bag on the beach. The process evoked a kind priest passing out bread to the local peasants.

My singing prowess became well known in grade school during the Stations of the Cross. For those who didn't have a decently-fledged Catholic upbringing, the Stations of the Cross is when Jesus took the cross and carried it to where he passed away (Editor's Note: I was informed that 'passed away' might be downplaying what happened).

My school would put on a reproduction of the Stations of the Cross featuring actors playing the iconic roles of Jesus, Mary Magdalene, and Mother Mary. There was always drama about who was going to be cast as Jesus. One year, a classmate who couldn't act, got the role solely due to how he looked like Jesus —

specifically, he had a six-pack. Jesus bares all as we recall. It's crucial he looks ripped on the crucifix in his final moments.

When I was younger, I always felt quite entitled to my solo in this performance: the final verse of *Mary Did You Know?* It was as if the minister or monk who had written that song had always envisioned me closing it with a harrowing baritone '*ooooh Mary, did you know-ooo—ow*?' The impression I always got from those who witnessed the program was that my solo definitely made Mary know. Mary couldn't *not* know when I was executing the solo.

In high school, I joined the chorus immediately and was one of sixty vocalists. Most of the music we did in the chorus was related to the school being a Catholic school. I was always envious of public high school choirs who got to sing pop numbers and music that was from the last twenty years. In the fall, we would prepare for our winter showcase, filled with dreary religious Christmas songs. There was no room for a jazzy *Jingle Bells* or a flirty *Must Be Santa* — we would do a *Carol of the Bells* that would befit a Christmas murder and some ancient Christmas music that even the most fervent Christmas fan wasn't able to identify.

In the spring, we finally exercised some contemporary music, but it was usually old show tunes and obscure musicals that even the hardened theater lovers would not have heard of or would go, "*that's* the song you picked?"

To expand my horizons, I joined the A cappella club as a freshman. The club met for an hour after school on Mondays and I would stick with it all four years of high school. There was a more exclusive A cappella club, one that involved an audition process. I auditioned my freshman year and did not get in and vowed to make everyone rue that decision. Granted, freshmen were rarely invited into the elite club. But I have this terrible habit of seeing rejection and writing things off completely.

In my freshmen year of college, I tried to be a resident assistant and a tour guide and was rejected from both. Most people would try again as a sophomore — but I refused. They had a chance to have me, and now they would be forever unable to have me. Younger Matt must have assumed they'd feel that sting for the rest of their lives.

"Wait — Matt Hribar isn't applying?! We really want him, though!"

The tour guide was a slap in the face, mainly because of what I *do* for a living. Many tour guides couldn't successfully tour a family through a playground, yet *I* was denied the opportunity? I like to imagine that they thought I would be too truthful.

"Over here is our cafeteria," Tour Guide Matt would say to prospective students and their families. "The food is terrible, so we recommend always having a fridge during your time here. Next up, let's see a cinderblock dormitory and convince you that American dorm life is simply the *best*!"

My rivalry between the A cappella club and the elite A cappella club blossomed during my senior year of high school. I formed a third group — a show choir half-inspired by rivalry and half-inspired by *Glee* (True Gleeks know that glee clubs are founded on revenge and betrayal). So when we performed a jazzy rendition of *Telephone* as a glee club — it brought down the house. The elite A cappella club members watched on in jealousy as they performed outdated pop numbers like *Brown Eye Girl*.

The drama carried over into the regular chorus. Quite often, the tenors of the chorus would make fun of the baritone-bass section in a reverse bullying experience. The school trips were always hassles. One student's mom, who I'll call Mrs. Robinson, was hands down the worst chaperone on our spring break choir trips. Mrs. Robinson allowed her sociopathic son to run the court with some chorus members. She enjoyed being the cool mother who let her son and other boys run around the hotel after mandated curfew. While the rest of us had taped down doors to prevent us from successful sneaks, Mrs. Robinson would re-tape her son's door in the morning. All these dramas sucked out my desire to join any musical organization again.

My first concert was Christina Aguilera with Destiny's Child as an opener. I had won the tickets at a youth spaghetti-eating competition at a county fair. I have no memory of the concert, but I assume we had a fun time. Was it okay for my parents to allow a child to go to a concert that young? But then again, should I have been in a spaghetti-eating contest? The 90s were *undoubtedly* wild.

The earliest concert I remember seeing is Sugar Ray at the House of Blues with my mom and younger sister. I was somewhat familiar with Sugar Ray's hits — but most of the concert was just me vibing out to music at a young age. I became more interested in attending shows and volunteering at festivals as I became older.

"What's the best concert you've ever been to?" This is a difficult question for me to answer. If we're talking about the best performers, the best shows, and the best musician acting in a live setting — it's easy to answer. Susanne Sundfør, my favorite artist of all time, came stateside in 2019. Seeing her sing her way through a piano, a synthesizer, and a guitar, all solo and alone, was beautiful. It was also one of the rare concerts where I loved the opening artist and followed up with listening to more from the opener post-show.

A fun little moment was when Susanne asked the crowd where attendees were from. I, being weirdly pious, was silent. But my mom kicked in with a: "Cleveland." Susanne turned to our direction and asked, "Like the Family Guy character?" In this moment, I realized that perhaps Cleveland was not the international hub I had believed it to be.

Lady Gaga is my favorite pop artist. Her showmanship, flexibility, craft, iconic history, visual performances, aesthetics, evolution, vocals, choreography — it's everything that I incapsulate. The Killers always sound better live than the album. They're one of the few bands/artists who have always delivered on each album and never supply less than perfect.

Another favorite includes Tori Amos — who can perform on two different pianos simultaneously with that smoky alternative vibe. I've seen U2 twice — both shows were energetic with anthem power. My favorite DJ in concert was Alison Wonderland, who mixed her music with instruments and live vocals during a compelling and trippy set.

But if you asked me: "What's the best concert you've ever been to," with the implication that the show was unforgettable, the answer is different.

My mother got free tickets for Danity Kane and offered them to me. I took my friend Deanna down to the House of Blues; excited to hear the girl group behind a favorite hit single of mine, *Damaged,* and other various songs. The Downtown Cleveland House of Blues can fit a couple thousand. The first floor is devoted chiefly to a mosh pit. I had never before or since seen an emptier floor. Maybe fifty people or so — all of us pressed close to the stage.

I like a good view at a concert but I usually don't have the energy or attitude to bulldoze my way to the front. So being this close to Danity Kane felt undeserved. I was certainly unworthy of being this close to the cult's upper echelon. I was surrounded by tried and true Danity Kane fans — who was I but someone utilizing a free ticket?

The show commenced in a fog which in the balcony would have looked dazzling, but up close was like getting pepper-sprayed. The girls sauntered in costumes that mimicked youth gymnastics competitions. The prop budget seemed to be twenty dollars — the only props were baubles and those ribbons on strings. There was no need for expensive accruements when the girls sang their hearts off.

"Who wants to hear more about my new album?" One of the Danity Kane girls asked, which got a giant rouse out of the small but tight fanbase.

As the songs continued, my friend Deanna and I realized we were the only ones who didn't know any lyrics. Around us, people sang and chanted as if ordinary people were familiar with the Danity Kane album's deep cuts. We were so close to the stage that I knew the girls could see our faces when they walked by. We were not masked in the concert hall darkness.

So I began to ad-lib and pretended to mouth the lyrics because I didn't want the Danity Kane girls to feel badly that I was the only person in the venue who didn't know the music.

In my cloud of anxiety I thought about what might have happened if a Danity Kane member saw me silent amongst singing fans. Would they stop the show, even go so far as to *cancel* the show? Would a quiet me in the front be the last nail in the coffin? Would they retire altogether? Maybe they would get into a fight?

"It's okay that he didn't know!" One of the members would cry in upset. "Not everyone has to know every single damn song of ours!"

"He was in the *front* row!" Another member chimed in.

"EVERYONE WAS IN THE FRONT ROW!" another Dainty Kane member would snarl before shattering their wine glass on the floor.

There is one concert that I will never forget. Even if my mind goes, and my body barely supports itself one day, I will forever remember forever your girl Paula Adbul. Picture it, the 2018 Paula Abdul concert live at the MGM Northfield Park. For those unfamiliar with the suburban-rural Ohio casino scene, MGM Northfield is a slots-only casino that hosts many concerts and comedians — all usually in the C to D-list range. To enter one has to walk through a waft of nicotine smoke and the scent of well-level liquor. My mother had won free Paula Abdul tickets, so I joined her for an evening of 80s hits.

I didn't really have any expectations going into the show. When I don't have expectations, I settle on an okay performance. Knowing that people like me were present, Paula Abdul refused to surrender to just 'okay.' The show opened with a bang — featuring a biopic of Paula Abdul's life and how she was a cheerleader — cue the pompoms. Another sequence involved her having bad dreams on a raised mattress while it stormed. She did a Frank Sinatra tribute. All of these random things on their own seemed a little ludicrous but altogether formed a fantastic mesh of intrigue and entertainment.

The sets looked like they were created by high schoolers for an all-school assembly about drug abuse. One set was designed to look like a dirty alley that not even a heroin addict would find charming, displayed graffiti that said, *SkatKat Was Here*.

Straight Up was performed while dancers strutted around on ladders and Paula stood around the ladders in that technique artists do where it *looks* like they're moving because everyone around them is moving. The same thing happened during *Cold Hearted* where she was grabbed, repelled, spun, twisted, sashayed, and was catapulted in every direction you could think of by the dancers around her while remaining statuesque.

There was a five minute homage to Paula Abdul's time on American Idol. It was as if they aired one of those 'Best Paula Abdul American Idol Moments' videos you would see on Facebook. There was another scene which mimicked the plane injury Paula supposedly had but is not on record anywhere. To mix these concepts together was not just a jarring biographical feature — it was like being on acid for the first time.

Paula ended the show walking among the crowd, but you couldn't see her because she is so short. You just would hear her belted promise, *I'm forever your girl!* and guesstimated where in the audience she was coming from.

Another favorite MGM Northfield show was when we saw Men at Work. You might be wondering — why does that band sound familiar? You might be familiar with the song *Down Under* with the flute solo and the iconic line — *I come from the land Down Under!* It's quintessential eighties with a bit of flair and pompousness.

This is one of those shows where you don't know most of the music, and you're waiting for the encore to hear things you're familiar with. However, the most eye-catching moment of the night wasn't the singer, the lighting, or anything you would immediately think of when thinking of a concert.

"I can't stop watching that tambourine player," I whispered to my mother, who immediately stifled a chuckle.

"Oh, I'm *only* watching the tambourine player," my mother confirmed, proving once again I am my mother's son.

Commanding the stage in a fury of sound, flavor, and passion was a tambourine player who could make the most minimal instrument maximal in usage. She slapped the tambourine with every body part she could imagine. She even traded it out for maracas and other shaking sound devices. Her peak moment for me was when she held the maracas by the bulbous section and proceeded to shake them. I really appreciated her audaciousness.

"She has to be sleeping with the lead singer," my mother's friend Michelle explained. "She was super outrageous up there...."

Indeed — a quick Google search revealed that she was married to the one remaining member of Men at Work, and we all cheered like frat brothers who had discovered extra beer in the fridge.

The most aggressive crowd I've ever seen at a concert was when I went to see The Black Keys. It was shocking because I didn't expect fans of the Black Keys to be dicks. The band is bluesy, rock, and chill blended together. You'd think people who went to see The Black Keys would be relaxed hippies just looking for the nearest veggie melt sandwich.

The concert was at Blossom — a venue that would strike any northeast Ohioan with horror. The actual Blossom stage is a gorgeous amphitheater that acoustically wins many awards for its sound design. However, the parking lot is, in reality, fields of grass that are designated as laissez-faire. There are some parking attendants, but they're usually young high school and college kids who do not get paid enough to deal with parking control.

These wild fields of 'choose your own adventure' are amplified by the fact that Blossom shows are notorious for their pre-game culture. Coolers and six-packs get pulled out of the car, forming a little party around your vehicle. This pre-game palooza prepares you for the upcoming slog: half a mile to the venue to see the show. Imagine driving your car across grassy fields unsure of where to go while surrounded by drunks. Even *The Walking Dead* characters had better transportation circumstances.

My mother, Monica, our family friend Olivia, and I arrived at Blossom in backup traffic so bad even Los Angeles would reel in horror. We finally turned into a side field thinking we were moments away from absolution. Our slow crawl turned into a standstill. We popped our heads out of the car like curious prairie dogs.

"Let's go investigate," I told Monica.

"I'll tell people behind us to get back." Olivia nodded, using her background as a teacher to be parking logistics coordinator.

The three of us left my mother alone in her car. I moved forward, ready to write down a license plate if a vehicle blocked a clear thru exit. I wasn't sure what I was going to see. That's part of the reason I went to investigate.

"What are you doing?" Some white guy with a beard cried out as I moved forward.

"I'm just gonna take a look."

"You don't need to take a look!" He aggressively snarled.

I was immediately confused by the volatility. You would have thought I was trespassing on his property. Monica was a bit behind me but was coming up fast, having smelled the assholery like a shark's attraction to blood.

"Where did you graduate from? Asshole Academy?"

"Right here, actually, so maybe you should leave my town!"

I should have clapped back with, 'Really? You went to school at a concert venue in the middle of a national forest?' But I was so stunned that people acted like this that I didn't have my top-notch sass prepared. I fail in this regard; sometimes, I'm significantly taken aback and unable to return witty repertoire.

Monica arrived hoping to defuse drama, only to be caught in his anger. At some point, I flipped him off and kept walking. I believed a way out was blocked but it turned out that there was no official way out of the field. The cars had parked in such a way that there was no exit. The field and fencing blocked in this awkward row of parked cards. There was no way to fix it — oh wait, maybe having legitimate parking?

Later, after Olivia helped everyone escape, we walked to the venue up ahead. As we navigated through a labyrinth of cars, we saw the man who had been rude to Monica and me.

"Oh my gosh — that's him!"

Olivia and my mother whipped their heads quickly as humans are apt to do. Olivia gasped upon sight.

"He's with my cousin!" Olivia confessed. "He's with my cousin!"

It was a dramatic twist you only assume you'd see in a Netflix series about boring straight people.

"How does she know him?" I wondered if she was romantically intertwined with that hothead, and if so, why? I don't want to assume he was an abusive partner, but was she okay?

The Black Keys themselves were great but the crowd was a little too... cracked out.

"I'm actually perturbed about all these people," Monica confessed. "It's all in the *eyes*. They're really messed up."

Monica might not have studied sociology like me, but she had the hunger of a sociologist. Her eyes flared up with intrigue at the slightest movements of people around us. But she also reminded me of when Homer Simpson visited the lesbian bar and noticed the lack of proper fire safety.

"I'm sure they're doing things safely," I said, more to ease Monica. Truthfully, some of the people around us screamed "problematic situations." But Monica and I both get anxious in these situations, so I hoped to batten down our emotional hatches.

Moments later, a guy walked by as I was jamming out. He copied me, and I wasn't sure if it was respectful or disrespectful.

"I like your dancing!" He cheered on.

"Thanks, I'm kind of an artist." What was I, an influencer at Coachella?

"Is that what you do?"

I told him more about what I did, which felt like artist adjacent. He began to look at me wide-eyed.

"I do marketing! For a company!"

"That's great!" I genuinely remarked.

"Do you know what I'm scared of?"

My eyebrows shot up quicker than the glass elevator at the end of *Charlie and the Chocolate Factory*.

"Um, no?" I wondered what could be bothering this poor white man who works in marketing and was definitely drunk, if not high, at a Black Keys concert.

"Have you seen the AI that can do creative things?"

"I have; it's cool."

"It's scary because it will take jobs away from creatives like us!"

This discussion was much better than the 'Mexicans stole our jobs narrative.'

"The idea is that AI will do that in *all* sectors, but creativity has been the last hurdle." I added.

"But it's *doing* it."

"It's doing what you're telling it to do," I explained.

"No — it's making it up altogether." The man gave an example of how he had given AI the keywords 'Bigfoot,' and 'Art Deco.' AI was able to come out with legitimate drawings of a regal Sasquatch.

"But humans are still the ones creating the concepts," I explained.

Meanwhile, my favorite Black Keys song was being played, and I was missing it to talk to some guy about his fear that creative AI would destroy livelihoods. That was the most upsetting part of this conversation, not the chat, but the *one* song I wanted to hear was being drowned out by this man.

"But the AI wouldn't know fully original ideas," I added. "It *knows* what Bigfoot is and what Art Deco is. But is it able to fully create something new?"

The man continued to worry about marketing jobs, so I remained pretty passive. He eventually had to go pee.

"I was so confused at what was happening," Monica said. "I was standing so close, but the two of you stared into each other and didn't notice me. Was he into you?"

"Well — I wouldn't mind that." I sighed.

We decided to leave early; none of us were married to the idea of staying long just to see the Black Keys. The walk was probably just as long as the walk of shame that Ceresi does in HBO's *Game of Thrones*. Except instead of people throwing rotten fruits and a bell of shame, there was just clouds of weed and drunk yips and shouts. The rock paths had giant boulders that caused me to trip a few times. And before you assume, no, I was *not* drunk. I do believe whoever designed Blossom was a sadist.

We soon returned to the car like a bunch of rejects. My mother was driving and came upon an intersection where cars were pulled to the side of the road. Red and blue lights flashed; it looked like we were stumbling upon an emergency.

"What is happening?" My mother said on behalf of us all. A man in poorly tinted neon was standing in the middle of the road.

"Left or right?" The man snapped.

"What—" My mom didn't realize he was acting in place of a stop sign.

"Pick a damn side! Where's the blinker?"

My mom quickly put her right blinker on.

"There we fucking go!" The man snarled as we turned right. I could see a sheriff's name on his uniform.

"Who is that prick!?" My mom asked moments later as we continued on our journey. We joined in on the insanity from that officer of the law. But it was Olivia who tied the pieces together.

"I think he was part of the park's security team; I don't think he's a real cop!" Olivia said in a Sherlock Holmes deduction.

"He can go investigate some roadkill." My mother sassily clapped back — causing Olivia, Monica, and I to howl with laughter.

Audioaddict ii
(Pop Star Incoming)

    One of my most profound life desires has been that I always wanted to be a pop star. Not because of the groupies and drugs, but because of the visuals, the eras, and the creation. I wanted to be the male version of Madonna, except not as sensual and sexual. I wanted to tell stories, craft moments, and titillate the masses like any good pop star.
    My mother told me that I concocted shimmery pop lyrics from a young age. *On The Right Side* was apparently the first song I ever wrote in kindergarten according to my mother.

"You didn't know how to type so you had to sing your lyrics and I would type them out." My mother explained.

My uncle and I did a couple collaborations when I was young — including my mother's favorite song, *Millennium Force Is My Source*, which was an ode to Cedar Point. Between my limited memory and young age, I don't have much memory of these songs, but my mother has kept the rare CD release.

So in 2010, I finally decided to screw what society said and chose to overlook my current limitations. I had grown up singing, having been trained religiously and classically. I was a writer at heart, so crafting lyrics and songs involved little to no work for me. The dancing part — well, that was *fine*. I was certainly no Michael Jackson. But with the right training, I could impress at a dance club or even make it backstage at a broadway show, just maybe not on stage.

The mixture was present. It was just piecing the puzzle. I found an online music maker and spent hours piecing together beat pads and selections. My first four albums were mainly created with loops. Eventually, I would begin to wade into the school of music production. All my projects have been done in-house — from mixing and mastering to executing the graphics and marketing. Even within the *rougher* moments of my career, there was a level of authenticity.

Breaking out into pop music was my Hannah Montana becoming Miley Cyrus moment. I was shedding behind the choir tracks of *Ave Maria* for my debut single, *Electric* — where I crooned, *Ey-Ey-Ey, Ey-Ey-Electric* over an EDM beat that could be best described as the musical equivalent of cafeteria cardboard pizza. Like electricity, my high school buzzed over the release. Even now, some classmates chant the chorus. This, to me, was a confirmation that, if anything, I could write catchy music.

I wanted to showcase variety, so following *Electric* came the rap track *Ring Ring*. The song featured obnoxious phone sounds over what could be best described as Soundcloud rap. I continued to confuse my fan base with the third single, a torching piano ballad, *Drowning World*. The fourth single (who did I think I was to have this many singles *before* an album) was a rock track called *Zephyr*. *Zephyr* was inspired by Madonna's *Ray of Light* song, and my mother was immediately concerned.

"That sounds like a copyright issue." My mother pointed out one time when I was telling her about it.

"A copyright issue?" I questioned.

"Yes, you're stealing her lyrics."

"No!" I gasped — offended that anyone would think I would plagiarize art. "I'm just inspired by the *word* zephyr."

"Just don't get sued," my mother said — imagining the worst, which was an impossible situation.

My mother, over the years, has always kept an eye on my music career the way I assume the Queen of England eyed her grandchildren. She referenced it once while I was on the hunt for a job.

"Are they going to look into your social media and see *Hot Intern* and all that crap?" My mother said, which caused me to gasp the way people did when they saw Madonna roll around in a "wedding dress" on the MTV VMAs.

"*Crap?*" I questioned.

"Well, you know what I meant!" My mother said with a hurt expression as if *I* had insulted *her* original music. "Just...like that *stuff*."

The fifth and last single before my debut album was the title track: *Beautiful, Amazing*. Yes — my first album was called *Beautiful, Amazing*. The fantastic and beautiful thing about that title was that I didn't consider myself either of those things back then. I was decently insecure, as most high school boys are.

But that's the beauty of having a pop artist persona — you can become the things you lack. I lacked that incredible sensation of self and beauty I would later claim stake within. I didn't feel beautiful or amazing in my ordinary life. But under cover of Hribstar, I was whatever I wanted to be. It was like starring in karaoke every single day.

I would perform live at a school open mic and miniature concerts in Mr. Murphy's Latin class. I don't think I held myself too seriously — and I think some people thought they were laughing *at* me. But I maintain that they were laughing *with* me. I've always been powerful, even when I was not strong. I'm a storyteller and entertainer at heart; even in moments where I'm singing alongside the instrumental in front of a Smartboard on the second floor of my high school building. I was always in charge of everything.

I started working on my second album immediately after *Beautiful, Amazing* hit the internet by storm. By storm, the kind where they say it's 20% chance of rain. Originally the second album was going to be called *Dark, Insane* — an inversion of *Beautiful, Amazing*. The pop music expert in me knew that my sophomore release had to continue my persona but provide something different. From my limited memory, I remember writing some really dark pop tracks. One title, called *Bisect,* comes to mind. This album was quickly scrapped for a different concept album called *Wunderbar*. I don't remember where I heard the word, but I instantly fell in love. It was a play on the German word for wonderful and sounded like my last name Hribar.

Wunderbar was a bit darker and featured my inner demons pictured with various masks. These masked demons were the personas of Manufactured Matt, Chaotic Matt, Conformity Matt, and Defensive Matt. In retrospect, my artistry was therapy. I was feeling very conflicted during this period. Even with this upped popular status, I was clearly an outsider in high school. I was maybe royalty when it came to the outsiders, but I was *still* an outsider.

Funnily enough, I think that theme didn't communicate itself through the singles and music video campaign. But there is a song on the album called *5V1* with a Marvel/news-broadcaster music bed. The four different insecurities each deliver a rap in a Nicki-Minaj-inspired personality battle. The song is absolutely a wash, but it was pretty creative. Most of my life can be summarized similarly.

The lead single for *Wunderbar* also became my first music video, *DFR (Dangerous Frisky Risky)*. The song had surging bass and arpeggio — where I almost channeled The Weeknd (although this was before his arrival on the scene). *'Dangerous and frisky, definitely risky, I'm a party animal in the club'* from a sixteen-year-old who had never stepped foot inside a club, bar, or any party attraction, felt disingenuous. But weirdly this song felt legendary, considering the inaccuracy of the lived experience in the song.

The music video for *DFR* was *epic*. I couldn't even tell you who helped, but it involved me being stoned to death for my wicked ways. It was a cliche that I still utilize in my music and art today. I'm a sucker for a martyr. Although it looks like people are throwing rocks at me in the music video, people were actually throwing grapes. I can't even imagine what the school staff thought had they caught the scene in action.

The second single, *Can't Mess With This*, caused a lot of buzz when scenes of me in the chapel leaked. It was one of the biggest scandals of the fall semester. Thankfully I got the weakest slap on the wrist ever. I just had to make sure to take down the music video. They had to create a new rule about art and media creation in the school chapel. The video also featured shots of me putting pins in a mannequin head blended with the chapel scenes and *was* slightly disturbing.

The dark visuals continued with the third single and music video, *The Return*. The song was a ballad, and I wanted to feature visuals without me in them. I created two cityscapes out of cardboard. The plan was to flood one within this old aquarium my family never used and then set fire to the other one within the old aquarium. It was actually a beautiful idea — and the mix of cardboard set against the rising tide of water and the increasing flames turned out to be one of my favorite videos I've ever done — even if the song doesn't hold for the rest of time.

My sister helped, and I remember being very concerned for fire safety. So we had just a bucket of water ready for when the fire got *too* dangerous, frisky, and risky. The fire seemed in control until it cracked part of the glass. Immediately we doused it with water.

My film teacher loved the video and showed it to our film class.

"The cinematography is top-notch." He told the room at large, which stirred up both pride and embarrassment. Eventually, we would watch *72 Hours* in his class, and I would pass out, only to be brought to life in the hallway with some water.

In revisiting *Wunderbar* over ten years later, I didn't realize how much rock and alternative sounds were all over my early work. There were plenty of lyrics that I could easily see being reincorporated into a rock band. "*You were an innocent pretender, and I cannot even remember what it was like when you were my friend." "People just don't understand what they call contraband." "You made me your rival, and our lives began to spiral, because you seek power."*

My third album, *Reflections*, was released only a couple months later. At that point, I was really inspired by Bjork, so I leaned experimental with songs called *Catalyst, Shatter, Transparency, Prism,* and *Crystallization*. A couple of the tracks leaned on alternative rock, which is still a genre I have not fully explored. I have to hand it to myself, even in my more avant-garde and wildly unlistenable moments (*Reflections* was a six-minute song that revolved around a harp), the concepts themselves were entertaining.

"I want to be reflections of my former self," with a harp and minimal electro beat sounds like something Lorde would have loved. Some lyrics would elevate a Katy Perry pop track: *"We can unite, we can bring the color. I'll be the light, if you'll be the prism."* There were even some attempts to harmonize on *Prism*, which was...ambitious. The funniest thing I noticed when listening back to *Reflections* is that I had labeled it under the new age genre. If this is genuinely new age music, then we can condemn contemporary music.

While certain songs absolutely escape me, others are like stepping into a warm bath. *Winter* — the last track of the original print of *Reflections*, is one hundred percent inspired by U2's song *White As Snow,* both thematically and in production.

There was a period during my senior year when I was working on a collaborative EP with my friend and fellow classmate Craig. But a problem developed when Craig realized I had no proper musical background. I was a pop music puppet trying to figure things out, while Craig was a bit more of a legit musician. Craig was expecting bourbon, and I was only capable of apple juice.

Following an experimental album, it was time to double down on my pop roots with a concept club mix album called *M&F*. Although my mother thought M&F stood for 'Motherfucker,' M&F stood for *Masculinity and Femininity,* the album concept was about perfection. I had a delicious backstory on why the title connected to the album concept. But now I feel like it was a bit...

try-hard of young Matt, although still appreciated. Even now I don't understand why the title is *M&F*.

You could feel the theme of perfection through the names of the album singles alone: *Can't Be What You Want Me To Be, Becoming Human, What My Dancing Heart Shed,* and *Running Away From The World*. And if those don't make you think I was dealing with the concept of perfection, maybe titles like *Indestructible Castle, Didn't Succeed, Freefall, Rising Blood, Don't Fall For Pretty Pictures,* and *Invisible (It's Better This Way)* provide that context.

This was the second rebrand of the original Hribstar stage name. I had gone by Hrib*r in a move that was inspired by Kesha. But for this album, I simply went by an asterisk (*). It was a Prince-type strategy — but doubling down on how easy it was for me to tear things apart.

The four singles got music videos which were pretty easy and tame, except for my favorite: *Becoming Human*. The song is about how it feels like a failure to showcase human imperfection. It involved a chase sequence where an animal-masked intruder was tracking me down. By the end of the video, the masked animal man had tackled me to the ground. He unveiled it to reveal it was myself behind the mask before donning maskless Matt with a mask. Pretty neat and a little predictable.

M&F had one of my favorite album rollouts because this was still when CDs were a primary method of sharing music. I had burned thirty copies of the album, complete with printed-out album covers, and passed them out to the biggest fans. I rolled around campus with CDs like I was delivering Valentine's chocolate instead of subpar pop music.

The first four albums had been unoriginal productions that I tried piecing together. But utilizing my Mac laptop's GarageBand and Logic Pro applications, I began to push myself into original production, chord arrangements, and sounds. I remember being fascinated with these programs and playing around with synthesizers and drum kits around the clock. Part of the reason I developed six albums over that year was that I spent every second learning about production.

My subsequent two albums come out that summer following high school graduation. I struggled between my poetic nature and comedic side, which I still do. I often find myself juxtaposed between leaning into happy, funny concepts or deep poetic concepts.

The fifth project, *Southern Gentleman*, was dubbed my first 'mixtape' and featured a rougher persona. This was where the gloves came off. Whereas before, I had danced in vagueness and explored myself and the general society around me, I was now airing all sorts of laundry, clean and dirty.

The lead single, *Stalk My Tweets*, was based on someone's complaints about my Twitter account. The chorus feels like a modern digital media nursery rhyme: *'Stalk my tweets, stalk them well, make sure that you go and tell.'* Imagine singing that to your child to have them fall asleep. *Stalk My Tweets* marked a significant lyrical and attitudinal change from the earlier albums. It was also sonically a bit different than my earlier works.

The *Stalk My Tweets* music video features the introduction of Mary Lou Sanders, a concerned resident inspired by the person who tries to report Matt. The video has many highlights, including a collection of me posing by various street signs, Mary Lou purposefully looking for art to ban, and a group of sassy tweets that honestly are concerning.

The second single was *Assassinate,* in which a seventeen-year-old Matt sings, *'Come and assassinate, Caesar, Lincoln, Kennedy — all controversial, all killed like me.'* It's a bold choice for a teenager who has never been assaulted or threatened with death.

The music video is an excellent forage in storytelling: concerned resident Mary Lou Sanders returns, but this time she's too frustrated and tries to hire various assassins to kill *me* Matt Hribar. Naturally, I play the trio of assassins, all who fail and end up dead from incompetence. Thankfully, the music video labels the characters accordingly. Otherwise, it would be easy to confuse me, with me, with me, and with me.

The best scene in the *Assassinate* video is when one assassin plants a bomb within a soccer ball and rolls it toward me. I end up kicking the soccer ball right into the hands of the assassin. The screen cuts to stock footage of an explosion so fake for the narrative that you can't help but appreciate how cheesy it is.

I look back on the tracks of *Southern Gentleman*, and I'm just... confused. There are songs called *Bring It!* and *Bull* which make sense for some cocky attitude over rap beats. But there's a 49-second interlude called *Mrs. Grendel*, who I assume was about some older lady.

My sixth album, *Explicator*, combined orchestral sounds with rock and alternative pop. An explicator is "someone who makes clear the meaning of; an explainer." The album includes *Hollywood*, an easy admonishment of fame culture; *Renegade*, which labels me as such; and *Streetcrosser*, a dark number invoking my love of the night. I don't think young Matt knew what 'streetcrosser' actually meant. Analyzing *Explicator* years later, I think I was interested in storytelling. Thematically there was a lot about religion, so bells and church-esque instrumentals were mixed into a lot of the tracks.

The album also features my foray into long songs. There is the six-minute *Confessions*, a loaded-up organ and staccato mess. The seven-minute song *Regicide and Deicide* about a king who thought he was a god. And, of course, the 8:53 long track *Illusions / Revelations*, two songs that sound like a dramatic overture for a sad indie movie.

The videos took place at iconic scenic institutions around Downtown Cleveland, Shaker Square, and my parent's house. My favorite song would have to be *History Personalized*, a piece about how we embody the history of the world and ourselves to become the person we presently are. It's a deep song that's delivered with shallow production.

The most popular video for *Explicator* was for the sixth single (sixth!!!!) called *Cheater / Liar*. Sequences of the film were shot at the Ideastream building in Downtown Cleveland. Parts of my body were wrapped up in cords. It was a dual metaphor for the ties of a relationship and how cheaters use digital communications. For a legitimate pop star, this is a great visual for the album.

"I just love the chorus," one classmate from college told me before yodeling the refrain: "*Cheeeeeattterrr, Cheeeeatttter!*"

It was not one of my memorable choruses — but you can't deny the howling 'cheater' over and over like some acid trip psychic isn't a vibe.

Heading into college, I was propelled into working on two sister projects. The first was *Spirits* — an ambient, soft electronica that featured a lot of poetics. *Elliptical Orbit* was about a pseudo-relationship where two people continued to orbit around each other. The song received a music video of me on a dark stage, singing along to the lyrics — simple and classy. *Grave* was...a video of me walking around a graveyard. That one was one of my more 'on the nose moments.'

Spirits had a lot of tracks that just smell of incoming pretentiousness: *Binding Bounds* (okay?), *Dangerous Faith* (that title alone screams homosexual), *Higher Movements* (okay, scale it back, e.e. cummings), *Under The Bells* (sounds like a terrible place to be), *Beautiful Wounds* (another Lana Del Rey moment), *Diadem* (it's just a crown), and maybe my favorite crazy title: *Heaven Is Limestone*.

While *Spirits* was spiritual and about the world with very faint sounds and ambiance, *Core* was the opposite. *Core* was hard electronics — not danceable but grimy and violent and filled with personal introspection. It was divided into three acts: the opening song, *Crust*, the middle track of the album *Mantle*, and the last song *Core*. It was sort of a Dante's Inferno but with questionable pop music.

The lead single, *Langolier* — was taken from a Stephen King book about alien creatures and a story about monsters in Chardon, Ohio. The song told a story about people who got murdered in words — a la Cabin in the Woods. The chorus built up to a catchy but grammatical fail: "*We are gone, We are gone, You may not, never know.*" In the video, I was kidnapped, a ghost appeared, and stock images were glued onto straws that became memorial crosses. We printed out Google common rights images of people and pretended they had been abducted and killed in the song.

The darker visuals and sound continued with *Blood, Flesh, Bone* — a video that featured me holding a pumpkin and masquerading as a drug dealer on campus. I can't believe I suckered tens of people to play my various clients, who agreed to be filmed with me passing them bags of drugs which were spices that I bought at the corner CVS store. *Of Blood, Flesh, and Bone — you will not grow, you will not live forever.*" I entered my Hot Topic phase with some straightforward honesty.

The first two singles leaned into a darker concept, so *Group Ambush* was chosen as the third single. Where the former two depicted dark truths and stories, this song was simply about the times I socially ambushed friends and family. The video features me literally getting into a fight with someone.

The last single remains a cult favorite — *How I'll Eat Your Heart* pushed the boundaries and sound for my image. The song was anchored by a guitar riff and opened with the lyric, "*When you leave me feeling dead, When you take my love and bed.*" Significantly as the guitar cut into a swirling synth, I shrieked, "How I'll eat your hea-a-art, How I'll eat your heart-a-art!" the pop persona would have made you think that I had been heartbroken (I don't even think I had gone on a single date in my life at this point).

The video was...stark. It featured an opening monologue as you follow the curves of my body to find out that I've been tied up on a plank of wood over a mattress. It served Fifty *Shades of Grey* before the movie and books hit the mainstream market. It ends with a bandana stuffed into my limp mouth with another monologue voice over (because why not).

When I revisited *Core*, this being my eighth album, I could tell that some progression was happening. Things were slowly getting tightened up — and we were only two years deep into this musical exploration. There were a couple of songs that could be reworked into something decent if you squinted your ears. *Spirits* and *Core* had acoustic EPs of the songs — probably some of the worst work I've ever distributed. Those songs did *not* need acoustic versions — it was like trying to take Dollar Tree macaroni and cheese and pass it off as high-end pasta.

With eight albums to my name, there was only one thing to do: release a greatest hits album with new material. The album cover featured three Matts posed in sexy (clothed) positions — all with bandanas and dorm keys wrapped in a necklace around my neck. The lead single and new song, *Break*, was a five-minute thumping anthem that featured distorted beats that would sound good if polished up. With a synth topper, I command in the refrain: "*Will your heart break in my crashing wake? Will your heart break, this is what I'll take.*"

One of the reasons I love the music video is because it featured choreography with some friends. I really must be charming for them to agree to execute some backwater dance moves that I had concocted.

However, things had been too happy, and thus we were thrown into darkness again on my ninth album: *Volatile*. If there's a piece of early work that represents some of my favorite moments, it would be *Volatile*. There were some depressing songs and some dark imagery, but it had a bit more prowess than earlier songs. Most of *Volatile* featured piano, and the songs were built around the piano sections. I think it's the closest I've ever come to being Tori Amos or some other pianist who writes poetry.

The lead single, *Vitality*, was about my struggles with beauty. The topic is presented harshly, utilizing eating issues and workouts to represent the visual of perhaps one of my more bleak choruses: "*To win in this contest, you need to sacrifice everything you've possibly considered. Character is fine, same with personality, but to adapt to attract to find perfect vitality.*"

Analyzing this song a decade later — I think there's more being said in that line than I realized. The direct implication is that looking beautiful was the most essential part of the 'contest' of dating. But underneath, there's this connection of health with love — as if just being in love or being with someone was automatically healthier than singleness.

I wish to say that was the darkest theme on the album. Nevertheless, tracks like *I Hate Loneliness, Loneliness Loves Me, Never Find (A Lover), Friendless,* and *Oblivion* are the equivalent of tying yourself to a boulder and jumping into a pond. Some people were worried about me, but even in my darkest moments, I didn't think I was a risk to myself or others. I just find that art is a place to express these small baubles of emotions that might feel unwanted or troubling out of the context of art.

Volatile's themes of loneliness and anxieties open up with a pretty piano ballad called *Biopic*, which starts the album out with: "*Pretty little pictures, flutter all around me, smother my own lifeline, never let me be.*" It's almost a call to explosive social media that can decimate self-image. This album came out a couple months before I decided to reinvent myself: cutting off my mopish hair and trading bulky glasses for contacts. It's almost like I pulled a *'The Simpsons* writing staff moment' in predicting my issues in real-time.

Even with one of the harshest song titles I've ever had, *Never Find (A Lover)* has some of the most gorgeous synth lines of my early work. It also features some of the heaviest lyrics I've ever put out: *I can be what you want (desperation), I can be what you need (dissipation), I'll make you worth a home run (deliberation)."* Oomph, talk about (desperation!) Upon listening to the song recently, one line jumped out: *Inside, I love who I am, but externally, I want to slash it out.* I hear these lyrics now and, thankfully, don't relate to them as much anymore.

Some of the other songs were dark without a subtle direct context. *Wolves Howl Alone* was a piece comparing myself to a lone wolf figure. *Deny* was about a crush that I felt was a denial: *You hate yourself, but I could love what you hate.* I look back on that lyric as an older human and can't help but roll my eyes at what eighteen-year-old Matt believed. *Riptide* followed a favorite subject matter of mine — water. *Baby, you're a riptide, cutting me down to size, force me to tell you lies.* Not my best rhyme scheme, but haunting when delivered with lush aquatic synth pads.

Treason was a story about two lovers escaping their unsupportive hometown: *One main road with four side paths, clutching on a lot of a building of wrath. There's only one shop, they don't get by, baby in this town, our love is going to die.* I almost imagine this dusty wild town left to abandon. The song evolves into this explosive chorus: *If this is treason, we'll have our reason; let's run away before we're martyred at the stake.*

Another powerful song: *Convenience For Nothing*, was written about two friends dating who totally wrong for each other. I grew frustrated and wrote the initial draft about this idea that they were dating out of convenience. It's both a song about how I would never want such a relationship but how those in convenient relationships aren't allowing themselves whats's best for them. *"You have convenience, but is that what you want?"*

After fourteen mostly depressing songs, *Volatile* ends on a song called *By The End of the Night*. This album is filled with sadness, stickiness, uncertainty, lonely pain, and inexperience dripping from a teenager on the cusp of adulthood. But it all melts away with the final song, a string ladened power ballad about letting it shed off of you: *Everything you've ever learned with go, empty your head, chop all you know. I give you more than I ever did, from my adolescence, adulthood, when I was a kid. By the end of the night, we'll be feeling alright.* It's a little clunky — but the image is there.

If there was one older album I could re-up, it would have to be *Volatile*. There are tricky and complex themes but dark beauty within its messages of volatility and loneliness. I've actually gone back and played with some of the concepts of *Volatile* in my modern music. The song *Stranded Islands* would be referenced in a track called *Tsunami* off my 2020 album *Mountainfaller*: "All these stranded islands on the sea have turned me kind of lonely."

After *Volatile,* which dripped with depression and verged on being impalpable, the following three projects invited some lightness. The next album, *Eager and Passionate Hearts Club*, was a nod to *Sergeant Pepper's Lonely Hearts Club*. While *Volatile* commiserated my lack of suitors and glaring singleness, *Eager and Passionate Hearts Club* embraced it. We weren't lonely. We weren't sad. We were eager and passionate — totally different.

The lead single was one of the more sensual innuendos in my career. *I Want Your Six* was designed to shock audiences, but the lyrics talk about wanting six things from someone. Those six things are not explained — bad storytelling on my part. The song itself was dark and murky — with deep-pitch vocals saying 'six' in the background. But it sounded more like the word it was masking...

The video features me on top of a rolled-up carpet -- an ingenious move on my part to utilize natural construction. It also features a futon scene, a scene with a ladder, and a white wall with multiple Matts existing at the same time. All in black and white noir — as if I was emulating Madonna's *Erotica* era.

The second single was the title track — one of my more forgettable songs and music videos. A loud guitar riff cuts through the track, while the video featured blurred faces and me 'teaching' people about club membership.

The third single, *4 Hearts*, was about a ruined relationship that ended in heartbreak. But the plot twist was that I had more than one heart — so even if you broke one heart, three others were waiting there. The chorus softly yet powerfully chanted: *I got four hearts wrapped in cellophane, four hearts that destroy all my pain.* The video featured different versions of myself in cellophane and aluminum — as well as a search for my four hearts. The video opens with a warning text message from a friend that my hearts are being sought after. So I must recapture them. One heart was located in the book *Cloudy With A Chance of Meatballs*. Another heart was in a brochure, another in a woman's sock drawer, and another behind a Mac. And before you say "was that intentional... or?" I have no clue.

The last video was for a song called *Obsessive,* about an obsessive partner. It featured me playing the stalked and the obsessive partner outfitted with the bold-glasses-fake-mustache combination. "*You're so obsessive, making me regressive; ooh-ooh-obsessive*" is crooned over a cheap EDM beat.

Eager and Passionate Hearts Club had twenty-two songs that balanced between bops like *You Will Lose Me, Lucky Duck, Sweet, Salty, Sour* and some really somber ballads like *Win Lose Win, Heartroots, I Could (Learn To Love You).*

While it's arguably one of the worst songs I've ever done, my song *If I Looked Like Sarah Jessica Parker*, was about looking like Sarah Jessica Parker and thus ensnaring people with my beauty. I don't know why I wrote that song after Sarah Jessica Parker. I was, and still am, unfamiliar with her personality and work.

My favorite songs on the album come down to: *Thunder Thighs* — which sampled Blanche Devereaux from *The Golden Girls. Thursday Night Special,* in which I promise to be someone's Thursday Night Special (take it as you will, whether that's a stripper reference or maybe a Thursday night wing special).

The song that takes the cake is *McDonalds' Wedding* which I wrote about the frustrations of people casually approaching marriage. "*Marriage never lasts anyway; it won't be a day you retain onto, McDonalds can cater all of your affairs before secret lovers and arguments do.*" Ouch! I would become inspired by the sociological theory of McDonaldization — which talks about how the qualities of fast food have soaked into our overall existence. That would become a much more polished song called *Fast Food Love Style* released in 2021.

Songs for Teatime was a small project that featured what some friends consider my Magnus Opus: *Sorry Mama (I'm In Love With A Republican)*. The song was inspired by my friend group's conversation in the college cafeteria.

"I could *never* date a Republican," my friend Jade told the table at large. "*Never!*"

This was back in 2013 — a *slightly* different era for Republicans than the current one.

"I dunno, I might be able to," I said, more so to rally against the ultimatum than to personally find out.

The conversation spun out with many opinions — but I went back to write this sultry bop about someone who had to confess to their mother that they were marrying a Republican. Immediately I wanted to cast my friend Jade as the mother character for the video. In video, I visit 'momma' in her apartment (which was a dorm room). My character had taken the train in and had left the ring behind because of 'train theft.'

"Mama, there's something I have to tell you. I've sinned," my character says, with a flare of anxiety.

"Tell me, what's wrong?" Jade asked.

"Mama... I'm getting married...to a republican."

There's a dramatic pause while momma takes in the news before yelling, "OH HELL NO," and rips me down to the floor. The rest of the footage involves her beating me to death, intercut with stairwell and shower scenes for visual flair. When I think of the top videos of my pop music career, this one ranks top three.

"It's so realistic — you look like you're being injured for real!" Friends would say, after watching the video.

"I really was though," I muttered. Jade was actually beating me to a pulp in that video.

In one of my more 'reachy moments,' there was a song on *Songs For Teatime* called *Quinnipiac Love Song*. I had a brief encounter with someone from Quinnipiac and thus wrote this passionate could have been love story for the album. Sometimes I wonder if I'm *too* emotional — and I see songs like that and go, 'oh, I'm *really* off the chain.'

Album twelve, *Hydra*, was considered my second mixtape project. It had twenty-seven tracks, the most I've ever had on one album. Many songs were quick interludes or choruses surrounded by long rap verses. By this point, I had discovered that having more potent recording equipment made more sense. When I released *Hydra*, I felt more confident in my abilities than before, even though I still had a long way to go.

Hydra had a lot of innovation both in subjects and sounds. A bold song called *In Yo Mouth* featured three female rappers (or friends that could rap), and *Baked In A Pie* sampled a nursery song about people being baked into pies. *Belligerent* featured deep-reverbed vocals over my favorite concept of being a controversial figurehead. There's a song called *I'm On A Conference Call* that samples phone calls and rings with lines like, "*You're in my business, it's like getting called on Christmas.*"

My favorite songs would be towards the back of the album. *Girls* is about relating to the feelings of the women in my life. I have some...concerns. It's a song that could use a bit of editing and rewriting. *Girls are just like me, we fall apart at the seams* (oomph — a little mansplaining meets generalizing there), *But we separate into teams* (ahh — women who don't uplift women?) *Our lives are echoes of our dreams* (okay, I can dig into that. It does feel like a feminist anthem that needs a bit of touch-up.

A minimalist psychedelic track called *Highway 71* pines for freedom and exploration with a partner. "*Empty like ego, fried like Crisco, got less in me than a glass of espresso.*" That's actually a decent line!

A dreamy, floaty song called *Burn My Pyre* continues to double down on this theme of being an attacked public figure: "*He will die tonight, mostly because he's mostly right. He's too honest for me, so I'll burn his pyre for all to see.*" Did I think I was Jesus or something for putting out outrageous music?

Another bottom-level song: *Rap For The Children,* closes out the album. Nothing I've ever created should be shown to children. Also — what child asked for a rap? It's a bold assumption.

Album thirteen, *Echleyon*, was actually instrumentals from an abandoned project called *Solstice*. It was the first and only project that didn't feature my vocals. The songs tended to lean on breathy synthesizers and acoustic elements.

I took two years off of music after Echleyon. I wanted to explore other projects — like the second season of my reality show, *Hribcam*. But then, even my YouTube channel went inactive for a while. I remember producing music at this time but sitting on it. Maybe a bit embarrassed by the constant output of material that wasn't often received well?

Over the years, there have been many 'forgotten' albums. Albums I made and created and never shared or finished. Albums that got deleted or improperly stored — existing only in memory. I did a lot of work on two albums called *Affect* and *Effect*, which blended social issues and psychological themes. I had an album mapped out called *Have You Had It?* Which was very suggestive with tracks like *Electroshock*, in which I compare a relationship to electroshock therapy. There was another project called *Ministry* — a concept album about a government takeover a la George Orwell's 1984. That project involved a lot of dubstep. One track, called *Excalibur*, contained many tongue twirls over dub baselines. Another project — called *Schism of the Night* — featured dance beats, twinkling bells, chimes, and synths (no *Under The Bells* happening here!)

I returned in 2015 with my fourteenth album, *Father Time*, which was created simply because we had a Greek Life talent show, and I was practically the only one in the fraternity who had anything of talent that could be harnessed on the stage. The EP featured five songs: *Father Time* about being a master of time, *What's Your Major?*, a song about people demanding to know your major (which I would interpolate for a future song called *Where's The Manager?*). There was *2 Good 4 U*, a sassy anthem that I recently recreated. *Politico*, a rap with the thesis that your butt is so wack that it's politico (which is wack cause it's Politico). The album ends with a ballad, *Passionmark*, which compares an ending of a relationship to hickeys. I promise the song holds up better than the explanation.

And then, I went on a hiatus for three years. I don't know why I stopped writing music again — I was still writing but was focused on stories and scripts. I can't remember the exact song that I wrote first after this break, but I think it was *Grenadine*. *Grenadine* was a song about dreams and *Grenadine* would became the title for my 15th album that I released in 2018.

Diving into my more contemporary era of music feels a little self-indulgent. It's exciting to turn ancient concepts into new things. Old ideas evolve into new images. Songs designed for a nudisco album called *My Personal Disco* rolled into my sociological album *Social Detective*. I had a few leftover beats and lyrics from my *Game Over* album which morphed into the *Bop City* album.

And there are so many albums that I wish to make. I would love to do a folktronica concept album about a cult. A really aggressive electronic concept album about nuclear fallout. I'd love to do a sports-themed album, a philosophy pop album, an actual house album, an 8bit album... collecting genres like little tattoos. It's not even about how good they are, it's just about doing them. Would I complain if a song blew up on TikTok and rocketed me into some weird vein of comedic sexy pop music? Trust me, I'd close a club down if such a thing happened. But realistically, I don't expect accolades, cash, or notoriety for what I do. I just do it. But don't tell Nike I said that. They might sue me.

Savanthood

"I don't know — I'm already *over* the city." Billiam tossed the comment away like a piece of gum as we walked through Chicago.

"You moved here two weeks ago."

"Yeah," Billiam mused, as if two weeks were enough to entirely consume and digest a massive city like Chicago. "But I don't think I'll be able to do two years here...."

I suggested three years which caused him to pucker up in horror.

"I *definitely* couldn't do three years," Billiam gasped, as if instead of sentencing him to a fun life in Chicago, I was condemning him to a Peruvian jail cell with no temperature control and a perpetual flow of men. The temperature control would be problematic — Billiam liked controlling his environment like how a business executive controllingly trimmed their bonsai plant. But I doubt Billiam would hate the men.

Billiam found himself moving to Chicago after two years in Austin. He's the first person to admit that he quickly becomes bored with a city. He has lived in stunning American cities and even internationally for time gaps. But Billiam was horrified by the idea of being stagnant in a town. When it came to city-dwelling monogamy, Billiam was not one to commit.

"Well, after Chicago, where do you go?" I questioned. "I guess New York, Los Angeles...maybe London, Paris, Toyko?"

Billiam had never shown interest in New York and Los Angeles. And if I had to bet where he was going next, it was London. Billiam prided himself on his ability to change with cities. He wore cities like fancy coats before depositing them off at the local charities after their fashion had gone out of vogue. Mint was *so* last year. I thought about Billiam's preference of phoenixing himself into a new city every two years. It seemed exciting and luxurious — but was it possible to fully experience a large city in such a short time? And wouldn't Billiam run out of big metropolises before he turned forty?

I enjoy the benefits of living in Cleveland while being able to travel quickly to more expensive cities like Toronto and Chicago. Meals that cost thirty bucks in Chicago or Toronto would cost fifteen in Cleveland. I get a bit of a thrill when I tell Chicagoans how cheap my mortgage is. I never fail to receive gasps of astonishment. They'd ask about the culture in Cleveland and I'd have examples of districts, festivals, shops, and scenes that would leave even the most hardened Torontonian and Chicagoan impressed.

Billiam had no desire to ever relocate back home again. If I had grown up in a small town away from the world, I could imagine the desire for Chicago, New York, and Toronto. But from a young age, I had always been active in the Downtown Cleveland scene. My high school was blocks away from West 25th, a Cleveland staple. And my involvement in programs and services had me active at institutions and organizations that dotted the downtown.

Our conversation about cities occurred during a Labor Day weekend hang-out. Billiam had invited me and two others to share his one-bedroom apartment in Chicago for the weekend. The projected vibe was fun and boozy — a celebration and vacation. Billiam had just moved, I was starting a new job, John was returning to Chicago for the first time since pre-COVID, and Colin...well, he was excited to drink.

John and I powered through a Friday afternoon drive from Cleveland. Our arrival was met with Billiam's demands that we start drinking immediately.

"I have to get ready!" I exclaimed, tossing my luggage open and pulling clothes out like a maniac.

"So? Get drinking!" Billiam made a chop-chop motion with his hands like I was being paid on the clock to work and was moving too slowly.

The group included: me, the artistic philosopher who enjoyed a good conversation; Billiam, the social media guru with a taste of luxury; John, the smart, preppy one with a well of conversational topics; and Colin, the subdued guy next door with a flair for fun and charm. Together, we were like the Golden Girls of Chicago except probably too much to air for cable television. Netflix or Hulu, if you're reading this, I can field your calls on bringing this show to life.

Billiam lived north of downtown in a district called Boystown, which sounds like a lousy musical that couldn't make it onto Broadway. Boystown was filled with cute, gentrified goodies like "Juice Rx," "Sugar Daddy's Bakery," and "Eggsperience." There were glimpses of the old-rough-and-tumble Midwest in convenience stores and businesses with battered exteriors but phenomenal products like a secret Cadbury interior.

As we crossed nighttime Chicago to hit the bars, I couldn't help but absorb the city. Quite often, media outlets like to paint Chicago as rough and downtrodden. But my night journey was a glimmer of an urban utopia. I felt like a grown-up version of Dorothy from *The Wizard of Oz*. Who needs Kansas when you have *this?*

The first bar we went to was called Side Track where each room donned a different aesthetic involving neon, fake turf, and... sporting equipment? The name must have been inspired by the sidetracked decor.

I ran into an old classmate, not-his-real-name Terry. Terry was at the bar with his boyfriend and we slid into a comfortable remembrance.

"You owe me your music career!" Terry pointed out. "I was the one to give you your first name."

I laughed in agreement. Terry and I had this awfully bitter man for an English teacher — as well as a very stern (but in my opinion lovely) Biology teacher who gave me a probably undeserved B in his class. Terry and I continued to catch up, and I felt powerful emotions. It was like finding out your favorite character got a good ending at the show's end. High school had been burdensome, so seeing people thrive in their post-school life was beautiful.

The tranquil recollection was quickly cut short due to Billiam, who had been vaping on the outdoor rooftop patio. The busboy passed by Billiam and picked up the table's prominent 'no vaping' sign. The sign had been three feet away from Billiam the entire time. The busboy held the sign in a tone that read, "are you stupid?" Billiam believed the busboy was a friend of the group and decided to 'jokingly' take a hit and blew the smoke in the busboy's face. It was a moment that made my blood freeze and my brain implode.

"That's it, you're out of here," the busboy immediately went from 10mph to 100mph. The busboy had probably been too nice to people in the past. We witnessed a newly minted man who had vowed to never be taken advantage of again. There had perhaps been an incident that mirrored Billiam's behavior which had previously been the busboy's reason for his lost faith in customers.

"Are you serious? I thought you were joking!" Billiam looked around to see if we would say anything in his defense. We all turned, sipping our drinks in silence. Even Terry and his boyfriend eyed the walls as if we were at an art gallery (not that I've seen art hung up on the ceiling before).

This moment could only be best described by the memes of drag queens and Real Housewives who would sit in silence to avoid the hanging question. One of the most significant bar rules was that you never aligned yourself with someone getting kicked out of the establishment. The only exception was if you were married to that person. But even then, why should you be penalized for your loved one's mistakes? In a joke that became a prophecy later, I earlier had informed the group that I would pretend not to know them if they started a bar fight.

The busboy dragged Billiam out of the club. I was glad that Billiam didn't put up much of a fight. Billiam is known for having *spicy* moments. Colin, John, and I eyed each other with half-full drinks.

"We'll go outside after we finish our drinks," I suggested to a consensus. I was not about to abandon liquor for someone's personal inability to read a 'do not vape' sign. Moments later, we met Billiam outside. He was more prickly than a cactus in a needle, porcupine, and tacks store.

"Let's go to Roscoe's," John suggested. "It was always my favorite bar."

Roscoe's turned out to be my favorite bar of the entire trip. The front was classy with luxurious velvet and dark black metallic tones. It was sensual without being explicit or too obvious. While the front kept it professional, the back room was a dance floor with a stage that resembled a boxing ring. It was the fashion equivalent of a mullet, crisp in the front, party in the back.

Billiam was not happy with this place. He wanted to go clubbing and considered the venue a dive bar. At his insistence, we moved over to a third bar called Splash. Splash borrowed heavily from the aesthetics of Mattel and Barbie — pink and turquoise paint and manic lightning splashed the walls. There was even a doll box perfect for Instagram. By this point, I was about six or seven drinks in and was enjoying the night. I was surprised that John and I were keeping up. We had busy mornings and a long road trip, but we were now dancing and popping it in the back room of a dirty club. That night I saw a flicker of John's true, unabashed self. It was like seeing hidden treasure unearthed before it was returned away from the public eye.

"I need to take Colin back," Billiam said, pointing to Colin, who looked like a rag-doll on weak puppet strings. We walked back to Billiam's apartment, and Colin almost walked right into the street. I was a bit bummed that we were leaving. I had a lot of energy that night.

John and I had skipped an actual dinner and found ourselves craving a late-night snack. Billiam, worried that Colin would get hit by a car, decided to take Colin back immediately.

"Get me fries," Billiam demanded as we momentarily separated.

"Aren't you on a diet?" John asked sincerely. Billiam had told us many times that evening that he was cutting calories. He was like a South Carolina housewife trying to impress her husband.

"I'll just have some fries," Billiam said with a shrug, as if fries had the exact calorie count and fat amount as arugula.

John and I ordered quickly, more bent on getting sustenance than being picky. I got fries with my meal, specifically for Billiam to eat later. We sat in silence, not a bitter or awkward kind. At that moment my poetic candor recalled the flashes of the "free" John; moments I can't find myself truthfully remembering or writing about here anyway. I wondered, *what did John think of me*? I ask this often to strangers, acquaintances, friends, and family. I am motivated by criticism, fueled by criticism, and ruined by criticism. I feel that I disturb peaceful moments by constantly ladling these burdens of thoughts.

"Should I get cheesy fries?" John was eyeing the menu board with glittering eyes that reminded me of a panda who had found the perfect bamboo.

"Of course," I smiled. "You deserve it."

John ordered his cheesy fries, and I watched on with a subtle grin. So many people would have tried justifying or denying their cravings. Especially gay men in Chicago. But there was beauty in not even a response to the justification that cheesy fries were alright. And a part of me was thankful that even when my artistic spatial mind errs on the side of emotional philosophical stress — there will always be events or people that remind me to live simply in the moment. The moment was the superb late-night food on Billiam's couch. Billiam cleared out the fries quicker than spoiled, ungrateful children would clear out their parents' estate.

By Saturday morning, I was already feeling the tired creeping claws of a stormy night of sleep and the hurt from yesterday. I had slept like a leaf in a rapid river filled with rocks. And while that might sound peaceful to someone watching the river, I'll remind you that *I* am the *leaf* in this example.

Billiam had demanded that we be awake by 8am like soldiers returning from war only to go back to battle. John and I were awake at 8am, but Billiam had slept through his appointed alarm clock. Colin, who looked like someone from a 'do not drink' PSA, was sprawled out in a discomforting sleep position.

"Let's go get coffee," John sighed. "I'm awake at the time that I was *supposed* to be. Unlike some people..."

Remind me never to disappoint John. Ever.

Last night before bed, Billiam had recommended that we do a Saturday morning walk and maybe hit a coffee shop. He had mentioned a coffee shop nearby called Intelligensia. Phone and wallet in hand, John and I crossed a few blocks for coffee. I, the giant burly ginger lumberjack daddy, got my coffee with extra cream. While John went straight for black coffee — no thrills about it. Coffee, for me, was an art of flavor and enjoyment, while John viewed coffee as a utilitarian caffeination process devoid of hubbub.

"This was a good recommendation," I mused while I sipped my six dollar with tip cold brew.

"Shocking for Billiam," John joked.

We left Intelligensia and stopped at Walgreens to pick up essentials — water and face cream. John even picked up a few cheap razors.

"I just *hate* how my beard gets without shaving," John said, pointing to beard hair that hadn't even reached a half-centimeter.

I hadn't known John much besides an Italian dinner a couple of months ago and yesterday's road trip turned dance party. And while I liked John, I think this moment was where I unlocked a vast understanding of John. He was here, enjoying a three-day vacation to Chicago, and felt like he had no choice but to buy shaving equipment to tone down the one o'clock shadow growing on his face. We were quite different — and I appreciate surrounding myself with people like John, who like making solid plans and needed to shave the tiny specs of hair off his face during a weekend getaway.

While checking out enough hygienic equipment to host a frat house, Billiam called with panic that we had been kidnapped from his apartment.

"We're fine; we're at Walgreens," I explained.

"Oh good, I was just so scared," Billiam sounded like a mother over the phone, who was still potentially worried that we might have been kidnapped, but this time at Walgreens.

"Is Billiam scared that we were doing something fun without him?" John mused at the register.

Billiam and John had very similar mental modus operandi — strong personalities. The difference was that Billiam operated out of anxiety while John chose to operate over self-preservation. This would eventually lead to a minor clash between them — and I'll admit, even I couldn't sit on the sidelines for that upcoming incident.

"What did you guys do exactly?" Billiam asked as we returned to his apartment. He sounded like the woman in the television series who thinks her husband is cheating on her.

"We got coffee," I said, holding up my almost empty cup.

"We went to that place that you recommended," John said in a simple add-on.

"What recommendation?" Billiam's face broke out into his classic confused look.

"Last night, you said we should check out Intelligentsia," John said, a bit thrown back. "Do you not remember?"

"I absolutely *didn't* recommend a coffee place. I don't even *know* that place, and I don't drink coffee," Billiam stared at both of us like we were fabricating a story.

"You definitely said we'd wake up and get coffee," I said. "That I remember."

"Billiam recommended Intelligentsia — how else did we know to go there?" John pointed out.

That was some excellent evidence. We *had* left Billiam's apartment specifically for that coffee shop and hadn't just randomly attended the establishment. The only person who could recommend a place would be Billiam. John had previously lived in Chicago for a hot minute but hadn't lived in this neighborhood. The only suspect that *would have known* about Intelligentsia would have been Billiam.

"I don't know about this *Intergalaxy*," Billiam sneered, purposefully saying the name wrong as if that made it seem like he was disconnected from the establishment. Billiam called it the wrong name, so he has nothing to do with it. This case is closed!

"It's called *Intelligenstia*," I stressed as if the whole point of the issue was Billiam's inability to correctly pronounce the name of the coffee shop.

"I don't know it," Billiam tossed his hands like we were asking for an alibi from a random day last year. I could tell that John was feeling a bit of heat — his face was beginning to show more flush than an MLB stadium bathroom.

"Billiam — you might have *forgotten* that you recommended the place to us, but you did," John barked, trying to offer leeway through justice and understanding. John's politeness was a thin layer of cellophane over a giant passive-aggressive casserole. It was his way of saying, 'you're wrong, honey.'

"And we loved the place — so it's a compliment to your taste Billiam!" I chimed in, offering praise through love and truth. I was definitely the good cop during this exchange.

Billiam double-downed that he had never heard of 'Intersection' and how he doesn't drink coffee, so anything coffee-related was so off his submarine radar that the news hadn't come from his ocean. John and I pressed a little but decided to back off and go hunting for post-night-out ravaging.

We attended a good brunch spot that was severely expensive. It was the place that donned simple foods with truffle oil and included kimchi in an Asian-inspired breakfast dish. I would staked my hard-earned savings account that a white man obsessed with Japan owned the business.

John had asked for a patio seating situation which had me instantly worried about the onset of the sun. We arrived at a minimally shaded patio, and my psychic prediction came true. I ended up being face-first in a sun that was taking no prisoners. While everyone else had shade and their backs to the sun, I allowed the sun to burn my white Irish skin into my skull. I felt like a torture victim who was being slowly teased with heat.

"Cheers for my dears!" The server said, as she popped by with drinks. After she left, Billiam turned to us with a shocked, delicious, horrified look. It was the kind of face someone might make when they are offended yet excited that the offense had happened in the first place.

"Did she say *cheers* for my *queers*?" Billiam questioned.

"NO!" John, Colin, and I shouted simultaneously.

After informing Billiam that he had misheard and that our waitress wasn't attacking us with slurs, I went to find the bathroom. I left the sun-trapped patio and walked inside to find a door labeled 'Water Closet.' I assumed that was a room where they stored liquid and soda station material, so I kept moving. On the other side of the restaurant was a second room labeled 'Water Closet.' At that point, I tested the handle and walked into a genderless bathroom.

I couldn't help but love and hate the ambiguity of a 'Water Closet.' I understand labeling the space in a manner that welcomes all humans. Who among us doesn't enjoy the benefits of a solitude shit. But the title of Water Closet was too abstract. I don't think of water when I think of bathrooms, at least not in a direct way. Why not label the space as "The Refreshing Room," "The Oopsie Room," "The #1 or #2 Room," or maybe "You're Dropping Something Behind Room."

I returned to our partially-shaded table to find a peaceful silence. Sweat trickled down my face like I was Elvis eating fried peanut butter in Death Valley during peak sun hours. Billiam, who believes that silence means boredom, decided to break some ice.

"Colin," Billiam turned his body like he was Oprah Winfrey, prepared to ask the tough questions for the viewers at home. At that moment, I wished Billiam was Oprah so I could ask for a car.

"Colin, what's it like growing up in Idaho?"

Colin, who had been looking at his phone, looked up at Billiam with a glazed-over stare.

"Billiam, you're just asking that so we can fill the silence."

Billiam was offended — but smiling as if he loved the accusation all the same.

"I was curious! It's *Idaho!*" Billiam stressed Idaho as if it were Mars or a dimensional distant future version of the real minimal Idaho. Thankfully the food arrived shortly after that to minimize more questions about Idaho.

After leaving the brunch spot, we passed by Intelligentsia, the coffee shop Billiam disavowed.

"That's the place we went to," I said, pointing firmly to prove its existence to Billiam.

"Oh, I *have* been there," Billiam said in a dozy recollection.

A small word spatter rang out between John, Billiam, and me. We probably sounded like three large birds squeaking and shrieking in public. Billiam still didn't believe he had brought up '*Insurgence*,' while John and I felt more confident in the truth than ever before. Dozens of strangers passing by must have heard some part of the argument over whether or not Billiam had recommended a coffee shop.

"This is the dumbest fight I ever heard," Colin said, hand to his temple to shield himself from our stupidity. It didn't matter who was right in that argument — Colin was the actual winner.

Upon returning from brunch, I noticed John pulling out his credit card.

"Buying something?" I asked casually, trying to look curious but not gossipy.

"Yeah, a hotel room."

John had slept on a cheap couch for one night and immediately decided to book a hotel room for the remaining two days. John spent at least 500 *per* night - which meant that couch must have been so soul-sucking. I'd rather spend a night in hell than pay that steep price. The sofa had been a test of suffering for John, so it was time for a hotel.

"John does this *all* the time," Billiam told me later. "He always booking a hotel instead of staying at the provided accommodations."

Billiam told me how John once left a party to drive back to his house. The drive was an hour and a half away. The motivation to drive home came from the desire to sleep in a comfortable bed. There's been plenty of offers in my life where people have clamored to provide me with sleeping space. But sometimes you really want to go home to your own bed.

While I was too cheap to relate to John's credit card statement, I could also understand John's desire to escape a tight space with so many people around. Four people in a small apartment just wasn't optimal. Certain things, such as a private bathroom moment to oneself, were downright impossible. Nobody wanted to let loose when the other three could hear every second of your bathroom experience.

"I want to be on vacation, you know?" John clarified this to me while finalizing the details. "I'm grateful to Billiam for offering his apartment. But I know I would be happier booking a hotel. Besides, it's my own money."

Billiam was initially a little miffed that John would not stay in his apartment for sleeping arrangements. Personally, as a host, if you're not happy with the accommodations, you are more than welcome to pay for alternative methods.

After John checked into his new hotel, we stopped at the Chicago River for pictures. The streets were covered and surrounded by pigeons and tourists. Many adults were masquerading with their children around under the pretense of selling chocolate for various school causes. One kid, in particular, was a bit husky and told me and some other tourists as we walked by that the chocolates he was selling "supported their basketball program."

I was skeptical because the kid didn't look like he would respond well if I brought out a hoop and a ball. Once the kid was out of earshot, a stranger behind me muttered to their friend:

"I don't think that kid plays basketball."

I immediately spun on my feet like I had just witnessed a hit and run by Tom Hanks. My face spread open like a Picasso painting as I sheepishly gasped:

"I felt the same way!"

While the adults using their children for financial gain on the street felt seedy, the loitering pigeons didn't know any better. Cleveland pigeons are skittish, but Chicago pigeons feel like they belong at your table. When you reserve an outdoor patio table in downtown Chicago, you must add a +1 to your table reservations for the flock of pigeons.

One pigeon was nibbling on John's leather shoe. Maybe the pigeon mistook the leather for food? Or was the pigeon so desperate for food that it tried the leather? Or was this an attack on John in demand for food. One of the gays at the table behind us pulled out a folding fan and clapped the fan so hard that all the pigeons in the nearby area flew away. Most of the restaurant patrons looked shaken — as if they had heard a series of gunshots or a giant crash. The fan did not do much in the long term, as pigeons returned five minutes later.

I had ordered the gyro on the server's recommendation, only to be mediocrely happy with the dish. It felt like a gyro that anyone could make — even myself. And that wasn't a compliment. John ordered a large hog dog and cut it in half with a knife. The same table with the fan-holding gay guy had all four members watching on in fascination and disgust.

"JUST Eat it! It's a hot dog!" The one gay guy cried out to our table.

John did a politician's smile that was friendly on the exterior but interiorly was a 'screw you' mentality.

"We are definitely *those* types of white gays," I told the neighbor table, who cackled in delight. "Any other time, he wouldn't complain about having that large of a wiener — but suddenly, at the restaurant, it's impossible."

Moments later, they asked if we had seen Harry Styles and other tables chimed in to talk about how hot Harry Styles was.

Colin arrived, as he had been so far absent from the Downtown trip. He looked only *slightly* more refreshed. For most of the trip, we performed *Weekend At Bernie's* with Colin's booze-soaked limp body. But for now, he had decently collected himself.

"Are you okay?" I asked as Colin nursed a beer. Colin's beer wasn't a fun drink, more so a potion to lessen the pain.

"I'll be fine," Colin said behind sunglasses that were shading eyes eager for rest. We made our way to Londonhouse for rooftop drinks. Colin was the one who pointed out that we only had a little time left in our schedule.

"Don't worry about it," Billiam said as he booked our name for a table. When Billiam says not to worry about it, that's usually a sign that I should worry about it.

"We don't need a table," I said, to the nods from Colin and John. I prefer to grab a drink and stand at the rooftop's edge to see the skyline.

"Well, why not just *ask* for a table?" Billiam questioned like he was posing a question of morality. To be, or not to be, a table?

The wait for a table was twenty minutes — but four twenty-somethings in their quest for their next drink couldn't wait that long. Cocktails were eighteen dollars a pop — and between that and a tip, my credit card practically hit three digits in a single cocktail round order. The host escorted us over to an open table. I felt confident that we would have to order things at the table — which was confirmed when Billiam tried to tell the waitress we didn't want food.

"You do know that sitting here means you have to order food and things?" the waitress said with a soft look of displeasure caked across her face. We quickly ordered food and the second round of drinks to appease the waitress.

"We're really cutting it close on time," Colin kept pointing out. The grand chef-d'oeuvre of the evening was Billiam's obligations at a pub for the OSU game that night. Proud OSU graduate Billiam was making an appearance and dragging us along. It was the only rigid plan for the weekend. I had specifically bought a fifteen-dollar OSU shirt for this event.

Suddenly, we were 'running late,' according to Billiam. Colin did a quick round of 'I told you so' as we burrowed into an elevator. For some reason, the elevator kept opening on every single level downward in a non-sensical glitchy mannerism. From the twenty-first floor, we stopped on floors eighteen, fifteen, twelve, ten, and eight... every stop was more confusing and frustrating than the last. It was as if the elevator was getting revenge on us for hogging a table while paying for minimal food.

John tried his best to help us find a train. But between Billiam's anxiety, Colin's hangover, and my non-confrontational nature, we appeared to be running in circles around Downtown Chicago. Finally, we ordered an Uber while John headed back to his hotel.

Climbing into the Uber, we started a somber topic considering we were exhausted from an afternoon of day drinking that was about to vault into night plans. We talked about cheaters, cheating, morality...you name it. Colin had discovered that a friend was cheating on their boyfriend, another friend of Colin's. Colin had broken the news about the cheater to the guy who had been cheated on. This made the cheater pissed at Colin for ruining the secret as if it was a surprise birthday and not an act of adultery. I couldn't tell how the Uber driver felt about the topic — had he heard worse, was he not interested, or did we enthrall him all the way to Billiam's apartment?

We returned to Billiam's apartment and began pouring drinks and tossing clothes around like we were reenacting *Sex and The City* on HBO Max.

"We are going to go out after the game," Billiam explained.

"Then I'm not going to wear this OSU shirt," I said, changing quickly before the Uber arrived. Welp, there goes the fifteen dollars I spent on the specialty OSU shirt. I was already a solid six-seven out of ten compared to the gorgeous people of Chicago. And no offense to a long-sleeve OSU shirt, but that would not help my physical game.

Another Telsa arrived as our Uber. Did people buy Telsas, realize how expensive they were, and decide to freelance as an Uber drive? The party was happening at an ordinary pub that was decked out with OSU colors and team jerseys. A welcome table had been erected in the front of the bar.

"This is where you'll be!" The manager walked us five feet to the table as if giving us a tour a la *Pimp My Ride*. "You can help people get raffle tickets right here."

For the entire week leading up to the trip, and until I stepped into the bar, I was under the impression that we would *hang*-out at a table. I thought this was a social call, something the OSU debutantes of Chicago did during a football game. I imagined OSU alumni tweaking their walrus mustaches while swirling bourbon over ice and saying, "yes, how debonaire."

Instead, Billiam was doing some assistant marketing and events volunteer gig for the OSU Chicago Alumni branch. I was considered one of the 'helpers' at the table. Most people might be agitated to be hoodwinked into volunteerism. I wasn't salty — because I knew I wouldn't lift a finger while letting Billiam run the event.

Billiam began to unroll the ticket roll for the 50-50 while I played on my phone.

"Which ticket do I keep?" Billiam asked, raising the roll of tickets as if it was the packet of Kool-Aid mix he wanted me to prepare.

"Well, it doesn't really matter," I shrugged. "Maybe you can keep the side that says 'Keep This Ticket?' It would remind you to keep that ticket, ya know?"

"And what's a 50-50?"

"You don't know what a 50-50 is?"

Billiam gave me a half-smile, half-blank expression of silence that let me know that he didn't appreciate my line of questioning.

"Half of your sales go to the organization, and the other half goes to the winner," I summarized.

"Ooh, that makes sense," Billiam shook his head as if he had known the entire time and had been testing me.

The manager of the bar came over to ask some questions.

"Wait — how does a 50-50 work?" The manager asked Billiam. Billiam turned his face to me as if I was about to speak about a tricky philosophical question like, "If a tree falls and no one hears it, does it make a sound?" The manager followed Billiam's lead, and suddenly I had two slightly confused people running this event starring at me.

"Half goes to the winner, half to the organization," I repeated, wondering if I was on *Candid Camera*.

The football game started, and it was evident that John was going to be running late.

"Can you text John?" Billiam asked me. "He'll answer you."

John replied to my text with a picture of delicious pasta and wine.

"He's...on the way," I gritted through my teeth.

As the game continued, Billiam sold tickets for the 50-50. Colin once again managed to become drunk on two White Claws. I don't *physically* envy skinny guys like Colin. But I am envious of their ability to become cheaply inebriated.

We kept ordering White Claw Buckets for the table. Nobody else cared to notice or was too drunk to see, but most of these White Claw buckets had lime White Claw. I have nothing against *lime* White Claw — I had three of them that night alone. But you'd think they would jazz up the flavors a bit more. Ordering a bucket of five White Claws and getting three in a distinct flavor felt *off* to me. Had I been a server or bartender, I would have probably tried to be more equitable with the flavor distribution.

I mentioned this lime-ification of the buckets to Colin, who drunkenly nodded. When I informed Billiam about the surplus of lime seltzer and the ratio of lime to non-lime feeling off, he stared at me as if I had just killed a dog for fun.

Another weird observation that night was that the bathroom's lone urinal was under construction. Not just roped off with a taped piece of paper that said 'broken.' A handyman was fixing the urinal at seven on a Saturday night. Saturday's prime time seemed like the worst time to tweak a urinal for the establishment and the contractor. Who wants to be down fixing the urinal bowl while tens of men come in to splash the toilet next to the urinal? This work could be done during the morning or afternoon or even pushed off till Monday.

I kept this observation to myself — worried I would be judged for noticing such details. I had just been branded a serial killer for observing the massive influx of lime. On a personal note, I am glad we are moving away from mass walls of metal troughs for men to pee in. I prefer the sense of privacy and leisure between the urinal and myself. Later that night — I would try and pee in a urinal and found myself unable to do so.

"Oh, he had to *heave it!*" A guy called out to me as I threw myself back into my pants to wait for the lone stall.

"I try my best." I sheepishly said, hoping God could take me right where I stood. I don't know why I sometimes bother to pee in a urinal if the bathroom is busy. I feel like an animal who cannot perform its duties. A bee who can't make honey, a cow who can't graze, a man who can't pee in a urinal if other people are circling like dogs on a bone.

Billiam will remember the most obscure parts of my identity in a way that no other friend can. Billiam met a girl exploring sub/dom play and enjoyed her time as an amateur dominatrix.

"You have to meet Matt," Billiam turned to me. "He did his research on sex and stuff in college."

Love and sex fascinate me — but even the deeper elements of communication, dating, hook-up culture, monogamy, marriage normative culture, kinks, and other romantic and sexual sundries. My self-appointed sociological independent study was about love styles and expressions. For my master's degree, I investigated attitudes between those who use dating apps versus those that don't.

This woman explained how she enjoyed being a dominatrix.

"I don't think it's *all* of my identity. I just have fun with it."

"And the guy you're seeing now is into it?" I questioned.

"No, he's the dominating one," she sighed, thinking back to her enjoyment of swapped roles.

"And I bet there's no communication — it's just an unspoken normality."

Her eyes got so vast I thought they were about to detonate like bombs.

"YES! That's what I love about LGBT relationships. There's *so* much communication involved."

Way too much communication. And this comes from someone who likes to communicate. Sometimes it feels like we're preparing for a thesis with a list of bullet-pointed checkmarks. Position? Cuddle position? Do you even want to cuddle? Kinks? Monogamy or poly? Open or closed? Semi-open? What do you define a 'relationship' as? It's healthy to lay this out on the line —

but sometimes it erodes the human connection. Let's get to some of the more essential details after we've chatted for a little bit? Unless you're way too strict or uptight on something — that might be important to note. And yes, I'm shading gay men who refuse to do anything more than act like a product you can currently get at Target for fifteen dollars.

"Okay — where is John?" Billiam asked, an hour deep into the OSU game. Billiam could be having tea with the Prime Minister of Finland and still be anxious about whether or not we needed dinner reservations at Subway across the street.

"He's probably coming." At this point I believed that John might be out for the count. Pasta, wine, and a bath? Talk about the perfect Saturday night in. I was surprised when John arrived; the game was slowly coming to a grand finale. Upon sight, John and Billiam went into a rendition of the *Real Housewives of Chicago* — which caused me to act as a mediator. Colin was on the sidelines, drunker than an entire moonshine distribution center.

"I deserve some *me* time," John explained. "I just wanted a nice dinner. I watched some tennis..."

"You could have *told* me that," Billiam clapped back. "I was worried."

"You don't have to worry. I'm an adult."

"You canceled your Uber — we got the texts —."

"I shouldn't have filled you in on that Uber ride then." John had texted us that he was on his way but had canceled the original Uber. "If this vibe will be the rest of the night, then I'll go back to my hotel."

I sucked in my breath because John's threat to leave threatened my night out. John was my social buddy. I didn't know Colin well, so it made sense that Billiam and Colin coupled up on our nights out while I spent the most time with John. Without John, it would be like trying to navigate space physics with the background of a space farmer.

Billiam left the table to handle the 50-50, and I casually told John to ease up on Billiam.

"I didn't even know we were part of the marketing committee," John quipped, looking at our little table.

"Trust me, they can't afford my marketing skills," I said loudly, which got laughter from the table of girls next to me. The table gave me some of their spinach dip, so that was a perk. Our tab was apparently going to be covered. But it ended up *not* being covered (don't get me started on that). Billiam returned, and John ran to the bathroom. I wondered if it was because of Billiam or a wayward pasta situation. Now it was my time to cool Billiam down.

"We just need to respect John's boundaries," I explained. "Sure, he should have texted us a bit more about what he was up to. But it's okay that he's late."

"I just get worried," Billiam responded. I didn't worry about John — he was eating pasta in an expensive hotel. If there was anything to worry about, it was the wine pairing with John's fettuccine.

I went to stand outside the bathroom to wait for John. John arrived in the hallway when Billiam swooped in with apologies. The two of them made up, declared we were heading out, and we exited the establishment.

We crossed Chicago in the beautiful twinkling nighttime. I took the lead directionally given my background with maps and diagrams. I talked with John about how proud I was of his progress, random drunk chatter with Colin, and got into a few 'no, it's this way' directional moments with Billiam. We arrived outside the bar but turned to find that John had vanished like a girl in a true-crime mystery podcast.

"Where did he go?" Billiam turned dramatically.

"I have no clue," I commented. "John was behind me, and now he isn't."

I felt like John had fallen in battle, and we didn't have time to mourn him. Instead, we had to continue our quest to get to Splash. I initially thought that John had climbed into one of the nearby bars for a quick break from the rest of the group. I just hoped I wasn't part of why John had to escape. Did John think of us as the 3 Stooges?

"I wonder if he's been kidnapped," Billiam seriously considered. He was way too quick to pull out the kidnapping card.

"I doubt a kidnapper would be so bold," I shrugged. "Maybe he went back to the hotel."

We ended back up at Splash like a predictable Nicholas Spark movie plot line. Billiam continued to network in the city, quickly schmoozing with bar patrons.

"Hi, I just moved here, I work *here*, I do *this*..."

Billiam and I approach our social butterfly moments differently. Billiam feels like a mechanical questionnaire. He wants to find out as much as he can as quickly as he can. Billiam wants to understand the gist and refuses to entertain any rigamarole. He'll promptly pass up on you like yesterday's mint, but he'll linger if he can smell a possibility for connection. It's a bold strategy — but Billiam is a master at identifying whether or not he could be friends with someone.

I don't initially assume connection or disconnection with someone. I'm intrigued by questions and motivations, and I look for tessellations within people. I'll hand over genuine compliments, ask them random questions, and hunt for quirks and unique stories like an ideologist truffle pig. I'm more motivated by people's quirks and remarkable stories. I wish I embodied more of Billiam's stylization — a bit more casual and quick. He is a bullet train, and I am an air balloon. And sometimes, you want to enjoy the ride, but other times you want to get there quick.

At this point in the night, Splash had turned antagonist on me. I had been chugging along for almost seventeen hours with only five hours of insufficient sleep. There had been no nap, twelve hours of booze, and too many altercations to keep it easy. I usually max out at eight hours of drinking, so it was a miracle that I was still functioning.

Dancing groups surrounded us as the DJ continuously played jam after jam. Had I been adequately rested, I probably would have kept up the energy but I was fading like an eighties song. I felt like a grumpy cat who couldn't appreciate cat nip. Even Colin, who usually seemed to keep up with the party, was retiring against the wall. His pretty flower self was slowly wilting away as if planted far from the sun and given no water. The latter part of that metaphor seemed apt — the man needed Advil, sleep, and water.

I hate being the first person to chicken out during a night out. I try hard to meet the expectations my friends have for evening plans. I feel like I let my friends down when I tell them I'm too tired to do something or to continue. But the second Colin said he wanted to leave, I took that opening and ran for it.

"Do you mind if I stay behind?" Billiam asked after I conveyed that Colin and I were retiring.

"Of course not, stay behind! I'll take Colin home."

Colin and I left the club and began the quick trek back to Billiam's apartment.

"I don't think you recovered from Friday's night out," I muttered, trying to make sure Colin didn't fall into the street again. Art took inspiration from life itself.

"I haven't," Colin confirmed. I wouldn't describe Colin as quiet, but drunk Colin preferred a simple slur of words rather than winding explanations.

"I wrote a poem in Splash — do you wanna hear it?"

Yes — when I'm bored or moody, I tend to write poems. Even in the middle of a club on a Saturday night. There was no verbal confirmation from Colin, just an amused smile. Or maybe it was an 'oh, this bitch thinks he's a writer' smile. I grew to like Colin, but I can't say he was an easy read. Quite often I could read people like a restaurant menu; some were a bit more complex, like a Cheesecake Factory menu. Reading Colin was like reading *Beowulf*.

So I read out loud a poem to Colin and Chicago:

I glide between obsession and possession,
For things I do not own and barely know.
Taking ink and splashing it into symbols I think are letters
Forming languages I think others can read
The only thing legible is a sense of unsound logic reeking with desperation.
Smelling like rotted raccoon piss,
Decaying quickly under nihilist sun.

A bloody wound and a bullet,
Make an assumption of a gunshot victim.
But if you didn't witness the tearing violence,
How does one be sure?

I finished reading the poem, and Colin, head nodding, spoke out a decaying:
"Oh."
I actually laughed out loud in a moment of levity. My stories are filled with fantasy and whimsy, my lyrics are stupid and sexy, and my scripts are comedic and sharp. But my poetry tends to key into depression, anger, sadness, disgust, and revolt. The poems tend to shock people — because it goes against the happy, go-lucky dancing monkey people see in me. But even the most optimistic people have tinges of sadness, slowly uncovering our veneer. I sometimes feel soft clouds of depression — they linger in weird cases, like when I'm not having fun and I'm surrounded by people who are.

For all I know, Colin didn't hear a single word of that poem and said, "oh," so he said *something*. Or maybe he heard it and didn't understand it. Colin might have listened to the poem, understood it, and found it terrible. Had the poem struck a deep chord within him? Hit something so rooted and profound in Colin that tugging upon that vine would result in so much displacement? '*Oh*' was more manageable than admitting your body was a stack of books ready to fall. Who wanted to play with emotions when you didn't have to?

I was looking for validation. I was fishing like your grandfather used to and still brags about. And instead of receiving anything constructive, complimentary, happy, or sad — I received a neutral o*h*. I had deserved such Switzerland neutrality. I had invited emotion into the mind of a drunk man who just wanted to sleep off vodka and dream of cute boys. I was the town witch that purposefully exposed the sleepy, peaceful town to all the terrible things happening outside their village.

But I like to believe — the keyword here is *believe*, that Colin was impressed to the point where words failed him. Even drunk and stumbling through Chicago like a three-legged kitchen table, Colin couldn't find anything close to his emotions in that poetry. But who knows? I'll have to ask him one day. Colin might even say:
"Matt, I honestly don't remember that night at all."

As soon as we arrived back at Billiam's apartment — Colin rolled into Billiam's bed as if preparing for his own funeral deathbed. It usually takes me at least ten or twenty minutes to doze off, but I was unconscious in mere seconds. As soon as I laid down on the stiff couch, my body gave up. My body was an underpaid retail worker ready to shut the store down, locking the front door minutes before closing.

Billiam stomped into the apartment around two in the morning. I wasn't upset that Billiam woke me up. There have been many times in my life when I gladly sacrificed total comfort for the ability to save money. While John was spending money to have a high-end relaxing experience, I was willing to splash through a free stay if that meant a 2am wake-up alarm of Billiam stumbling into the room.

"Did I wake you up?" Billiam asked, concerned. I imagine Billiam looking at me: my limp body curled up into a fetus on a couch with my face buried so deep in a pillow you'd think I was trying to suffocate myself to sleep.

"Yeah, it's okay."

Billiam tip-toped into the bathroom, and I immediately went back to sleep. Moments later, Billiam screamed something like, "hey boyyyy." I remember turning to face him, still clutching the pillow I was burying myself in.

"I'm TRYING to SLEEP!" I shrieked in an offended tone that reeked of an older, privileged white lady.

Billiam immediately pulled back, and I fell into a sleep that lasted longer than Friday's. The next day, Billiam confessed to me a shocking statement:

"Oh, the guy I was talking with at Splash did *not* like you or Colin."

"What?" I gasped — one of my most significant anxiety factors was not knowing *why* someone hated me. I could name a plethora of valid reasons why someone *would* hate me: I'm too loud, I think I'm funnier than I really am, and I'm sometimes a wise ass. I don't mind hearing that someone hates me. But *not* knowing why someone hated me is a mystery I can't let go of. I'm aware that receiving closure wasn't always possible. But could my haters at least answer a survey question or two? The worst thing is to tell me that you hate me sans context.

"Yeah," Billiam's eyes were so broad as if I had done something last night that was so egregious it explained why a complete stranger would hate me. Did my mystery hater dislike people chilling in the back of the bar? Did he think I was being standoffish when I was, in reality, tired?

"*And* he said you and Colin were ugly."

Now, that I could get. I am unconventional beauty — a ginger lumberjack tank with a great smile, a symmetrical face, and a pleasant personality. I wasn't for everyone, but those who liked the vibe loved the product. I was confused why Colin had been labeled as ugly. He was handsome in that Abercrombie model with the blue eyes way. He had light scruff and an exposed navel that could make straight guys shrug and say,   "*fine*, yeah, he's cute."

"Why?" I doubled down on my inquisition. "Why did he hate Colin and me? Why does he think we're ugly?"

"I dunno, that's just what he said," Billiam said with a flippant hand.

"Wow..." I whistled. "I think that might make me a bit homophobic."

"He was hitting on me, so..." Billiam said with a jazzy shoulder move as if we should overlook someone's nasty opinions so Billiam can have a date. "Don't worry, I blocked him already."

Only one mandatory event left was on the docket — Sunday morning drag brunch. I was worried we might end up working the host podium instead of just attending. We were herded like cows into a giant hall with dozens of other guests. For sixty bucks and a tip, you were treated to a full-out drag show, unlimited drinks for an hour and a half, and brunch food. The drinks included mimosas, beers, and well spirits with energy drinks — all strong enough to leave you stumbling outside by noon. The event was legal, but unlimited drinks that early on a Sunday morning should come with a mandatory 'this is not advised' message.

The server came over with an iced-tea pitcher of mimosa alongside a whole extra bottle of champagne.

"I brought over an extra bottle of champagne just in case," Our server said with a mischievous smile.

"Is that just juice?" Billiam asked as I poured and sipped on the pitcher of mimosas.

"Nope, it's a mimosa," I confirmed, eyeing the extra bottle that was more incriminating than when your illicit acts are caught on video.

We ended up trying the Watermelon Mimosa and the Tropical Mimosa — both of which Billiam disliked. I mixed champagne, juice, vodka, and Redbull, which made me feel like an actual booze garbage disposal. I'm not a binge drinker — I tend to drink heavy drinks moderately quickly. I could probably finish a Long Island in ten minutes if it was an emergency. But it only took two or three Long Islands for me to feel the tipsiness and call it a day. Swigging down gallons of juice and champagne is different. It's a heavy lurch to the stomach and almost feels like you're flooding your body.

I thought eating food would help my poisoning — but the food didn't seem to absorb much. The food included the breakfast classic combination of eggs, Costco-style bulk frozen tater tots, bacon, and over-fried French toast balls. The lunch component was a sad-looking pile of arugula over bread with chipotle aioli. The aioli was drizzled haphazardly over the plate like an elderly driver who should hand over their license. I assumed this dish was to ensure this event could be denoted as brunch and not breakfast.

"People don't come here for the food," Billiam explained as if the soggy eggs and brick-hard spheres of toast decay indicated that the food was the main meal.

"Clearly," I said — still shuffling eggs down my throat like a pelican who was giving up on an un-openable Mcdonalds' brown bag in the parking lot and settling for rotting fish on the beach.

A few times I could feel my stomach surge with things making their way up my esophagus. I managed to force it all back down. Billiam and Colin were staring at me like I had cursed out the entire restaurant.

"If you're going to...*do that*, you should go outside," Billiam couldn't even bear to bring himself to say the word vomit. And I'm glad he didn't — it might have made me upchuck over the unlimited mimosas. Once everyone had been primed with booze, the show was over, and we were forced to clear out so they could prepare for a second performance. We tried doing a bar after — but it was too early for people to be out.

Colin, who was using his airline employment feature to get free plane trips, was worried that he would be stuck if he didn't take the 6pm flight. So he left a bit earlier than intended. Billiam was a bit upset, but I related to Colin's anxiety over transportation. Colin had never gained back a second wind this weekend.

"I guess it's you and me for dinner," Billiam explained. "Unless John is around..."

I knew John hadn't left the city — but I figured John had plans to see friends. John had previously lived in Chicago, and I could see him fitting in various visits to friends he might not have seen in over two years.

The promise of dinner was scratched out when Billiam told me we would meet his friends at Roscoe's.

"I'm actually *really* excited to see Roscoe's," Billiam said with an excitable grin.

"You *have* seen it," I pointed out. "We were there on Friday, and you hated it."

"I did?" Billiam paused, and I decided to void the issue. I didn't want a round two of Intelligentsia.

We trudged onward — back to the nearby bar district. Billiam's friends arrived late, so we got drinks and danced before mingling with them. It turned out to be a tumultuously emotional night for me. Billiam got struck by the bathroom monster and left me alone in the corner of the bar for a half-hour. A deep wave of depression slammed into me. I reminisced about the times I had been left alone, placed in a corner, and subjugated. All these beautiful, happy people around me seemed like real-life social media. I knew they were facing their own problems and negativity, but I felt alone in a pit. This was an extension of yesterday's emotions. I was the only one *not* enjoying myself, surrounded by those who were. What was wrong with me?

Billiam returned later and I snapped.

"You *left* me *alone*," I complained, my face breaking out in rage and sadness.

"I was in the bathroom—." I could tell that Billiam was thrown off by my 180.

"I just— I have to leave."

I am no saint. I stormed off, leaving behind Billiam, Roscoe's, and all the happy people. I was still determining what I wanted from Billiam. A text message explaining how sorry he was? Being dragged along to the bathroom in the first place? Something that proved he understood all the nuances I was exhibiting?

Italian food helped me recollect the pieces. I joked for a second to myself that maybe I was hungry. But now, a tinge of guilt was kicking in. Had my actions seemed rooted in some legitimacy? I knew my emotions were valid, but they were expressed messily. It was like performing Shakespeare with bad actors — ruining this poignant piece with subpar performers. And there was so much said: I threw issues like confetti which Billiam swept up in a similar motion, "I'm sorry, I'm sorry, I'm sorry."

The apology was quick at breakfast the following morning. We had both woken up politely and had walked down to Eggcellence. And as I peeled back the poached egg on my Benedict, and as Billiam danced around his food like the pickiest ballerina, I began to do the challenging yet necessary work regarding friendship.

"I'm sorry about last night," I began. "I should have...well, been better."

"It's okay," Billiam said, as if I had spilled white wine on vinyl flooring and not had an emotional outburst comparable to Vesuvius. "I love you, Reeby."

Reeby — a nickname that only Billiam uses, but a handle I like. It's quirky, it's artistic, it's casual. Last night I spouted some sensitive questions, some out of line. But there are moments, such as when Billiam pulls his own personal nickname for me, that remind me that he is my brother. A brother I love, a brother I sometimes get incredulous over, but blood to me.

Sometimes the closer you are to someone, the easier it is to fall into the light dramatics. Because you unconditionally love those people in your life. You love them so much you overlook most of their quirks or frustrations. You ease their anxieties, disregard your personal preferences, and even adapt like a Koala in a jungle. With co-workers and acquaintances, you're painted up like a French madame — trying to act the most proper and collected for their sake. But for your friends, you wipe the make-up off, push your face forward and say, "*I am what I am.*" And what we are is frustrations over expectations and social obligations turned hem and haw. We are too many drinks and too many slips of the tongue. We are lashing at each other and praying over the damage we cause. We are imperfect for each other, and we hope we can improve things.

After breakfast, John appeared so we could return to Cleveland.

"I want to apologize," John began, immediately pulling Billiam into a hug. "I think we both had different expectations of this weekend."

Like a cheesy Lifetime original movie, there were hugs and promises of visits soon. Before I knew it, John and I were propelling through downtown Chicago, hugging Lake Michigan so close you could run into the lake in mere seconds.

"Something I thought of was how Billiam and I go back seven years — exactly seven," I pointed out. "Science says it takes seven years to truly know someone."

Did I feel like I knew Billiam? Did I even successfully know people who have been around in my life for a decade? Two decades? Considering I still feel unconfident in understanding the vast abyss in myself, could I summarize another's soul?

"And now that you know him, how do you feel?" John asked.

"I love him," I confirmed. "I didn't love going out three nights in a row."

John and I chuckled, and the conversation shifted onto the new tangent I had posed.

"I sometimes feel..." John began, pausing to think through the emotion, "...that I feel disconnected from others, kind of..."

"You feel elevated," I whispered, staring into the grey concrete blurring by. "And not in a pretentious way. Just..."

"In a mature way," John pointed out. "Like, we're getting older."

I was beginning to slightly discard the heavy drinking and partying lifestyle thanks to COVID-19 and my emerging adulthood. I still had moments where I wanted to go out. But I was beginning to feel different about what I wanted versus what I needed. I used to want to go out every single weekend night. And now, I don't need that anymore.

"And sometimes, I dunno..." John paused. "I feel like I just...*need* something more out of my friends lately."

John went on to talk about a long-time friend he had recently ended a friendship over due to feeling semi-excluded. His friend had new responsibilities and more prominent characters in her life. And suddenly, he had gone from a large land holding to some farmland tucked away in the corner of her country.

"They can't be close to me anymore. The way we used to be."

"You feel like a supporting role," I commented — having felt that way before.

"I don't want to be a supporting role. But...I feel bad. I want to reach out and apologize for how I acted the last time I saw her."

"But you don't want to reach out to reignite the friendship?"

"No, just...just to *end* it better."

Moments later, the conversation shifted again, and I cracked a joke with John.

"We're social savants."

"Savants!" John cackled. "Isn't that word like...used to denote you are 'special' or something?"

I Googled the definition — quite confident that it meant intellectual in a spiritual and scientific blend. Besides, I usually reclaim the first definition of words that get bent by society.

"It works then," John smiled. "Did you get something in Chicago that you don't get in Cleveland?" John asked behind sunglasses — staring ahead and singing along to a Faith Hill song.

"No," I quickly surmised. "The novelty of the city was fun, as it is visiting every new place. But I get everything in Cleveland."

I sometimes wonder what it would be like to reinvent myself — to vanish like some 1920s vagabond who could slip away from the world. I don't want to pull a Houdini — I love my life.

"I loved going back," John admitted to me. "But it confirmed I didn't need to be in Chicago. I loved my time there... and I'll go back again. But I love where I am in my life now."

All four of us took multiple lessons from that weekend. For Colin — it was probably something like proper rest and staggered drinking. For Billiam, I think it was something to do with managing expectations. For John, it reminded him of boundaries and confirmed that he was where he needed to be. For me, it was a lesson in the forgiveness of self and the forgiveness of others. It was a lesson I believed I would need to repeat like a mantra, perhaps even tattooed on myself as a constant epitaph. But if Billiam could forgive me casually over breakfast of eggs and ham, I could easily excuse myself. Forgiveness over how I treated people, how I treated the world, and how I treated myself.

A Collection of Random Notes Written In Passing (2019-2022)

I.

    I often find myself going through light obsessions. Sometimes it manifests in where I'm going to get groceries. I'll go exclusively to Trader Joe's or Aldi's for months on end before dropping them in favor of someone else. Sometimes my obsessions are habits — like what I do when I'm fiddling around on my phone. I might spend months obsessed on Reddit or playing a ridiculous video game. And then, finally, I move on like a vagabond passing the time.

    I exclusively watched one television program for weeks on end: TLC's show *Four Weddings*. And for those who don't know, *Four Weddings* is the show where four brides rate each other's weddings and the winner gets a honeymoon. You invite three strangers to your wedding to have them nitpick the shit out of the best day of your life.

    Every episode of *Four Weddings* opens up by introducing the brides. The producers do a great job finding brides who will not like each other. One bride will say, "I love glitter and sparkles and bright colors," and then the next bride will share, "I love black things that do not shimmer at all." Or one bride will say, "I love a country barn wedding," and the next girl comments, "if I get married outside, I will *MELT*." And then the editors really make the magic pop.

In the beginning, the producers have the girls meet for wine before the competition to quote 'meet the competitors.' And EVERY EPISODE has one bride who lifts her merlot and says to the women: "cheers, girls, good luck, but I'm going to win!" My theory is that the bride who threatens them with defeat on camera never wins. Let's be honest, we save the threats for our private confessionals.

We move on to the competition. To avoid 'bias,' the girls rate the overall experience out of ten and then rank the other three brides' weddings on food, dress, and venue. You'd think it would be easy, but you're inviting brides to quibble their way through an event. It's like having someone at your funeral going, "mmm, lilies? Looks a bit cheap...."

Here's a very valid and not over-exaggerated example of how the brides bring about their judgment:

"I enjoyed the ceremony...the candles were beautiful. And I liked the way the chairs felt for dinner. But the DJ sucked, the food was cold, the walk from the ceremony to the dinner was too long, and the color of the flowers in the entryway was ugly. So I'll give it a 5/10."

Or a bride will say:

"This *bitch* had the nerve to serve asparagus at her wedding!!! 2/10."

The first one feels excessively nitpicky, while the second one is malicious. But there's something about the disconnect between the third type of bride:

"I loved the ceremony. The couple looked so romantic, the dinner was excellent, the DJ was great...so I'll give it a 5/10".

A 5/10 is when the waiter spills your burnt entree on you, not when everything at the wedding is GORGEOUS. Does the bride think that 5/10 means immaculate?

If a bride is non-white, the other brides are like, 'I love how she showed her culture. I loved seeing her heritage.' A bride could legit display bowls of salsa at the cocktail lounge, and one of the brides would say something stupid like:

"I MUY liked the salsa; it was great to see the culture...."

Meanwhile, the catering staff is pouring Kirkland Signature mild salsa into the cocktail bowl.

After everyone's wedding has been judged, the girls gather back together where they don't *necessarily* lie but definitely *exaggerate* the truth:

"So I really loved the font used on the entrance sign. It was stunning."

And then the other girls bellow "*yessss, yesss, yesss*" squawking like seagulls on a brown paper bag. There's never any truth to their statements. They glide over the negative comments as if they weren't ripping into each other's best days. And then, finally, the limo rolls up, and it takes five minutes to find out who the winning groom is, and there's a winner and a full-point breakdown.

I don't know why *Four Weddings* fulfills so many of my entertainment needs. There is natural drama in any reality show, but something about reducing one's wedding day into a critique feels maliciously delicious. And I'm fascinated by those who decide to publicly share their wedding and have people rank them. I'd be mortified if I came in last place on the show. But then part of me uses this show as information, not that I'm anywhere close to being married. So, I suppose we can say that *Four Weddings* is educational?

II.

In 2019, I went to the Geauga County Fair for the first time in a hot minute. From a quick scan, I look like the average country fair attendant: boozy, white trash. But there's one thing that's becoming a bit apparent. I don't remember it as a child. And in retrospect, it was always there. The county fair is a breeding ground for right-wing extremism.

This realization does make me feel a bit stupid. It's as if saying: "I didn't expect caffeine in this coffee" or "I didn't expect homework in this college class." But a young child remembers the cute animals and the greasy food that probably didn't help with my childhood obesity. Another primary childhood memory of the fair experience is riding death-trap rides made with local scrap metal. But I did not remember the religious right. One stand featured a large sign that exclaimed: 'Are you sure you're in heaven?' All I could think was *Nope, I'm definitely currently in hell.*

III.

I have a consistent weekly gig hosting trivia. It's a fun job, pays decently, and it's perfect for someone who tries to make a living through talking. But the problem I've encountered is when a bar doesn't have regulars who want to do trivia. So that means I have to constantly pitch my trivia game like a salesman. I'm not great at social rejections, so this part of the process is probably why I get paid as much as I do. Imagine having this conversation multiple times over in quick succession:

"Hiiiiiii... would you like to play trivia? It's free, and it's fun, and it's only like an hour or so, and there are gift cards...."

And you have a variety of responses. Some of the older folks will keep sipping their beer and eyeing a sports game without drawing their face to me, just muttering a soft, displeasured no.

Some couples are into it, but it's usually the woman. She thinks it will be a great icebreaker situation with her boyfriend or husband, who realizes he's better going along with his wife's demands than fighting them. However, some couples look like I'm ruining their honeymoon anniversary dinner, as if I've pushed the violin player out of the way to accost them and spilled their award-winning bottle of champagne on ice to the ground. I'm hosting a weekday trivia game at a chicken wing restaurant two steps away from being a fast food chain. So let's roll back the melodrama. The families are also hit and miss. But what's shocking is the picture-ready magazine spread families who give me a look like I'm a solicitor asking for money to fund serial killers.

Lately, I've nailed down the correct process which minimizes rejection and keeps my anxiety under wraps. I'll approach most people but will avoid those who appear as if they will seriously murder me if I ask them about the weather, let alone about trivia. I quickly ask:

"Would you like to play trivia?"

If they say *no*, I say something like 'no worries' or 'next time,' and then move on. If they say *yes*, I vault into instructions with excited fervor. If they hesitate, I usually take that as a no. I'm not trying to convince people like a door-to-door religious zealot or a snake oil salesman. There are benefits of receiving a weekly rejection — it's truly kept me humble.

IV.

These are the five stages of going out to karaoke.

Stage One: Pregaming and Preparing. Even though the bar that hosts karaoke most likely serves three-dollar drinks, you need to save a little money. That means you're going to buy a large soda mixer from a Sheetz gas station and bring it over to your friend's house. If Dollar Tree is still open, you get a gallon of bubbly soda for under two dollars. You arrive with some kind of beverage unless you're a mooching friend who says they'll 'get people drinks at the bar' (Fact: this same mooching friend is the one who claims they'll buy a drink for whoever drives but will forget to bring cash).

While saving money and quickly downing drinks, you try to pick out what songs you should sing. It's hard to know what the vibe will be. Some would say it's better to play to the crowd. Others might argue that you should just sing what you want. There's never a wrong answer; determine if you're in the mood for a sultry bop or a sad ballad. If you're a decent singer with a decent range, you feel free to pursue a vast collection of classics. But then again, you don't have to be a good singer to do karaoke. If you had to be a good singer to do karaoke, half the people who regularly karaoked would be banned.

Having a few drinks means you shouldn't drive to the dive bar's karaoke night. So you decide to have a friend or Uber drive you. You're usually warming up with a fun Spotify playlist on the car ride. You're contemplating what potential dance moves you might add to the set. And you're testing your range. You're drunk, but sober enough to hit that high note.

Stage Two: Assessing The Scene. You and your friends arrive at the dive bar, and now you have to see what the deal is. What's the energy of the crowd? Is this dive bar, a country bar, a gay bar, a random hole in the wall, a place that probably shouldn't even be operating as a place of business? You listen to the songs others have chosen. Can you casually sneak your deep-cut Britney Spears or '80s one-hit wonder into the lineup? You must also check the book to see if they even have the instrumental you want. There's nothing more disappointing than picking a song in that earlier Uber ride that the DJ then doesn't have. You put your name and song in, grab a drink from the bar, and silently judge the other contestants. Because suddenly, it's not a casual karaoke night out; it's SPARTA, which means war. You pray that you're not up after the one local girl who definitely auditioned for *American Idol*. You hope you follow up the singer who bombs like French World War I warfare, 'cause even at your worst, you're better than that. Suddenly you just need one more drink, even though that drink might make your usual soprano go baritone.

Stage Three: Your Performance. The DJ calls your name and informs the room of your song selection. At this point, you can't change the song but scan the room to see the reaction. Are they happy with the song? Is there someone rolling their eyes due to the 'terrible selection?' Is anyone curious about what song you'll perform? But the instrumental kicks in, and you perform. You move with the rhythm, maybe closing your eyes so you don't have to see the sights lasered onto you. Suddenly you get to the bridge. Maybe there's a key change. Something bolts into you as you nail that final refrain. The DJ gives it up for you, and so does the room. You have successfully drunkenly karaoke'd.

Stage Four: Perform Again.

Stage Five: Wind It Down. Depending on how late it is, you might get a second or third performance. Another factor is the competition: how many stars and starlets demand their own throttle with the microphone? All that pregaming might mean that you show up to that bar late. You and your friends close the place down, singing obnoxiously to other people's songs, adding flair to pieces that don't need flair when sober, and promising to get "just one more drink." Finally, the bartenders physically communicate that they've had enough with this second-rate rundown version of *The Voice*, and declare last call. You hit the streets to find another place to drink while you and your friends lament over all the other songs you didn't get to butcher.

V.

You can tell a lot about someone by knowing their gym membership.

Planet Fitness membership: they're not here to brag about going to the gym. They just need a gym. They're tired, like a Viola Davis character being told some upsetting news.

YMCA membership: Family individual, always talking about 'having fun at the gym' but probably because they're taking the damn cooking classes and not working out.

Esporta nee LA Fitness membership: these fancy bitches want to let you know that they might pack their bags and move to Denver to smoke weed and drink kale all day at any point. They will run you over in the parking lot, get pulled over by a cop, and flirt their way out of a misdemeanor. They are not here for your pathetic-poor-person bullshit.

24/7 Fitness membership: Working out is not just a movement or lifestyle. It's a complete identity for them to illustrate and weaponize. Like their gym, they're always 24/7.

Home gym membership: Constantly talking about their home gym. You could talk about anything with them, and the conversation will eventually return to their home gym.

I'm not large, but I definitely am not the picture of health you'd see on the cover of *Health & Fitness*. Surprisingly, I am a member of a gym. I say surprisingly because often when I tell people I attend the gym, their first reaction is a slight surprise. My six-pack of abs retired back when I was seven, and while I can feel them underneath my walrus blubber, they have no interest in returning to duty. I can't say my abs went AWOL because what jacked seven-year-old has visible abs?

I work out at Planet Fitness, and I can honestly say I've never had pizza, bagels, Tootsie Pops, Tootsie Rolls, fried chicken, a giant sheet cake, a shovel of sugar, or whatever else that Planet Fitness leaves out for its members. And I don't mean to say I don't eat those foods. It's just that the whole point of me going to the gym is so I can justify having a slice of pizza. Eating that slice of pizza at the gym just feels like an immediately cancel-out situation. You would have burned more calories at home on the couch.

But having goodies is a smart strategy because it lowkey forces people to come back: they're not losing that much weight *and* because it's free food. And if there's anything motivational in life, it's free food. I could be in the middle of a torture interrogation by 1970's New York City corrupt cops, and suddenly they say, "Hey, do you want a taquito?" And I'd respond, "Oh my gosh, give me three!"

Lately, I haven't seen any food at Planet Fitness. I don't know if they've phased it out due to the criticism that a gym shouldn't be handing out free unhealthy snacks or if maybe it was a financial decision.

There are a lot of characters at the gym. There are people like me who are definitely people-watching the whole time. We're like those paintings in the old *Scooby Doo* mysteries where Shaggy goes, "Zion's, did that painting's eyes just move?" Yes, ma'am, I am looking at your chest, mainly because I'm trying to read the fancy script that proclaims you love Jesus.

There's this one guy at Planet Fitness who is ALWAYS there, but he's NEVER working out. He just stands around as if just by showing up to the gym, you can claim that you were at the gym.

"Hey, how was your day, Bob?"

"Well, I went to the gym for three hours today."

"That's impressive! What did you do at the gym?"

"I told you, Josh, I was *at the gym* for three hours."

This other guy just walks in giant circles around the facility like he's some single mother who lost her child at the supermarket and now has to like scour the aisles.

"Oh he has to be on the next aisle over, right? Oh geez, now I'm getting worried. Where are you, Nathanial James Clark Yorkshire Strawberry Caucasian Smith!?"

And to the guy walking circles, it's seventy degrees and gorgeous; if you want to walk, take an actual walk outside instead of squeezing between the equipment and almost knocking people around.

Another kind of person at the gym is one who really wants to use the equipment you're using. Usually, this person likes to cuts in front of people at the buffet because they don't need the current section you're at, and there's room in front of you. It's really obnoxious at the gym, just do some squats while you wait for a leg machine. And these people aren't just giving you a casual glance as they wait. Their mad eyes make you think, "oh he's going to kill me for this arm machine." Their next step is when they approach you and inquire, "SIR, I NEED TO USE THIS MACHINE. HOW MUCH LONGER ARE YOU GOING TO BE ON

IT?!" Me being the nice person says, "I'm almost done," even if I'm not.

The worst is when you start using a piece of equipment and from the depths of the gym comes: "I WAS USING THAT!" It's like the show *To Catch A Predator* when Chris Hansen comes out of nowhere with iced tea, and you're like, "Damn it, I thought I could handle that nice piece...of gym equipment." One time I sat down at a machine just for someone to run up to me from a different machine.

"Oh I'm using that." Their voice hostile.

I turned back over to the machine they had been at. Apparently he had an invisible twin brother using my machine and I had just sat on the twin's lap.

We could never forget that at Planet Fitness, there's no judgment. No judgment unless you drop weights and set off the Lunk Alarm. The Lunk Alarm is the equivalent of the alarm that goes off at the fire station when there's a fire. Except the Lunk Alarm usually sounds off when someone has dropped a five-pound weight. It's an obnoxious sound that's truly more ridiculous than the person who is being Lunk Alarm-ed. I remember one time a lady coughed a bit loudly, and the alarm went off.

VI.

I recently noticed that Cedar Point is super LGBT-friendly. Not in overt rainbow and g-strings, but just with their demographics of employees. It seemed as if every ride operator was a young gay twink summering away in Sandusky, and I was living for it. Internally, I couldn't help but exaggerate the employees:

"Girls, I need you to keep your hands and feet in the ride at all times. Can't you be grabbing onto the ride like the way I used to hold onto my ex-boyfriend Michael. We need phones in the pocket too, ladies and some of you...mmm, I can't tell if that's a phone or if we got a hard situation going on. I'm gonna place this bar tight on your lap, tight as the way I am without Michael these days...

"The ride is gonna get really bumpy. Wow, this whole ride reminds me of Michael...girls I'm going to have to take a second. It's just formidable to date here in Sandusky...alright, so the ride

will go up 169 feet...god damn it, Michael...okay, Lance, we got this. Okay, blue train, are you ready for the ride??? Alright, byeeeeeee."

VII.

    I'm so proud that everyone is finally admitting that we, as humans, love true crime. A decade ago, you'd say: "Why do you think he murdered so-and-so?" and someone would probably say, "GASP, why would you ever TALK ABOUT MURDER!?"

    Have you ever stayed up to watch one of those true crime shows? I love the shows where it's undeniable what happened. Take *Snapped*, for example, a show that revolves around murderous women who have 'snapped' into committing murder. Going into the show, you know that the murderer is probably a scorned wife. The answer is confirmed in the first ten seconds by the narrator:

    "They were a perfect couple. Until Tim was poisoned. Did his wife, Brenda, do this?"

    We know it's Brenda. We probably have an idea right then *why* Brenda killed him. But we'll still watch the show over the next hour to find out the whole story.

    I also love *Forensics Files* because it's a show you can just fall asleep to with that narrator's voice:

    "She decided it would be a divorce, but the only separation *he* was willing to do was to separate her dead body."

    It's a very smooth line delivered in that standard news-speak tone. Classic!

VIII.

    When you're the funny one in the friend group, there's so much pressure in *Cards Against Humanity*. You always want multiple black cards if you believe you're funny. Having only one — or worse, zero black cards — is a sign that you are not as amusing as you believe yourself to be.

    But sometimes, it's slanted. You get terrible playing cards with references from the '60s or stupid things that are never funny. Meanwhile, Doug, who is legitimately *not* funny, continues to get the nasty sex cards.

I was playing Quiplash — a cooler, digital version of *Cards Against Humanity*, and won two rounds back to back. Going into game three, there was so much pressure that I fumbled and landed fourth. The entire friend group is funny, but as the person who has staked professional and personal interests into comedy, it felt like Custard's Last Stand.

IX.

Everyone knows their stripper name but why don't people know their serial killer name? I think it should be your favorite city or location with the method you would use to kill someone. So mine would be The Cleveland Swordman Murderer. Or if I was really honest, The Dunkin' Donuts Drive Thru Smothered With Love and Affection That You Can't Handle Murderer.

Or, if we were exact in our geographic locations and more honest about how we would kill someone, mine would be the Fairview Park Accidental Murderer. That one feels like the Eeyore of serial killer names.

X.

Have you ever been in a love triangle? I'm in a love triangle with caffeine and melatonin right now. Caffeine wants me bouncing off the walls while Melatonin wants me comfy in bed, relaxing. It's truly like having a wife and seeing a mistress, how do you balance both of those? I realize I need to schedule them properly: having trysts with caffeine in the morning, and then blending with melatonin when nightfall cometh.

The best part is that caffeine definitely has the advantage because quite often I'm forced awake, and not necessarily looking to crash.

XI.

A conversation I overheard recently:
A waitress approaches a table.
Waitress: "Sorry if you've been waiting a while!"
Lady: "Well we have."
Waitress: "Sorry about that, we are slammed and understaffed."
Lady: "It wasn't like that last week!"

XII.
    Did you know that the Soviet Union was the first society to ban lobotomies? It's probably because Russians learned that they didn't need lobotomies to mess with people's heads. You can do just as much damage through torture, brutal punishment, and sharp words. Although people on television who have lobotomies are always sitting in rocking chairs and wearing cardigans. You have to admit, something is alluring about that idea. Just add some cookies and a cup of hot tea and you have an ideal fall Sunday.

XIII.
    I drove by a PSA poster for safe sex which said, *Sexually risky?,* next to a guy rolling a pair of die. The die had landed on seven, which any gambler would tell you is a great roll (I think). So, the safe sex worked out for them? What was the metaphor exactly? If the idea was to roll on something terrible, wouldn't they have landed on snake eyes? So if anything, they should've had the man land on snake eyes or a dice roll that was scary.

XIV.
    I would be a good murder victim because I'd leave behind so much DNA.

    Wanna figure out if you are the loser of your friend group? If your friend group went to the rollercoaster park, would you always be riding alone?
    "Poly but open to new dynamics." Dynamics? Is this like work talk for, "yes, this threesome is really raising our *surplus.*"

    I'm so cheap that I'm the kind of guy who stocks up on Target clearance soap. You visit me in July and say, "This Christmas Tree Snowdrop Soap is divine."

    Someone told me that seeing each other's faces makes us smile. Smile as in, "I'm happy to see you?" Or smile as in, "Your ugly face is so bad it makes me smile."

I got a message from the Taco Bell app that asked, "Are you craving a burrito in your mouth?" I'm relatively shocked, how does the Taco Bell app know about my lack of sex?

I logged onto Hulu recently and found out that my life was used as the inspiration for their new show: *Dating App Horrors: The Untold Story*.

Wanna save money? Order fruity drinks at the bar that come with garnish. Get your booze with free fruit!

Dangerous activity: peeing into a urinal while wearing sandals.

Ways to make young people feel old: the Nintendo Wii is considered a vintage piece of technology.

Some of my wealthy friends are like, "We're going to Italy this summer!" And I'm like, "Oh I *love* visiting Little Italy."

Has anyone ever left a penny in a *take a penny/leave a penny*? If you want to know who is going to heaven, it's people who leave their coins in that tray.

Do you ever get a news alert about a celebrity death and you're like, "Oh my gosh! ...Who?"

I love food products that will advertise how much PROTEIN they have. "This snack has 16 GRAMS OF PROTEIN per serving!" It makes you feel like it's healthier.
"Oh honey, look! This gallon of lard has extra protein! I'll grab two!"

Did anyone see that McDonald's engagement? Two employees at McDonald's got engaged at work. Which, I can't criticize too much, since I'm terribly single. But imagine visiting that McDonald's on the day of the engagement and wondering, "Okay, this is nice, but is my order done?"

Nothing is more ridiculous than the way we frame corporation branding. "This event is powered by D-Mobile!" *Powered*? Like they brought their official D-Mobile generator out of some storage locker to provide electricity? "This event is charged up by Molly's Soap and Shampoo!" So Molly's Soap and Shampoo is electrifying? Just say Molly gave you some money and now she gets a shoutout.

XV.

So I like to have my Indeed job alerts active because you never know when the dream jobs are going to show up. But because I consider myself a hungry but not starving artist, I have some weird notifications set up. Examples include: 'event hosts,' 'tour guides,' 'artists,' and even 'media teachers.' I got a notification that there was a new artist gig in Cleveland. Immediately, I swiped open my phone, wondering if it was an art medium that I dabbled in.

Turned out that the "artist" gig was for Subway. They were looking for a 'sandwich artist.' They have major audacity to use the word artist to describe the work. Can you imagine Subway hiring *actual* artists to creatively interpret sandwiches?

Customer: "So I wanted Mayo on my sandwich."

Subway employee: "I just *felt* like the *piece* didn't *need* Mayo."

XVI.

I love when people use the word 'stoic' as a compliment.

"Oh, Great Aunt Jean is a stoic woman."

So she was a bitch? Labeling something as stoic implies that the person is a bitch without *saying* the word bitch. If it's being used to describe something, it's not positive.

The same effect goes with phrases.

"Fred follows a drum to their own beat."

Not a positive compliment, it's just an excellent way of saying someone is a goddamn weirdo.

XVII.

When I enrolled in a Catholic school for grad school, I knew it would be religious. It's like going to a steakhouse and expecting steak. Well during orientation everyone kept talking about how God brought them to this program and class. I didn't have the heart to tell them that Google was the creator that bought me there. God might listen to what you need, but so does Google, and Google has a pretty optimized search engine.

XVIII.

There's *full* and there's *dessert full*. When experiencing the regular full, you can't eat any more pasta or savory dishes. But suddenly there's room when a dessert cart gets rolled out. You couldn't eat more salad, meat, cheese or bread. But there is definitely a higher threshold for full.

Dessert Full comes with multiple levels. Eventually, you get full of cake and solid desserts. At some point, the cookies that once could be squeezed into a gullet become un-tempting. You see cookies or cake and want to throw up. This is *Dessert Full: Solids*.

But then you can still cram liquid desserts like pudding and ice cream. Liquids, like water and booze, go down easier. There is always room to round out all the solid food with a splattering of liquid. This is *Dessert Full: Liquids*.

But there remains the top of the *Dessert Full* pyramid. It matters not whether you have solid, liquid, or gas. For there are fancy desserts like macrons, creme brûlée, and anything that you know you cannot make at home. These are desserts that are like rare species of animals in the wild.

"Look at that beauty." You might say as your eyes sparkle amongst the rare creature or dessert. You become a snake that unhinges its jaw, and you begin to hyperdigest things in your stomach. It's like evacuating the town from a flood — "*go and do not come back! The macrons come in unique flavors.*"

You thought you could no longer continue — and finally, after having the dessert of upper echelons, there is simply no room in the inn, no matter if the Jesus of desserts is before you. This is *Dessert Full: Rare Desserts*.

XIX.

I once went to a bar where the bartender told me:
"Tell me what you like and I can make you a custom drink."

I wouldn't say that I have trust issues, but I don't exactly like going blind to certain menu items or sashaying into creative off-menu interpretations. The worst example of this was when I ordered a drink at brunch that was sixteen dollars. It featured one liquor I didn't recognize and I shrugged it off, thinking it would be okay. That drink ended up being undrinkable and was wasted. Indeed a life lesson and arguably the most important thing I've ever learned in my life.

Deciding to be friendly, I played along with the bartender's desire to have fun.

"Sweet fruity vodka drinks," I explained to the bartender. I felt like this was an easy descriptor — I'd be happy with vodka with any juice sans grapefruit juice. What was the chance this place *had* grapefruit juice?

Moments later she comes over and serves a drink that at first glance looks neither fruity nor vodka-y. I took a sip and felt my throat clench in a gag.

"This is whiskey over rocks." My voice grew sour with a hint of rage. "Is it *Opposite Day*?"

When she returned I asked if she could do something to change the drink. Thankfully she added a half-gallon of simple syrup to remedy the situation. I still to this day don't understand how she fumbled that bag. I remain convinced she thought I was telling her what I hated and had served the exact opposite. Or maybe she believed that her whiskey over rocks was so tempting that it would convert me. Bartenders around the world, please don't be like this bartender. I don't need to be impressed with your skills or improv — just make me something I'll like, please.

XX.

Idea — Skin product with hydrochloric acid: the best kind of skin is *no skin*.

I realized that having a communications degree is knowing how to stalk for information but make it seem *academic*. I'm not just stalking to find this person's social media. I'm doing *research*. The second asset of having a communications degree: you're able to take great photos.

Polos are problematic for me. Because either you care enough to wear a button-up, or you don't care at all and you wear a shirt. Polos feel like you're coping with that vital decision. But then suddenly, soon after I turned twenty-eight, I ran into a polo on clearance. For some reason, my past attitude washed out of me. And now I own a polo — that looks really good on me.

Someone on Tinder asked me:
"Do you like crackhead energy in your life?"
And I said,
"No, I do not."
Do people answer that question in the affirmative? I'm curious if there are people among us who would have seen that message and started looking at wedding bands on Amazon.

My body is too stubborn to be allergic to anything. But then I found that I was allergic to something: love.

We posted an article about a Roomba deal at work and some Facebook follower commented '*not in my house.*' What on earth did a Roomba to do this woman to bring out such disdain?

I watched three seconds of local cable news today. The coming-up teaser was:
"Sad news! Hermit crabs are dying. Also, is Justin Timberlake a slut?"
That might be enough local cable news for the rest of the decade.

XXI.

My favorite moment in cooking shows is when the contestant is explaining their dish, and the editing crew has run out of room to write down their entire dish.
"I'm making a fried chicken risotto with buffalo mozzarella skewers, crispy tomato flanks, organic arugula, with a balsamic reduction glaze with hot honey."
And the graphics on the side of the screen just say *Risotto, Caprese.*

XXII.

Boys are kind of like breakfast diners.

Boys who are like First Watch are everything you would want but come at an expensive price. "Wow I can get avocado toast, cage-free eggs, and organic watermelon juice?" And then you realize the problem isn't with First Watch, it's that *you're* not good enough for First Watch. So you leave and hope you can afford to go again.

Boys who are like Cracker Barrel are at first all show. You see a lot of trinkets and exciting things, right? You walk into Cracker Barrel and say "Wow, a porcelain frog for the yard that doubles as a bird fountain?" These boys are like the Cracker Barrel store: giving you things you don't need and comes with a mediocre breakfast. But maybe you settle for that boy...the way you might settle down in that Cracker Barrel rocking chair!

Boys who are like Denny's...you try and hype them up but you know what you're really getting. You're getting the basics, and nothing more. You don't get no organic shit or Cracker Barrell store. You get your goddamn eggs and you will goddamn eat them. They might spit in your food or put cigarettes in your food and you're going to deal with it because you don't think you deserve more than that. No matter where we are, don't we all want breakfast food rather than starve?

XXIII.

I'm a sucker for body and life-improving apps. If my friends were to say that I need to be "focused" that I'm "destructive" or that I "don't live in logic," I'd be getting new friends. But when a life improvement app tells me I'm a hot mess, I reel backward with a gasp because suddenly it all makes sense. It's similar to when your mother gives you advice you don't take, but suddenly some friend says the same thing and you finally consider that advice valid.

I have an astrology app called *Co-Star* on my phone. The app sends me daily questions to muse over. Sometimes the questions can be easy: 'Did you stop and reflect?' I appreciate those kinds of questions. But most of the time, *Co-Star* pulls a "Germany in a world war" card and goes on the offensive. *Co-Star* will ask questions like: "Do you crave being the center of attention?" "Do you have an addiction to your ego?" If I wanted to be criticized and dehumanized, I'd still be working at my old job.

XXIV.

During the fall of 2020, I got a haircut and wore a mask during the procedure. I call it a procedure because my hair had reached a point where taking care of it *required* a *procedure*. And I loved wearing a mask because it meant I didn't have to do that forced smile that I usually do during a haircut. It's that polite "I better look like I'm happy with the service" type smile that you usually only give for a minute to the average retail employee. But spending twenty minutes *minimum* in a chair during a haircut means you keep that fake smile on for so long that I end up looking like the Joker and becoming just as psychotic.

The smile especially becomes hard to do when you're getting the *worst* haircut of your life and you have to pretend to at least look neutral. Possibly even worse is when the haircut is good, you really have to bring a grade-A smile to make sure the hairdresser knows it's the best haircut ever. But with a mask, the only thing my hairdresser can see is my cold dead eyes in the mirror.

Another time I got a haircut, the female hairdresser asked how I'd like my hair cut. I explained that usually I got my hair cut short on the sides because my curls get out of control. The hairdresser immediately blew up as if I had been a victim of society's expectations.

"NO, YOU HAVE TO LOVE YOURSELF! YOU HAVE TO LOVE YOURSELF!" She kept saying over and over while touching my hair and trying to put the spirit of confidence in my curls. You would have thought this was her clip submission to the Oscars. I didn't *hate* my hair, I just wanted a good haircut.

XXV.

Nothing good ever happens at a club called Rumor. First off, the only good rumor is the album *Rumors* by Fleetwood Mac. Naming your club Rumor is just inviting negativity into your bar. It's the linguistic equivalent of pulling out the Ouija Board. You'd never call your club *Gunshots* or *Attempted Murder*.

"Hey, where are you going tonight."

"I heard things are going to get really rowdy at *Gunshots* tonight."

"We should go to *Molesty Men Club*."

Okay, certain people might go to that establishment.

XXVI.

I'm inadequate at small talk. I usually prefer to jump right into what's happening, usually with significant questions and heavy themes. I'm the kind of guy who will get existential right off the bat, especially when I've been drinking.

"Hey, how are you, do you think purpose is what drives the contemporary man?"

Eighty percent of people hear me and internally think: '*oh fuck he's one of those people.*'

And it's not even the nature of handling small talk. I fail to remember the basics of those I'm trying to small talk and schmooze with. The other day I asked this acquaintance if he was still seeing that 'one guy.' And he goes:

"You mean my fiancé who I've been dating for six years?"

So I countered, trying to save my skin:

"I'm glad things are *finally* going well!"

XXVII.

Did you ever fall in love with someone and then they went and burned you? Ruined you with the fires of hell? That happened to me last weekend with fajitas. The restaurant we visited is the only place serving fajitas that doesn't put a glove on the fajita handle. So I grabbed the actual handle, thinking I would be protected by the mitten.

After burning my hand, eating the fajitas, finishing two margaritas, and paying my bill, I rolled over to the grocery store to get Jergen's aloe vera hand lotion and gloves. I felt like the pervy equivalent of the murderer who buys duct tape, plastic bags, lye, and bullets.

"Whatcha gonna do with that lotion and mittens?" The cashier asks with a massively raised eyebrow.

Even with slight burns on my hands, my friends still wanted to go out. If you're looking for a good ice-breaker with tipsy strangers, a large tub of Jergen's aloe vera hand lotion is a winner. EVERYONE is going to want to be your friend. You could look like a murderous creep who just left jail, but if you're passing out free expensive lotion at the bar, people will thank you and explain how their hands are "*sooooo dry!*"

XXVIII.
    One of the best feelings in human existence is when you beat the GPS's estimated time of arrival. How dare the maps function underestimate *my* driving skills. The robot told me that it would take 27 minutes and that I would arrive at 12:34. Instead, I did it in 24 minutes and arrived at 12:31. No better feeling than beating technology. Naturally, if the robots do uprise, my GPS would undoubtedly be one of the inventions rooting for my death.

XXIX.
    If you ever need to know how fancy your neighborhood is, check out the pans your neighbors keep in their cupboards. You know you're in a privileged community when you see wok pans, specialty cake pans, panini presses, and sous vide machines. Hell — I'm guilty of owning a wok pan. But then you look at the quality of my wok pan and realize, 'ah, he's not rich nor poor — he's just American middle-class dirty.'

XXX.
    The most significant piece of information I learned during quarantine is that Chuck E. Cheese had take-out and delivery. For twenty bucks you could get two pizzas and 800 tickets to cash in for a *future* visit. That's what I need to get through quarantine, a stockpile of tickets so I can go to Chuck E. Cheese God-knows when so I can stock up on cheap erasers and keychains. And naturally, get arrested for being a man in a venue that's for children.
    Imagine saying: "But officer, I got these tickets because I ordered take-out from Chuck E. Cheese during quarantine! I'm not here for the children!"

XXXI.
    I was house hunting with my friend Sam. Sam and I wanted different things. I wanted a good location and a cheap

price, and Sam wants stainless steel appliances and granite countertops.

So Sam tells me, 'listen, there's this place that's a great location and has stainless steel appliances and would only be a six hundred dollar rent.' Six hundred was cheap for Cleveland, but not cheap enough to be suspicious. Six hundred in Cleveland would be like two grand in an expensive city.

Feeling confident about this house, Sam and I drive up to the gateway to hell. You know the U2 song where 'the streets called Bono's name?' These streets were calling me to tell me to fuck off. The house Sam wanted to see on the outside looked like it had been built in the Home Depot Kids Kraft Corner. If these walls could talk, they'd just let out a painful whimper before collapsing.

Sure, the inside of the house was steel and granite city. But it's like they spent thirty grand on the inside of the house and then said:

"I don't think this house *needs* a lawn."

The true highlight came as we stood in the kitchen that even The Terminator would think had too much metal. In the backyard was a grill pit that had a sideways shopping cart that acted like the grill. Imagine cooking hamburgers for everyone on a side-turned shopping cart over a fire that didn't look like it met any safety standards.

I turned to Sam and pointed out the grill. Sam dared to say:

"But the stainless steel sink."

XXXII.

Documentaries usually do a great job preparing you for what you are about to watch. For example, they might tell you in the trailer that a woman has been murdered and her husband was the prime suspect. Going into most documentaries, you have an idea of what is going to be explored. No one is watching a documentary about Jeffery Dahmer and is surprised that it has to do with murder and true crime.

My coworker and I were watching the same documentary series, and she had finished it before I did.

"I'm excited to see the last three episodes," I told the coworker casually. Well, my coworker went on to spoil so many details that were awaiting me. Never had I ever had someone spoil a documentary for me. And once a documentary is spoiled for you, it's not fun anymore. Instead of guessing whether or not it was the shifty husband, you now *know* it was him. What's the fun in that?

This event reminded me of the time I was part of a book club where I was the *only* person who finished the book each month. Everyone else would be still powering their way through chapter two, or were maybe halfway done. In my opinion, why bother coming if you didn't finish the book? Even halfway through the book feels the most offensive. Do people really enjoy talking about books that they didn't finish, didn't read, and were highly likely to not finish after the book club met?

I never got a grasp on how to talk about a book when only a few people in the book club had read it. I always felt like I was dancing on eggshells because I didn't want to spoil a major revelation or death.

The best part was that the book club moderator would work with these book club attendees. She would promise not to spoil the book, but she would constantly fall.

"How did you feel when the main character died at the end?" The librarian would ask the room while the students issued a soft gasp, realizing what she had just done. The other attendees would tell the librarian it was okay, partially because they weren't that invested anyway.

XXXIII.

I thought about what a modern Stations of the Cross would look like.

"Girl, did you betray Jesus?" Asked one of the Disciples as they thumbed through Twitter.

"Yes, Lindsay, I betrayed Jesus for a brand new *silver* iPhone!" They hold up the iPhone to an audacious gasp.

The Last Supper would probably be at a chain restaurant — think Applebee's or Chili's. Some of the disciples would complain.

"Who picked *this* venue out?" One might say, looking at the menu as if they were being forced to eat insects. Another would comment about the lack of vegan options, while two would absolutely keep mentioning how they could have gotten good food at a local restaurant.

Later on, when Jesus was arrested, he would be safely brought to jail. Of course, this would only happen if Jesus was blonde and Caucasian.

During the crucifixion, I think the woman who wiped away Jesus' sweat wouldn't be happy.

"Jesus grabbed my Prada scarf and rubbed his face on it. What am I gonna wear to the next wine mixer?"

Skeptics would certainly be abound.

"I saw Jesus fall for the third time but I think he totally faked it. Like I did last night with Joel."

Jesus returns on the third day and asks the guard,

"I have returned from the dead, where is everyone?"

The guard, confused about who this guy is, explains to Jesus:

"Sir, this is a graveyard. Unless you have questions, please keep it moving."

The guard returns to his TikTok while Jesus looks into an imaginary camera to give a classic 2000's sitcom stare down.

XXXIV.

When I was contemplating getting my master's degree, I wondered if it would be possible to get an MBA in passive-aggressive emailing. Such as when a coworker doesn't do their job and you write, "Just following up with the email forward of you agreeing you'd get this done...what's the status?" Or when a co-worker lies on the email chain and you write, "Here's the previous communication we've shared where it proves you've misunderstood the work."

And I think my master's in passive-aggressive emailing can apply to dating apps: 'Per my last message, I do not think our company values blend and I will be revoking our contract. Thank you for your time.'

It could also apply when a friend is acting up at the bar. "Unfortunately, we are going to have to part ways at this time as you are unable to meet our demands.'

XXXV.

Monica and I were having a social distancing picnic the other week. While Monica and I chatted, this lady stopped by and gave us a six-pack of water. I assumed she thought we were homeless or something. We were just two young-somethings sitting on a lawn and looking scrubby. She must have been thinking, 'I'm going to give these poor souls some water.' But after she walked on, I realized she had donated cantaloupe grapefruit la Croix. Which feels like an insult to the homeless. If you're going to contribute a *flavored* water, please donate a good flavor.

XXXVI.

There is a particular problem in America that I have seen for decades that has received zero discussion. People are wearing glasses that do not work for them.

We all have a shirt that looks like crap on us, right? And we keep it around *just* in case we get to that point in our closet where we have no clothes left. But you're *stuck* with glasses. You might have a second pair if you can afford it. But you're constantly wearing the glasses.

This is why I propose that every glasses store needs to come with a highly trained honest glasses critic. The genuine glasses critic will simply tell you whether or not the frames you want match your face. The critics will be stationed at every place that sells eyeglasses. They can be scheduled for virtual appointments. Part of the critic's code is mandated honesty. Imagine a world where everyone is wearing the best glasses for their face. Soon after — world peace guaranteed.

XXXVII.

I was on a dating app and this rando goes, 'Do you party with tuna?' and at first, I imagined tuna fish at the club. Turns out he meant Tina, which made me question if I knew a Tina. And if I did know Tina, was she a partier? Finally, I found out Tina actually meant drugs. The answer that I sent back was, "no, I don't party with tuna fish, Tinas, or drugs."

Guys, we have to talk about what it means to call yourself a jock. Just because you're not fat doesn't mean you're a jock.

If I ever got sent to rehab that had a roommate situation...oomph. Put me in a rehab *for* rehabbers who had roommates at their last rehab.

A new study came out that gay men fat shame each other and did we *need* a survey for that fact? Feels like a waste of government research funding.

I don't like apps that shame me for not using them. "Where have you been?" the app asks. "Having a life?" I respond. Duolingo used to do that all the time. The app would announce, "yo soy not using Duolingo." I know I'm not using Duolingo because they definitely said that whole sentence in Spanish.

Thin cookies are stupid. I'll have one thick cookie cause that's a big boy. But thin cookies mean I can have three or five or twenty and I don't feel bad 'cause it's a light cookie. But then I end up eating twenty or thirty thin cookies because the size throws me off. At least I can adequately count and shame myself with one oversized cookie.

I was driving down the street and all of a sudden this crossing guard just branched out into the middle of the road ready to DIE on the job so some boy could cross the road. I don't know her salary, but I'm confident it is not worth it. If someone came to me and said that I'd get paid 15 bucks an hour but there was a chance I might be hit by a car — I'd probably turn the job down, unless it came with free food.

Sugar in the raw sounds like a euphemism for sex.
"Whatcha doing tonight?" Someone might ask.
"Having sugar in the raw!"
"*Oooh*, you're getting some."
"No, I'm just going to have a cup of coffee, pervert!"

My niece Ivy explained gender to me the other day. She said there are 'girls and train wrecks.' Honestly — not the worst explanation of gender I've ever heard in my life. And some good theories by a three-year-old.

There's nothing that a Long Island won't fix. Besides alcoholism.

I'm not intimated when it comes to avoiding "this place only" parking spots. Like what are you going to do about it? I know your store is already understaffed and nobody is out there in the parking lot confirming where the customers parked. And I parked in Chick-fil-A's "this place only" parking cause fuck you and also sadly they're way too busy taking pleasure from people to check the parking lot.

I hate having to return things, especially if they're expensive. I recently went to Best Buy cause this seventy-dollar input didn't work. And so I'm returning this item with a receipt and I'm feeling guilty. I keep having to justify to myself and the cashier why I'm returning the object. Like hey, "I thought I'd love this and cherish this but it doesn't work and I'm so sorry it doesn't work." It feels like breaking up with someone.

I like my coffee like I like my man. Burning so hot that it melts a hole in my heart.

List of people I don't trust: people who call themselves young professionals. People hunched over the steering wheel. Currently the end of my list.

A place the other day advertised that they sold *Warm gravy and queso*, as if those things would be served cold otherwise.

I've been sick so I've been using the plan B of cold medicine because I do not have time to be a painting of a medieval-plague-deathbed-patient.

I had a dream where there were a thousand light switches on the wall and it took forever to get the right switch, and then a serial killer was at the bottom of the steps. Also in the dream, I accidentally parked in a handicapped parking spot and was shamed with giant signs around my car a la *Scarlet Letter*. It was half horror and half embarrassment that feels like horror.

Sometimes I feel like I lay it on thick when I'm trying to be friendly to retail workers. There are so many rude people out there that I feel like being extra lovely is my way of atoning for the sins of the general public.
"Hello, how are you? Hope it's been going well. I love your polo. Oh, it's a mandated work polo? Well, you wear it well. Thank you so much, please, please, thank you, thank you. Have a great day, an excellent weekend, and a fabulous month. Happy holidays that are coming up in the next few months, and hope you have a great next year as well."
I guess it's better than being shitty, but maybe not by much.

A colleague told me that he enjoys the comment section for PornHub because people will have life tips and hacks like how to get certain stains out of shirts. I think I'll just keep to Google.

I had a dream about a killer who was after me. It turned out the killer was Donatella Versace. Then the dream did a nonsensical transition where I was using sage soap in the shower. The scariest part of the dream is truly the sage soap. Wouldn't that smell worse than my natural musk?

I was out with friends the other day and they asked if I was losing weight. I told them yes and proceeded to ask for someone to pass the appetizer fried foods basket.

Girl Scout Cookies now feature inspirational messages. So when you eat your cookie treat, you might get an inspirational quote or comment like, "stay strong." I want my cookies to tell me to stop being a fatass.

A friend of mine is a dispatcher and the other day they got a call that there was a "bush fire at Dick's." Usually, we call that crabs.

Do you ever get those alerts from apps that say, "hey sis, we've updated the privacy policy," and you're like, I used this app once....like what in the world is this? It's like after one date your date goes, "so when's the wedding?"

I think If I lose a limb, I want to have a funeral for it. "That left arm was so good at lifting things for me."

XXXVIII.

Regular people usually have an hour of weekly therapy and some light habit-building and possible medication to overcome their mental health problems. But rich people handle their mental health problems by going on a 'journey.'

You know the type of Instagram posts where rich people are on a beach with a caption saying: *I learned so much about myself, I shine bright.* Meanwhile, in the back of the photo, a turtle is choking on a straw. Going on vacation for months at a time would probably be very beneficial for my health problems. I wish I could go to Cancun and get massages and Mai Tais for a month for my mental health and call that a journey. But instead, I get to write and create art as a way to deal with my mental health.

If everyone who needed a 'journey' for mental health took a two-month siesta, America would be a ghost country. We'd all be on a beach somewhere wearing giant Jackie O sunglasses and on our third-morning cocktail.

"Where is everyone?"
"On a *journey* in Fiji!"

XXXIX.

There are so many questions that haunt me at night. One question is what happened to Quiznos? Quiznos used to be everywhere. You couldn't go a city block without seeing one. They served fresh squeezed lemonade. Buttery warm cookies alongside crisp bread. I think Quiznos even sponsored a Super Bowl or something. Close your eyes and imagine hearing, "this football game is brought to you by Quiznos."

There are so many bad catchphrases out in the world. But Quiznos' slogan feels apropos of the moment. 'Mmmm toasty' feels current, nostalgic, and timeless. It's the type of statement you might say after having their food, or after letting out a giant fart.

Cleveland has become void of Quiznos, but our nearby neighbors Lorain and Akron have them. I should have known that Lorain and Akron would be the beacons of legendary food choices.

XL.

There's a new season of *You* out on Netflix. *You* is like that friend who has nothing going on but you're still fascinated with them.

"What did you do today." I would ask, only for that friend to casually, if not say with a hint of sadness,

"Laundry."

"WOW, incredible!" My eyes dance with amazement.

For those unfamiliar, *You* is all about a psychopath trying to manipulate the world around him all in the name of love. Some people offered the question: *how would you feel if a psychopath was manipulating you into liking him*?

"At least someone is putting in effort when it comes to a relationship!" I'd answer. Especially when in the context of *You* — a brilliant, hot guy wants to be your boyfriend? As much as I want to say I'd stand firm, I would be easier to manipulate than folding a piece of thin paper.

XLI.

Recently I heard that a specific brand of plane isn't safe anymore. Internal reports from the airplane company show executives saying, "we wouldn't put our kids on our planes." I love those internal reports where executives are shitting on the product. I get why they don't have morals. But why would you leave that in writing? Writing which could be leaked or published?

When it comes to plane safety, I get really fed up. I didn't care when they stopped serving salty pretzels and peanuts which left me dehydrated. I didn't care when they began charging for complimentary soda. I didn't care when they charged 20 bucks for bad WiFi because Netflix lets me download shows straight to my tablet. But can we at least have a *plane*???

I wonder if there are airplane executives who question whether guests need seatbelts or if standing-only flights could be a future innovation. I bet they'd be willing to change every function for the worse, but they'd still leave us with that terrible in-flight airplane magazine. How else would they pedal the dredge of their sister companies?

XLII.

I'm constantly told that I should pursue more acting. But a lot of the paid gigs in Cleveland are modeling and commercial work. Contradictory to what my mother or best friends would say, I'm not handsome for modeling and commercial gigs. Nobody wants my face in the Old Navy commercial, they want me playing the fat funny guy or doing something with physical humor like falling into a vat of acid. My driver's license makes you want to call in a preemptive amber alert. Seeing my face on a product would be deflating to the average consumer.

Imagine seeing me on a product that describes itself as fat-free or slimming. You would be quick to assume that I didn't eat the product in my life, the product didn't work, or that if that picture was me slimmed down, what did I previously look like? If anything, I could leverage myself into doing gigs where I play the sexual predator in an HR commercial.

XLIII.

I'd love to see more New Year's Resolutions such as: "I want to gain weight," "I want to stay at my job," or "I want to be single." At least that's more interesting than the same old resolutions. So many people want to lose weight or find love — but where are the people that subverse those norms?

Usually, towards the end of the year, people post their favorite songs, shows, and photos. But now I've been seeing this increasing trend of people posting all the books they read during the year. I think they do it because they get away with the ability to brag about how much they've read. It's not about whether they enjoyed the books, what they learned, or even if they tried different genres or authors. It's just about the amount.

Truthfully, I may have read ten books in the last year. And by reading, I mean listening to ten audiobooks. I hate to sound like an old man who is blaming things that don't deserve blame, but modern society has ruined my ability to read a hard-covered book.

And the hard-covered books I do read are for work and research. Even now, there's a small pile on my desk about design theory. I'm intrigued to read about design theory, but it's not the same as a juicy narrative exposition.

I had someone in my life post on social media that they read ninety-five books in the last year and I'm just like *when* in this economy and Americana lifestyle did you manage that? That is almost two books a week. I just don't believe someone is doing that unless they're a bored house spouse who has no obligations at all. Maybe those ninety-five books were online fan fiction novels that were forty pages each? Maybe they read ninety-five poetry books by that famous poet who has five words spaced out across a page and calls it poetry? No offense, but some of those poetry books are like '*sadness ebbs. Life is blue.*' Next page. Blank page. Next page. "*Sunflower rose daisy and dew, I think I miss you.*" Next page. If I was reading a book that was designed in that way, I'd crank out 95 books a *week*.

XLIV.

Once in a while, I'll get a notification that I have a new match on Tinder. And then when I go on the app I find that the person has unmatched with me. It's like craving ice cream all day long and imagining ice cream in the freezer at home. You arrive home, ready to pull out the bowl and spoon, to find there's no ice cream in the fridge. There are just frozen sausage links and ice. Guess I'll have a sausage smoothie.

Dating is like Chipotle orders, where you handpick what you want and try and stuff it into a burrito shell which starts to explode as soon as things get too heavy. But gay dating is similar, just double meat and a massive load of sour cream.

Personally, I've looked at profiles of people on Tinder and instantly had a reaction that that person is a serial killer. Maybe I've been listening to too much true crime, but some profiles have crazy eyes or facial expressions that look like an alien used AI to decipher what human emotions should look like. I can just see the mannequins or giant pit in their basement just by staring deep into their soulless eyes.

Quite often dating apps like to inform you that you 'missed out on a match.' And I never regret swiping left on these 'missed matches.' I won't be shamed by a dating app for passing up someone like 'Hunter' who wants to cheat on his wife, 'Looking,' a blank profile that is looking for sex, or even 'Adam' who is obsessed with Disney as an adult.

I have a lot of demands from dating profiles. Some red flags include:

- All their pictures are in a group situation and you have no clue who it is you're talking to
- All their pictures are blurry as if taken with a computer from 1980
- "Looking for a good time, not a long time."
- You get one filtered Snapchat picture — *if* that
- All your photos are selfies that are cut off at weird angles. Am I going out with just half a face?
- Photos that are clearly dated by *years*
- Any mention of, "I'm looking for the Jim to my Pam," "I'm looking for the David to my Patrick," or any other sitcom-based relationship metaphors

Another pet peeve I have is when a profile says 'read my bio' and when I visit the bio, it says something idiotic like 'looking for something real.' Did that need to be a mandated read? It's like being summoned to the town square by a medieval knight who says, "hear ye, taxes are owed." If someone is going to bully me into reading their dating profile biography, please make it enjoyable.

Did you ever meet someone on their dating profile that reads, *'Oh I talk to everyone, :)*.' And then you message them and you don't get a response? Am I *that* ugly that the person who talks to everyone wants nothing to do with my ass? Don't pretend you are the Mother Theresa of chatting to everyone on dating apps and then refuse me your charity.

I don't really have high dating standards. But I guess I want someone as attentive as Google's security. Not a day goes by without Google telling me I'm in critical danger of someone hacking into my account. I can't even remember the last time a human made me feel secure, but damn it I can cuddle up in bed knowing Google cares. Unlike Facebook, stealing my damn data and selling it to my ex, Russia.

XLV.

My niece is in that stage where she says 'no' to things. So my sister would ask:
"Do you want to clean up your toys?"
And my niece expectedly goes:
"No."
And it goes for all sorts of things,
"Do you want to take a nap?"
"No."
I can't wait till my niece gets older and claims she wishes she had more naps. I'll politely sip my beverage of choice before reminiscing about how she refused naps as a child. Call me petty, I call it poetic justice.
The funniest thing about a child experiencing their "no phase" is that you could say anything to my niece and she'd still blurt out no.
"Wanna solve cancer?" I could question.
"No."
"Do you think that we're all here on this earth for a reason?" I could ponder.
"No."
"Do you think Jeffery Epstein committed suicide?" I could suggest.
"No."
She would be right on that last one, similar to how even monkeys can write Shakespeare (although I'm still waiting on the local zoo to deliver me that manuscript). But sometimes you have to learn how to manage in a world full of nos.
"Should Uncle Matt *not* have another milkshake?"
"No."
God forbid that's the day she decides to use yes.

XLVI.

One of my many anxieties in this world is when I have a messy car and I'm in a drive-thru at a restaurant. My car is filled with recycling, a little trash, clothes, books, and whatever leftover supplies I have from a project. My passenger is not human — it's a junk pile.

I purposely always drive a little past the window. This makes it so that I'm always reaching back to the employee. My arm is outstretched, my whole body hoping they don't see the mess. The funniest thing about my attempt to remain pure in the eyes of the restaurant employee is that I really doubt they care what my car looks like. But my anxiety manifests in the form of the one employee who sees my messy car and goes on to tell the staff.

"He had like *ten* large iced Panera Bread cups in his front seat. And all these gym supplements as if he *goes to the gym*!"

My recycling is so bad that recently a cop pulled me over and spent five minutes flashing his flashlight into my backseats. As if there was a body between my Propel water bottles and Starbucks cups. I legit was sweating because for all I knew, someone had hidden a body or a crime in my car and I just didn't know it. I wonder how well that would hold up in the police interview and the court of the law.

Hands down my favorite recycling moment is when I went to pick up my father and sister at the airport. I told them to please watch the recycling in the back and in the trunk. My father opened the trunk as if cracking open a crab leg. Tons of bottles, cups, and recycling flew out of the trunk and began flying across the airport.

"My *RECYCLING!*" I screamed, running around like a crazy maniac to re-collect the recycling. I was so upset that I didn't speak to them on the entire ride home.

XLVII.

Did you ever hear the name of an evil organization and go "...ok?"

Like I was watching a show and the evil organization is called the "Soothsayers." It sounds like someone got out of a dental procedure. The villains in James Bond had an organization called Spectre, which sounds like a gay bar. 'Girl we're going down to Spectre for drinks and drag bingo!' I've never played Resident Evil, but their villains are called Umbrella Corporation which sounds like they just...make umbrellas?

I love when evil people explain their plans in every single movie and tv show. It's so cliche but also so good at the same time. You know that I'd be that villain who's like:

"Sis listen, here's the tea, do you have your cup ready for what I'm about to pour in? I know you don't like me right now and I get that...but I have to tell *someone* what I'm up to..."

XLVIII.

The worst video games are the ones where you have to run a business. 'Can you run this pizza shop? Can you run this store? Can you run this college?' It just feels like an extension of my reality. I use video games as a way to escape for a second and become someone I have no chance of becoming. In real life, I could become a president of a college or a pizza shop. But I have no chance of owning Pokemon, scaling platforms and walls, owning and operating a sword, or being an actual jacked hero. Even the games where you have to run people's lives feel like too much work. As someone who is barely running my own life, what makes video game companies confident I can help this digital person?

XLIX

Some coupons have extreme limitations that make me wonder why they made the coupon in the first place.

"This coupon can't be used Monday through Sunday from 11-3 and 5-10. The coupon also can't be used with groups of 3, 5, 7, 9, and 11. Half the menu can't be ordered with that coupon."

Those kinds of coupons had to have been made by Mr. Burns from *The Simpsons*. I imagine some marketing expert shaking their hands maliciously, so proud of the fact that their coupon is entirely unusable. But then again, two dollars off a product is quite tempting, mainly because you're so poor. So you'll just have to use it at 4pm.

I remember my mother wanted to use a coupon, but the restaurant said it was a holiday and we couldn't use the coupon.

"What holiday is it?" My mother asked.

"It's Sweetest Day." The cashier said. Sweetest Day, a made-up holiday designed to rip people off of cash, feels like a stretch to designate as a day void of coupon use. It wasn't even like the establishment was busy with customers *and* it was lunch hour. Nobody goes on a romantic lunch, and if they do it's definitely coupon related.

Another time, my father handed me a coupon for a local Chinese restaurant. This was during year two of COVID, and I was worried about local restaurants.

"Should we use the coupon? Will they accept the coupon?" My moral quandary presented like a philosophical caper.

"They put this coupon in the weekly local coupon book." My father said with a shrug. "They wouldn't advertise the coupon if they didn't want people to use it."

I walked inside, feeling guilty for holding my 10% coupon. You would have thought I was a guilty train robber who was approaching the steam engine. I presented the coupon to the cashier who sighed, throwing himself dramatically backward.

"Well, we actually shouldn't be running this coupon." The man sighed. "We lose so much money from this coupon."

He sadly took 10% off the bill — and I returned to my parents, embarrassed for having nickled-and-dimed a man over his own coupon.

"They have to *pay* to have their coupon in the Valpak!" My father gasped, which made me only slightly less guilty.

A year later, we discovered that the restaurant had forever shuttered — most likely in conjunction with the coupon they paid to put out in the local coupon book which they secretly didn't want people to use.

L.

My friend told me that she's going to die in the next two years. I was baffled by her confession. She is not a boring friend, but it's not like she's constantly knocking at death's door. She's not addicted to drugs or extreme sports. She doesn't have a dangerous job like a sex worker or even a part-time volunteer cop. Now, if she was addicted to heroin and free-lanced as a sex worker, volunteer cop, and crab-fisher while competing in a dangerous sport, I would probably agree that she was more likely to die than the average person.

LI.

I have some friends who recently discovered the love of their lives. Upon discovering this recent fact, they ask — "is this weird?"

No love could be as weird as Romeo and Juliet. These two knew each other for three days before committing suicide. Imagine you went on two dates with someone and fell in love and then killed yourself once you discovered you can't be together. Romeo and Juliet were fourteen. To all those old people who say 'teens are overdramatic these days', newsflash, teens have always been overdramatic!

A weirder love is probably a murderous couple who kills children, that love is more unconventional. Or a couple deciding to raise a child in today's world, that is some bizarre love!

LII.

Part of living in a country that has a terrible healthcare system means that you occasionally research your illness systems on WebMD. You do it mainly because it's free and easy to Google with your phone. Ever since WebMD told me I was dying of cancer due to insistent coughing, I have been signed up for their email alerts. They send out newsletters and breaking medical information. The joke's on them, I only consider WebMD useful when it comes to diagnosing my cough for *free*.

I don't mind an occasional WebMD email. Sometimes it's nice to be told *why* I should eat kale. Like most people, I am eating kale because people are telling me to eat kale. I'm easily convinced I'm doing healthy habits simply from Instagram hotties with bodies. The problem isn't *why* WebMD is emailing me. It's WHEN WebMD emails me.

I got a notification from Gmail that WebMD had emailed me around midnight on a Saturday night out. The email was labeled with the subject line: 'Seven Signs You're Depressed.' Imagine being home alone on a Saturday night with no one to have social plans with. You're feeling sad already and WebMD emails you with the attitude of a sassy high school bully saying, "Hey girl... here are seven signs you're depressed. Thinking of you! This feels *just like you!*"

One time WebMD emailed me Friday night around 10pm with an email titled 'Five Reasons Not To Drink.' You better believe my drunk self was pre-gaming at that moment with a drink so strong that it violated several elements of the Geneva Convention. The email intern for WebMD probably cackled in her studio apartment.

LIV.

    I always envisioned myself as the sassy lawyer who'd announce in court, "Your honor, I present new evidence that proves my client is free. I'd like the charges to be dropped quickly so the prosecutor can get a new haircut."

    I'd be the type of lawyer who would saunter over to the jury with a peaceful jaunt and a solid opening line.

    "The prosecution would have you believe that my client was up to no good. But you know what's no good? The prosecution's case."

    This would be communicated with a thick Southern accent and a light sweat. I'm portly after all and I bet this courtroom is *stifling*. I'm an immense flirt, so I bet I'd use this time to lay down some major schmaltz with the jury. Even when the pressure is applied by the prosecution, I remain unbothered, while still acting friendly and lovely with everyone in the room.

    "Why, what will you have for lunch?" I might ask the court stenographer at some point.

    My cross-examinations would be very peaceful. I'd slowly get a witness for the prosecution to believe that I'm a nice man. I'm just here to look for the truth. But then I'd slowly get the witness to reveal their lie or misconception, and the whole court would gasp.

    But imagine going to law school just to be a dramatic-ass defense attorney who plays with emotions and did not actually have any understanding of the law. I suppose that's pretty similar to the current American justice system.

LV.

    My sister reserved a hotel room at Kalahari that coincided with her birthday weekend. Kalahari is a giant waterpark that makes your local pool appear as substantial as a mud-filled mosquito-ridden puddle. This was *huge*. Not because we were visiting Kalahari but because my sister was not really known for spending money on the members of my family. Granted at this time she was a stay-at-home mom who did odd petty jobs for petty cash. But even before the children and household responsibilities, she had always been The Giving Tree. And she was *not* the tree.

My parents had a period where they would haggle with me and my sister over items to auction on Facebook marketplace. My parents flirted with social media — my dad was mainly obsessed with TikTok and my mom was a social justice Twitter retweeter. Neither had Facebook and so had to rely on my sister and me, the former who posted on Facebook every two hours like a religious cathedral bell.

One item that my mom gave my sister sold for fifty dollars. Under the spoken but unwritten family Facebook marketplace contract, the two would split the fifty dollars. My mother had to work *tooth and nail* for that twenty-five dollars. My sister at first feigned ignorance, and then blamed my mother for not having a Venmo account. Finally, my sister bartered in a desperate bid to hold onto the cash the way ravens hoard shiny objects.

"I'll just buy you some groceries." My sister said with a casual shrug as if clearance cereal and 2-for-1 protein bars could substitute a meager yet sturdy twenty-five dollars. So yes — for a woman who would try to weasel out of handing twenty-five dollars to their own mother, buying the hotel room for a night at Kalahari for the family was historic.

My sister's birthday falls around Mother's Day. I recall that my sister mentioned this was part birthday celebration but also part Mother's Day festivities. I found that excuse pretty flimsy. Our mother hadn't entered a public pool since Y2K and avoided public people ponds in the way that Ancient Romans avoided beer. If this was a trip meant for my mother, it was another 'gift' masquerading as self-indulgence. These gifts often appeared in my family with the exception of my mother who remains the best gift-giver in the family. Everyone utilizes workplace discounts, 'group experiences,' and, a typical bar example, a bunch of soap and shampoo that was less a birthday gift for mom and more a coupon deal for the family bathroom. While we won't live down the presents of soap and hangers, we have made up with recent gifts for mothers. My sister gave my mother an air fryer to make up for decades of unsatisfying offerings (although, I'm sure a coupon and a workplace discount were involved in that decision).

My sister's fiancé was running by potential names for his new business. A trait that runs through the family is that we are always looking for ways to make money. The difference is, I look for jobs and paid experiences that will incite my passions. My father and future brother-in-law really could care less what they were doing as long as the money was right. The latest scheme involved power-wash supplies my sister's fiancé had purchased for 'practically nothing.' In my wallet, five grand was definitely *something*. But dropping noteworthy money like that was nothing in the eyes of my father and brother-in-law. If they could turn that five grand into six grand, they were aboard that ship. Even if that ship turned out to be the Titanic.

"What about Sham Daddy Power Wash?" My brother-in-law asked with a chuckle and steel seriousness. I felt a tinge of nausea run through my body from the name Sham Daddy Power Wash. It sounded like Scam Daddy, which made me think of an old man who scams people. And who wants to hire a Scam Daddy to do anything? Secondly, this was a power washing company *not* a Chippendales-themed car wash in Las Vegas. My sister agreed with me. While I was more concerned with outrageous creativity, my sister wanted to make sure the title was something that could bring in more money for her to spend and hoard like Smaug, the dragon from *The Lord of the Rings.*

Names continued to be tossed out as we entered the water resort. My sister's girls were 4 and 3, which meant we were limited to kid splash zones. Being an adult without a direct child in a splash zone always makes me feel uneasy. I have to go out of my way to make sure people around me recognize that I am truly connected to present children and not just some loser sitting suspiciously alone by a lilypad. Especially these days with heightened security — I can't imagine what the 1960s kids' splash pad looked like. Probably similar to cell block D down in county prison.

We did eventually get around to the lazy river and wave pool with the girls — but there was much more burden on the adults. The girls had to be held and managed in these exhibits. My work here feels similar to how the managers of Lindsey Lohan and

Paris Hilton must have felt in the early '00s: wild, carefree girls demanding experiences that make you hypersensitive to the environment around them.

The real shame is how *unlazy* Lazy Rivers have become. In magazines and in our minds, we picture the Lazy Rivers as relaxing and slow-paced. Lazy Rivers are supposed to be the old folks' home of the water park. If you want action and adventure, there are plenty of slides and pedophile-free splash pads. There's even a wave pool to test your cardio! The Lazy River was overrun with kids pushing and shoving as if racing to finish the course. I had ten-year-old kids force me and my inner-tube against the wall on multiple occasions. I suppose it's my fault — after all, why would I ever wish to relax in a Lazy River?

After doing three trips of a very Active River, we exited.

"How much is that pizza?" My father asked a couple who were holding a giant box of pizza. Their 'za reminded me of greasy school pizza where the cheese had melded to form a defensive shield over the underdone dough.

"Forty." The guy said with a bit of regret. Immediately our whole family gasped at the outrageous price. We were taught to barter, beg, and be frugal — traits that I forever stand by. My only exceptions are shoes and good food and drinks. And in case you're unsure, this pizza is not good food.

"Forty for *that?*" My father asked, pointing at the pizza in case there was any confusion on the item that was in question. In some other dimension, I'm sure the man laughed and said, "Oh I'm sorry, the pizza is actually ten dollars! I thought you meant my waterproof fancy watch..." Unfortunately, we were not in that dimension.

After an off-campus dinner, my father and I were itching for the hot tub — a delicacy to us the way salmon is to a household cat. We were excused from family time and made our way to the adult-only swim-up bar. They had a regular hot tub, but I'm not really 'excited' about the all-ages welcome hot tub bar. Like the lazy river, the hot tub is really supposed to be an 'unwinding.' There's nothing relaxing about being in a hot tub with kids splashing, seven-year-old Jared complaining to his father, or the lazy river inner-tube pushers, pushing through the hot tub.

On our way to the hot tub, we passed a room filled with teenagers.

"What is this — after prom?" I joked, a comment more for my dad than for me.

"It is!" The one girl said with a grin. "Wanna come party?"

I really want to believe that she was joking. After all, what group of teenagers want to party with a forty-seven-year-old penny-pincher and a scrubby twenty-six-year-old? But part of me thinks she wasn't joking. And perhaps, if we were white trash (or, more white trash than we are), we might have joined the after-prom committee. Instead, my father and I laughed, awkwardly made a comment about how we didn't have time for prison, and scrammed. We'll save the prison time for the weirdos at the splash pad.

In an epilogue that seemed predictable, I discovered my sister had only paid for half the room and my father paid for the other half.